The American Bombing of Libya

The American Bombing of Libya

A Study of the Force of Miscalculation in Reagan Foreign Policy

NICHOLAS LAHAM

McFarland & Company, Inc., Publishers
Jefferson, North Carolina, and London

LIBRARY OF CONGRESS CATALOGUING-IN-PUBLICATION DATA

Laham, Nicholas.
　　The American bombing of Libya : a study of the force of miscalculation in Reagan foreign policy / Nicholas Laham.
　　　　p.　　cm.
　　Includes bibliographical references and index.

　　ISBN-13: 978-0-7864-3185-4
　　softcover : 50# alkaline paper ∞

　　1. United States — Foreign relations — Libya.　2. Libya — Foreign relations — United States.　3. Reagan, Ronald. 4. Libya — History — Bombardment, 1986.　5. United States — Military policy.　6. United States — Foreign relations —1981–1989. I. Title.
E183.8.L75L34　　2008
327.730612 — dc22　　　　　　　　　　　　　　2007036504

British Library cataloguing data are available

©2008 Nicholas Laham. All rights reserved

No part of this book may be reproduced or transmitted in any form or by any means, electronic or mechanical, including photocopying or recording, or by any information storage and retrieval system, without permission in writing from the publisher.

Cover image ©2007 Alamy Ltd.; cover by TG Design

Manufactured in the United States of America

McFarland & Company, Inc., Publishers
　Box 611, Jefferson, North Carolina 28640
　　www.mcfarlandpub.com

To Haydee, Carmelita, and Ma. Ella,
with love and appreciation

Contents

Preface		1
Introduction		3
ONE	Reagan Pursues a Misguided Policy	9
TWO	The Reagan Administration Unsuccessfully Attempts to Isolate Libya	49
THREE	Heading Toward a Military Showdown	83
FOUR	Reagan Orders the Bombing	113
FIVE	International Condemnation of the Bombing	165
SIX	A Legitimate Response to Terrorism or a Demonstration of Power?	200
Notes		211
Bibliography		221
Index		223

Preface

This book is based almost exclusively on research I conducted at the Ronald Reagan Presidential Library in Simi Valley, California. The Presidential Records Act of 1978 makes all White House records, beginning with those of Reagan, the property of the federal government. The records are to be opened upon public request under the Freedom of Information Act, subject to certain restrictions, the most important being national security, five years following the president's retirement from office. Three researchers, including Joseph T. Stanik, who has written perhaps the most authoritative book thus far on the American bombing of Libya, and I made Freedom of Information Act requests for presidential records pertaining to the air strikes. The Reagan Library processed 2,635 pages of records in response to those requests, opening 682 pages of material. The remaining records are classified almost without exception for national security reasons. In response to another Freedom of Information request, the Reagan Library processed 628 pages pertaining to the multinational force (MNF), 127 of which are open, and the remaining classified, once again due to national security considerations. In response to additional Freedom of Information requests, the Reagan Library processed 1,957 records pertaining to either the American bombing of Libya or the MNF, 605 of which are open. The bases of this book are the presidential records pertaining to the American bombing of Libya, and to a lesser extent, the MNF. The records are based on the files of selected members of the White House staff, all of whom were members of the National Security Council (NSC) during the Reagan presidency.

I would like to take this opportunity to acknowledge the contributions of a number of individuals whose invaluable contributions made this book possible. My first words of thanks go to the excellent archival staff at the Ronald Reagan Presidential Library. I would like to thank Lisa Jones and Catherine Sewell in particular for directing me to the presidential records upon which the research for this book is based, David Bridge and Jennifer Sternaman for supervising my photocopying of this material, Mike Duggan for processing my Freedom of Information Act request for documents pertaining to the American bombing of Libya, and Shelly Jacobs for managing my request.

Finally, I want to acknowledge a tremendous debt of gratitude to my wife, Haydee Valencia, for all the joy and happiness she has given to me during our marriage. I want to express my deepest appreciation to Haydee for making our marriage a truly wonderful and exhilarating experience. I also want to thank my mother-in-law, Carmelita Valencia, and daughter, Ma. Ella, for their indispensable contributions to our marriage.

Introduction

Given the horrific nature of the terrorist attacks that struck the United States on September 11, 2001, it is easy to forget that the war against international terrorism that Washington launched on that infamous date was actually the second, not the first, such response of its kind. On January 27, 1981, President Ronald Reagan chose the welcoming ceremony for the newly-freed American hostages, who had been held in captivity by Iran for 444 days, as his venue for declaring Washington's first war against international terrorism, promising that the United States would pursue "swift and effective retribution" against the forces of global terrorism. Reminding us of Reagan's long-forgotten war against international terrorism, which all but faded from public memory in the wake of 9-11, Joseph T. Stanik notes, "Reagan and his advisers regarded international terrorism as an issue of vital national importance, and combating it became one of the new administration's highest priorities."[1]

On April 14, 1986, Reagan, for the first and only time in his presidency, fully implemented his policy of "swift and effective retribution" against the forces of international terrorism when he ordered the American bombing of Libya. The air strikes were in retaliation for the bombing of a disco in West Berlin on April 5, which killed an American soldier and a Turkish civilian, and wounded 230 others, including fifty American military personnel. In his national television address from the Oval Office announcing the air strikes, Reagan placed responsibility for the bombing squarely on the shoulders of Libya's mercurial leader — Muammar Qaddafi. In justifying the American air strikes against Libya, Reagan noted that the bombing of the disco was the latest action in a coordinated international terrorist campaign Qaddafi had organized and launched since the United States severed diplomatic relations with Libya after demonstrators sacked and burned the American Embassy in Tripoli in 1979 with the acquiescence of the renegade leader of Libya.

This book argues that the American bombing of Libya was the result of a severe loss of credibility the United States suffered in the Arab world arising from Reagan's decision to draw Washington closer to Tel Aviv than it had previously been. The strengthening of relations between the United States and Israel resulted from Reagan's disastrously ill-fated decision, which the president announced on August 20, 1982, to establish the multinational force (MNF) in Beirut, composed of token contingents of troops from the United States, France, and Italy, which were later joined by a small British unit. The decision came following the Israeli invasion of Lebanon on June 6, which resulted in the successful expulsion of members of the Palestine Liberation Organization (PLO) from Beirut and the southern part of Lebanon.

The original mission of the MNF was to ensure the safe and peaceful withdrawal of members of the PLO from Beirut, which was successfully completed on September 1, 1982. However, following the massacres of residents of the Palestinian refugee camps of Sabra and Shatila in Beirut by militiamen of Lebanon's fiercely nationalist Phalange Party, on September 20 Reagan announced the establishment of a new MNF in the battle-scarred capital of Lebanon with an expanded, twofold mission: first, to facilitate the restoration of the sovereignty of the Lebanese government throughout its territory; and second, to secure the withdrawal of all foreign forces from Lebanon. However, the mission of the MNF was doomed from the moment Reagan announced its establishment: the force fell far short of the troop levels required to achieve its ambitious objectives.

The MNF languished aimlessly in Beirut for one year, incapable of taking any meaningful step toward fulfilling its mission. On October 23, 1983, the MNF suffered a fatal blow when terrorists, in a well-coordinated pair of suicide bombings, destroyed barracks housing American and French members of the force, killing 241 American Marines and fifty-eight French paratroopers. Reagan responded to the bombings by vowing to maintain the American military presence in Beirut, declaring that the United States would not be intimidated by terrorist violence. However, following a four-day resurgence of street fighting, Shiite and Druze militiamen seized control of West Beirut on February 6, 1984, resulting in the collapse of the Lebanese government. With the dramatic deterioration of security conditions in Beirut, Reagan ordered the withdrawal of the American Marines from the capital the next day, and the evacuation of French, Italian, and British troops soon followed, bringing an abrupt end to their ill-fated military mission.

By vowing to maintain the American military presence in Beirut, only to abruptly reverse course and order the withdrawal of the Marines from

Beirut three months later, Reagan came across as an indecisive, irresolute, and vacillating president who had pursued an uncertain, incomprehensible, and self-contradictory policy in Lebanon. This image was exacerbated by Reagan's ineffective efforts to link the MNF mission in Beirut to the peace process in the Middle East. Hours following the withdrawal of members of the PLO from Beirut, Reagan unveiled his peace plan for the Middle East, hoping that he could capitalize on Israel's success in expelling the organization from Beirut by jump-starting the stalled peace process in the region. However, Reagan immediately shelved his peace plan after it met vehement and vociferous denunciation from Israel. The Jewish state flatly rejected Reagan's demand for an Israeli withdrawal from occupied Arab territories as a critical element of the president's peace plan. Reagan's decision to abandon his peace plan in the face of Israeli rejection only added to the image of the president as indecisive, irresolute, and vacillating.

Reagan's unfortunate decision to send troops to Beirut, and his unsuccessful effort to link the mission of the MNF to the peace process, inexorably led him to commit his supreme miscalculation in pursuing American policy in the Middle East: the decision to draw the United States closer to Israel in the wake of the bombing of the Marine barracks in Beirut. Guided by the firm belief that Israel was a strategic asset to the United States in the Middle East, Reagan reckoned that he could use the Jewish state as a counterweight to the efforts of radical forces in Lebanon to drive the Marines from Beirut. In a summit meeting with Prime Minister Yitzhak Shamir held in Washington one month following the bombing of the Marine barracks in Beirut, Reagan announced the he was formalizing the strategic alliance between the United States and Israel.

As an additional gesture of support for Israel, in 1985 Reagan scuttled an initiative Jordan and the PLO launched that was designed to revive the moribund peace process in the Middle East. Reagan rejected the PLO's demand that the United States recognize the right of the Palestinians to exercise self-determination as a condition for the organization's agreement to meet American terms for entering into a dialogue. This came in response to a public relations campaign launched by the American Israel Public Affairs Committee (AIPAC) in 1985 to persuade Reagan not to lift the prohibition against American contacts with the PLO that President Gerald Ford had imposed a decade earlier.

Reagan's pro–Israel policy in the Middle East substantially undermined the credibility of the United States in the Arab world. By the end of 1985, that credibility had sunk to a new low with Reagan's decision to scuttle the Jordanian-Palestinian peace initiative. The collapse of this initiative coincided with a major change of Qaddafi's international terrorist tactics. Until the end of 1985, those tactics mostly involved assassinations and murder attempts against exiled Libyan dissidents. After that period those tactics focused on targeting Western European facilities, frequented by Americans, for terrorist attacks. These new tactics were more deadly and menacing as they involved the random targeting of innocent civilians of any national origin for a terrorist attack. Qaddafi's new and more deadly form of international terrorism was unveiled on December 27, 1985, when Libyan-sponsored Palestinian terrorists launched a pair of brutal attacks, designed to indiscriminately kill as many innocent civilians as possible at the international airports at Rome and Vienna.

Qaddafi had every reason to believe two things: first, his new international terrorist tactics would inexorably lead him on a collision course with the United States; and second, in the inevitable military confrontation between Washington and Tripoli which would ensue, the moderate Arab nations would support the irrepressible leader of Libya against the president residing in the White House. The reason for the second belief was simple: as much as the moderate Arab nations disdained Qaddafi, they found Reagan's embrace of Israel to be even more distasteful. Indeed, when forced to choose between Reagan and Qaddafi in the wake of the American bombing of Libya, moderate Arab leaders opted to support their fellow Arab head of state, an ardent enemy of Israel, rather than the pro–Israel president of the United States: the moderate Arab nations roundly condemned the air strikes.

The nations of Western Europe played a critical role in the evolution of the acrimonious conflict between the United States and Libya. Reagan's hand against Qaddafi was severely weakened by the dissension and disarray between the two sides of the Atlantic regarding the most appropriate means to respond to the challenge of Libyan-sponsored international terrorism: the United States favored a get-tough policy against Tripoli, which conflicted with the determination of the nations of Western Europe to preserve their friendly relations with Libya. Qaddafi exploited this division to successfully thwart American efforts to isolate Libya from the rest of the international community.

However, the American bombing of Libya galvanized the nations of Western Europe to adopt a hard-line policy against Tripoli. The nations of Western Europe fully recognized that additional American military action against Libya was certain unless Qaddafi immediately abandoned his involvement in international terrorism. Such action was certain to have a devastating impact upon the extensive and lucrative economic interests the nations of Western Europe enjoyed in oil-rich Libya. Though the nations of Western Europe, with the notable exceptions of the United Kingdom and West Germany, condemned the American bombing of Libya, they were not oblivious to the threat Qaddafi posed to the international community. To deprive Reagan of any pretext to order additional military action against Libya, the nations of Western Europe responded to the American bombing of Tripoli and Benghazi by expelling over 100 Libyan diplomats and businessmen from Western Europe.

Through the mass expulsion of Libyans from Western Europe, the nations of the region hoped to impress upon Qaddafi that they were prepared to sever their economic relations with his regime unless he immediately abandoned his involvement in international terrorism. Qaddafi finally reckoned that the costs to him of his continued involvement in international terrorism exceeded the benefits. There were no additional acts of Libyan-sponsored international terrorism in the weeks and months following the American bombing of Tripoli and Benghazi.

While scholars generally defend the American bombing of Tripoli and Benghazi as having dealt a devastating blow to Libyan-sponsored international terrorism, the air strikes came after the United States had suffered a severe erosion of its credibility in the Arab world. That Reagan felt the need to order the bombing as a means to regain that lost credibility suggests the conventional view of the air strikes—as a legitimate American response to Libyan-sponsored international terrorism—is true, but only to a point. Rather, the air strikes can more accurately be seen ultimately as an act of desperation: by the spring of 1986 Reagan saw no alternative to defend American strategic interests against the challenge Qaddafi posed than to order the bombing. In the end, Reagan attempted to restore America's lost credibility in the Arab world, not through the pursuit of creative and enlightened diplomacy designed to advance the peace process, but by impressing upon the Arab world that the United States remained a global superpower, willing to defend its strategic interests by using military force against its enemies. Qaddafi would serve as an example of what was in store for any Arab leader who chose to challenge American power in the Middle East, thereby making it clear to Washington's enemies in the region that they stood to pay a high price should they choose to follow in the footsteps of the revolutionary firebrand of Libya in confronting the United States.

CHAPTER ONE

Reagan Pursues a Misguided Policy

> *It is hard not to conclude that Reagan's disengaged style as President, his lack of curiosity, and his passivity on issues related to the Middle East were impediments to creative U.S. peace diplomacy.*[1]
> — William B. Quandt, political scientist

The American bombing of Libya can ultimately be viewed as the culmination of a misguided American policy in the Middle East Reagan had pursued during the first five years of his presidency. Reagan entered the White House determined to pursue a pro–Israel policy in the Middle East. Presidents Richard Nixon, Gerald Ford, and Jimmy Carter had felt the need to conceal American support for Israel under the guise of step-by-step diplomacy designed to create the illusion, though not the reality, of creating a sustained momentum toward peace in the Middle East. Reagan was determined to dispense with the niceties of step-by-step diplomacy and make American support for Israel open, honest, and explicit.

The Israeli invasion of Lebanon, which resulted in the Jewish state's successful expulsion of members of the PLO from Beirut and the southern part of the war-torn nation, created new opportunities for peace. Lebanon represented the last base of military operations from which the PLO could mount terrorist attacks against Israel. Having lost its military base in Lebanon, the PLO could no longer achieve its aim of destroying Israel through terrorist violence, but would instead have to pursue a negotiated peace settlement with the Jewish state.

Reagan attempted to fully exploit the opportunities for peace created through the expulsion of members of the PLO from Beirut and South Lebanon. He attempted to do so through the peace plan he unveiled in a nationwide television address delivered from the KNBC studios in Burbank hours after members of the PLO departed Beirut on September 1, 1982. However, Reagan quietly shelved his peace plan after Israel flatly rejected his demand that the Jewish state withdraw from occupied Arab territories, a requirement which represented a central element of his proposal. Reagan followed the collapse of his peace plan with the establishment of the MNF designed to restore political stability to Lebanon which had been engulfed in a violent and bloody civil war since 1975. Reagan hoped that newfound stability in Lebanon would provide Israel incentives to make the political and territorial concessions required to achieve a just and lasting peace in the Middle East.

However, Reagan's hope of linking the MNF to his broader objective of reviving the moribund peace process in the Middle East was dealt a fatal blow by the bombing of the Marine barracks in Beirut on October 23, 1983. Reagan responded to the bombing in a confused, uncertain, and self-contradictory manner: He vowed to maintain the American military presence in Beirut, only to abruptly change course and order the withdrawal of the Marines when a resurgence in street fighting resulted in the seizure of control of the western half of the war-ravaged capital of Lebanon by Shiite and Druze militiamen. The bombing only reinforced Reagan's determination to pursue a pro–Israel policy in the Middle East. One month following the bombing, Reagan acted to formalize the strategic alliance between the United States and Israel, hoping to use the Jewish state as a counterweight against the efforts of radical forces to eliminate the American military presence in Beirut.

Reagan pursued his pro–Israel policy in the Middle East by scuttling a peace initiative Jordan and the PLO launched in 1985 designed to break the stalemate in the stalled peace process. Reagan flatly rejected PLO demands that the United States recognize the right of the Palestinians to exercise self-determination as a condition for lifting the prohibition Ford had imposed in 1975 against American contacts with the organization. Reagan's action came in response to a public relations campaign AIPAC launched in 1985 warning against any American contacts with the PLO.

By the end of 1985, American credibility in the Arab world had been sufficiently eroded by Reagan's pro–Israel policy in the Middle East that Washington's enemies in the region, led by Qaddafi, felt free to launch an international terrorist campaign in Western Europe, specifically targeted against facilities frequented by Americans. This campaign inexorably led the United States and Libya on a collision course, which culminated in the American bombing of Tripoli and Benghazi. The bombing is conventionally viewed as a legitimate American response to Libyan-sponsored international terrorism, and there is certainly substantial credence in this view. But the bombing can perhaps be more accurately viewed as an act of desperation by Reagan to resuscitate the loss of credibility the United States suffered in the Arab world through the pro–Israel policy in the Middle East the president had pursued. Reagan's strategy for restoring that lost credibility was based, not upon the pursuit of creative and enlightened diplomacy designed to advance the peace process, but through the president's determination to exercise and demonstrate the capability of the United States to use overwhelming military power to punish its enemies in the region, with America's foremost nemesis, Muammar Qaddafi, serving as the target. Qaddafi would serve as an example of what was in store for Washington's enemies who sought to challenge American power and influence in the Middle East. In the end, Reagan's efforts to restore America's lost credibility in the Arab world relied upon the use of military force against Qaddafi, and not the pursuit of evenhanded diplomacy designed to achieve a just and lasting peace in the Middle East.

Reagan Moves American Policy in the Middle East Further in Favor of Israel

During the 1970s the United States felt compelled to preserve the illusion, though not the reality, of pursuing an evenhanded policy in the Middle East in order to appease the Arab sheiks of the Persian Gulf who joined Iraq and Libya in imposing an oil embargo against Washington in retaliation for its support for Israel during the Yom Kippur War of 1973. American support for Israel was concealed under the guise of Washington's pursuit of step-by-step diplomacy Nixon initiated following the end of the 1973 conflict; the effort was designed to break the stalemate in the stalled peace process, which had languished since the Six-Day War of 1967. However, Reagan was determined to dispense with maintaining the appearance of pursuing an evenhanded American policy in the Middle East which his three predecessors had adopted. Rather, Reagan was committed to pursuing a policy based upon the provision of blunt, open, honest, and explicit support for Israel, without even maintaining the illusion of a sustained momentum toward peace which step-by-step diplomacy had created.

Reagan changed the direction of American policy in the Middle East in favor of Israel in two major ways. First, during the 1980 presidential campaign Reagan condemned the PLO as a terrorist organization, reversing long-standing American policy which was ambiguous on the issue of whether to characterize the group in this harsh and negative manner.[2] Second, following his assumption of the presidency, Reagan proclaimed that Israeli settlements in the occupied Arab territories were not illegal, reversing longstanding American policy which considered their establishment to represent a direct violation of international law.³ By essentially sanctioning Israeli settlements in the occupied Arab territories, Reagan, whether inadvertently or not, gave the Jewish state the green light to expand the pace of its settlement activity which Tel Aviv had undertaken following the Likud Party's assumption of power in 1977 under the leadership of Prime Minister Menachem Begin. As Noam Chomsky aptly notes, "Settlement was accelerated when Begin took power in 1977. There was further substantial expansion in the settlement program after President Reagan announced that he regarded West Bank settlements as 'legal.' This reversal of American policy (at least on a rhetorical level) set off a huge 'land grab' operation on the West Bank."⁴

The settlements were designed as a fait accompli which Israel would use to lay an irreversible claim to occupied Arab territories, thereby making a just and lasting peace in the Middle East politically impossible. Reagan's strong and unswerving support for Israel essentially resulted in the abrogation of America's traditional and longstanding role, however disingenuously it may have been performed, as an honest broker committed to a fair and balanced resolution of the Arab-Israeli conflict. By compromising America's position in this manner, Reagan failed to advance the peace process during the first two years of his presidency.

Despite his staunch and unequivocal support for Israel, Reagan remained committed to advancing the peace process. Consistent with the view of every president who has served in office since 1967, Reagan recognized that the Arab-Israeli conflict represented the major source of political instability in the Middle East. The Israeli invasion of Lebanon provided Reagan an opportunity to advance the peace process. By removing the PLO from Beirut and South Lebanon, the invasion had deprived the organization of its major base of operations from which to launch terrorist attacks against Israel.

The greater security afforded Israel from the military blow the Jewish state had inflicted upon the PLO in Lebanon would theoretically provide Tel Aviv the strategic incentives it needed to make the political and territorial concessions required to achieve a just and lasting peace in the Middle East. Operating upon this assumption, Reagan pursued a two-step initiative designed to jump-start the stalled peace process. First, on August 20, 1982, Reagan announced the establishment of the MNF, composed of token contingents of troops from the United States, France, and Italy.⁵ The mission of the MNF would be to ensure the safe and peaceful withdrawal of members of the PLO from Beirut. Second, on September 1 Reagan unveiled his peace plan for the Middle East hours after the withdrawal was successfully completed.

However, Israel flatly rejected Reagan's call for the withdrawal of the Jewish state from occupied Arab territories which represented a vital element of the president's peace plan. Reagan responded by quietly shelving his peace plan in deference to the objections of Israel. The Reagan Plan represented an effort to achieve a fair and balanced approach to the Arab-Israeli conflict, calling upon Israel to withdraw from occupied Arab territories in exchange for the recognition by its Arab neighbors of the right of the Jewish state to exist within secure and recognized borders. But Reagan's decision to drop his peace plan reflected the fact that his newly found commitment to the peace process had not resulted in any discernable change in American policy in the Middle Easxt which remained based upon the provision of firm and unyielding American support for the Jewish state.[6]

Reagan Announces Formation of the MNF in Beirut

On September 14, 1982, Beirut became engulfed in a new spasm of political violence when a 400-pound bomb destroyed the headquarters building of the Phalange Party, where the commander of its militia, Bashir Gemayel, who had been elected to the presidency of Lebanon and was awaiting his swearing in to office, was addressing a gathering of members of his organization. Gemayel was killed in the blast. On September 15 Israel responded to Gemayel's assassination by ordering its troops to occupy West Beirut, where they permitted Phalangist militiamen, enraged over the assassination of their leader, to enter the Palestinian refugee camps of Sabra and Shatila in Beirut.

Having spearheaded a seven-year military offensive to drive the PLO from Lebanon, which had fueled its bloody and internecine civil war, the Phalange Party had developed a strong enmity against the Palestinians. Not surprisingly, once they entered Sabra and Shatila, Phalangist militiamen proceeded to engage in the systematic massacre of hundreds of residents of the refugee camps during September 16–18, 1982. The grisly scenes of slaughter from the refugee camps were broadcast to a worldwide television audience.[7]

In response to the shock and horror over the Sabra and Shatila massacres which reverberated worldwide, Reagan decided to take action in order to restore political stability to Lebanon. To this end, on September 20, 1982,

Reagan delivered a nationwide television address from the Oval Office in which he announced the formation of a new MNF composed of token contingents of troops from the United States, France, Italy, and the United Kingdom. The mission of this newly reconstituted MNF was twofold: first, to facilitate the restoration of the sovereignty of the Lebanese government throughout its territory; and second, to ensure the withdrawal of all foreign military forces from the war-torn nation.[8]

The strategic assumption underlying the newly expanded mission of the MNF was that Israel would not make the political and territorial concessions for peace unless political stability was restored to Lebanon. In 1976 Syria had invaded Lebanon in an effort to end its bloody and internecine civil war which had erupted the previous year.[9] With Lebanon having fallen under Syrian and Israeli occupation, a very real potential existed for the outbreak of war between the two enemies for control of their small and weak neighbor. Reagan reckoned that if he could use the MNF to facilitate the restoration of the sovereignty of the Lebanese government throughout its territory, it would provide the political foundation upon which both Israel and Syria would see it in their mutual interests to withdraw. With the potential of a regional war between Israel and Syria for control of Lebanon defused, the Jewish state would feel sufficiently secure to make the political and territorial concessions required to establish a just and lasting peace in the Middle East. For Reagan, the road to peace in the Middle East went through Lebanon, and the president was willing to take the risks of sending Marines to Beirut because he believed it would reap substantial political dividends for the United States in advancing the peace process.

The Bombing of the American Embassy in Beirut

On April 18, 1983, the United States suffered a devastating blow in its effort to restore political stability to Lebanon when a delivery van carrying a ton of explosives detonated on the grounds of the American Embassy in Beirut. The midsection of the eight-story building collapsed, killing sixty-three individuals, including seventeen Americans. The explosion occurred as Robert C. Ames, the chief analyst of Middle East affairs for the Central Intelligence Agency (CIA), was convening a meeting with seven of his colleagues at the embassy. All eight CIA officials were killed in the explosion.[10]

Hours after the bombing, Amin Gemayel, whom the Lebanese Parliament had elected to the presidency to succeed his assassinated brother, Bashir, called Reagan to express his condemnation of the terrorist attack. The six-minute phone conversation concluded at 11:20 a.m. EST on April 18, 1983. The NSC produced a memorandum, marked "secret," which summarized the conversation. On May 23, 2000, the National Archives and Records Administration (NARA) declassified the memorandum, which reads as follows:

Gemayel: Hello?
Reagan: Mr. President. Good morning.
Gemayel: Good morning. How are you?
Reagan: Just fine.
Gemayel: I wanted to tell you how sorry I am, Mr. President, for the tragedy that happened to the embassy this noon [Beirut time].
Reagan: Well, I appreciate that very much, Mr. President, and I, of course, feel very badly myself and [about] what has happened, but I realize that that's the climate we're trying to solve.
Gemayel: Yes. You know there is no doubt that your courageous efforts to restore peace here in Lebanon has made some extremist unhappy. There is always a price for courage, as you know.
Reagan: Yes.
Gemayel: But I am confident also that such acts will not in any way discourage you from continuing to push for your peace initiative [in the Middle East] for which we are completely with you in this peace initiative.
Reagan: Well, rest assured, Mr. President, we're not going to retreat. We're going to continue [with the Reagan Plan].
Gemayel: We'll be together, sir. We'll be with you.
Reagan: Well, I appreciate that very much and we shall continue to fight to bring peace to the area.
Gemayel: Thank you. I wish to express also in my name and in the name of the Lebanese people my deepest condolences to you and the families of the victims.
Reagan: Well, thank you very much. I appreciate that very much. I appreciate that.
Gemayel: Thank you.
Reagan: Alright, and I shall pass that word on to them.
Gemayel: Thank you, goodbye.
Reagan: Alright, goodbye Mr. President.[11]

The bombing of the American Embassy in Beirut was designed to force an American withdrawal from the war-torn capital of Lebanon. However, if there were any illusions that a withdrawal might occur in response to the bombing, they were quickly put to rest when Reagan appeared in the Rose Garden and issued a statement on the terrorist incident at 11:50 a.m. EST on April 18, 1983, a half-hour following the conclusion of his conversation with Gemayel. The statement represented Reagan's first official response to the bombing. In his statement, Reagan vowed that the bombing would not deter the United States from pursuing its goals in Lebanon.

> We ... remain committed to the recovery by the Lebanese government of full sovereignty throughout all its territory. The people of Lebanon must be given a chance to resume their efforts to lead a normal life, free from violence, without the presence of unauthorized forces on their soil. And to this noble end, I rededicate the efforts of the United States.[12]

Through his statement, Reagan made it clear that the American military presence in Beirut would continue until the United States had achieved its two primary goals in Lebanon: the restoration of sovereignty of its government throughout its territory and the withdrawal of all foreign military forces from the war-torn nation.

On April 19, 1983, Howard J. Teicher, special assistant to the president and senior director of political-military affairs for the NSC, sent a memorandum to William P. Clark, assistant to the president for national security affairs, informing him, "Per Bud McFarlane's [a member of the NSC staff] request, a memo for Secretary [of State George P.] Shultz is attached asking [the] State [Department] to lead a presidential mission to Beirut to recover the bodies of Americans killed in Monday's [April 18] terrorist attack." Teicher recommended to Clark, "That you sign the memo." Clark marked the line under the word "Approve" and sent the memorandum, which the White House national security adviser received from Teicher, to Shultz.[13] In the memorandum, Clark informed Shultz:

> The President has directed that a presidential mission be dispatched in Beirut to retrieve the remains of Americans killed in the April 18 terrorist bombing of our embassy. It is requested that the mission be led by the Under Secretary of State (Political Affairs) and be composed of parent agencies and the National Security Council staff. A special air missions aircraft will be provided.[14]

On April 19, 1983, John M. Poindexter, deputy assistant to the president for national security affairs, sent a memorandum to Frederick J. Ryan, director of Presidential Appointments and Scheduling. In his memorandum, Poindexter recommended "that the President attend the arrival ceremony, to be organized by the military district of Washington, for the return of Americans killed in Beirut." Poindexter explained that the purpose of Reagan's attendance at the ceremony would be "to receive and honor the remains of the fallen Americans, to console the next of kin and recognize the contributions of their loved ones, to reiterate the U.S. commitment to our objectives in Lebanon, and to speak out against terrorism." Poindexter noted:

The tragedy in Beirut comes at a time when radical forces in the Middle East are trying to undermine the President's peace initiative. Given our stakes in the area, the President's involvement in Mid-East diplomacy, and the enormity of the tragedy, the President's participation would give special meaning to the arrival ceremony.[15]

Teicher quickly responded to Poindexter's request through a memorandum he sent to the deputy White House national security advisor. In his memorandum, Teicher informed Poindexter, "Per your request, attached is a schedule proposal for the President to attend the arrival ceremony at Andrews Air Force Base when the presidential delegation returns with the fallen Americans from Lebanon." Teicher recommended to Poindexter "that you sign the schedule proposal."[16]

Poindexter approved the schedule which would govern Reagan's attendance at the arrival ceremony at Andrews Air Force Base for the bodies of the Americans killed in the bombing of the American Embassy in Beirut. The ceremony was held on April 23, 1983. Reagan delivered a brief address at the ceremony.[17] In a nationwide radio address broadcast earlier in the day, Reagan reiterated that the bombing of the American Embassy in Beirut would not deter the United States from pursuing its mission to restore political stability to Lebanon: "More than ever, we're committed to giving the people of Lebanon the chance they deserve to lead normal lives, free from violence and the presence of all unwanted foreign forces on their soil. And we remain committed to the Lebanese government's recovery of full sovereignty throughout its territory."[18]

The Bombing of the Marine Barracks in Beirut

The bombing of the American Embassy in Beirut served as a prelude to the most severe terrorist attack the United States suffered until 9–11: the explosion at the Marine barracks in the war-torn capital of Lebanon. At 6:22 a.m. Beirut time on October 23, 1983, a driver rammed a truck carrying six tons of explosives into the four-story building serving as headquarters for American members of the MNF, destroying the concrete structure.[19] A total of 241 Marines were killed in the blast. Shortly thereafter, a bomb planted in a truck exploded near a nine-story building serving as headquarters for French members of the MNF, also destroying that concrete structure. Fifty-eight French paratroopers were killed in the blast.

The bombing of the American Marine barracks in Beirut occurred at 12:22 a.m. ET on October 23, 1983, while Reagan slept in the Eisenhower

Cottage of the Augusta National Golf Club, where he was spending the weekend. Two hours later Reagan was awakened by a call from Robert C. McFarlane, assistant to the president for national security affairs, who informed him of the bombing. Reagan responded to the news of the bombing by quickly flying back to Washington.[20] Upon his arrival at the White House, Reagan delivered his first public statement on the bombing eight hours following the terrorist attack.[21]

On the evening of October 23, Larry M. Speakes, assistant to the president and principal deputy press secretary, appeared in the White House Briefing Room and issued a statement to reporters announcing, "The President held extensive meetings today with his senior advisers to consider the United States response to the deliberate and heinous acts of international terrorism in Beirut against American and French forces." Speakes affirmed that the bombings of the headquarters buildings of the American and French members of the MNF, respectively, would not alter Reagan's commitment to maintain the presence of Marines in Beirut until their mission of restoring political stability to Lebanon was fully completed.

> One thing is clear: Those who sponsor these outrages believe they can intimidate the government of Lebanon, its people, and friends in the international community. They are wrong. We will not yield to international terrorism, because we know that, if we do, the civilized world will suffer and our values will be fair game for those who seek to destroy all we stand for.[22]

On October 24, Reagan called French president Francois Mitterrand to discuss the tragic events of the previous day. The White House prepared talking points for the call, marked "secret." On May 23, 2000, NARA declassified the talking points.

In those, Reagan was to have expressed to Mitterrand, "I hope you received the message I sent last evening. Allow me to express my deep sorrow over the loss of French lives in Lebanon. We have suffered terrible losses ourselves, but we remain committed to the search for peace and reconciliation in Lebanon." Reagan confirmed to Mitterrand the information Speakes had provided to reporters the previous day that the president had held extensive meetings with his national security advisers following his return to the White House hours after the bombing of the Marine barracks in Beirut: "I met with my national security advisers for over five hours yesterday. We conducted a detailed review of the situation in Lebanon and the broader security issues in the Middle East and the [Persian] Gulf." Reagan vowed to Mitterrand that the United States would take retaliatory military action in response to the bombing of the Marine barracks in Beirut: "For our part, we plan to retaliate ... once we have determined who perpetrated this heinous crime."

In his talking points, Reagan was to have assured Mitterrand that the United States would cooperate closely with France in order to ensure that the mission of the MNF — to restore political stability to Lebanon — was successfully completed.

> I have asked General [P.X.] Kelly, Commandant of the U.S. Marine Corps, who is leading our special mission to Lebanon, to consult closely with your mission about security in Lebanon. As noted in my message, I have asked George Shultz to discuss with his counterparts the possibility of an MNF foreign ministers' meeting later this week to review the situation and possible future steps.
> On the margins of this meeting, I would like George Shultz to discuss with [French Foreign] Minister [Claude] Cheysson in a most private manner how we could cooperate more closely to prevent future attacks on our forces. I would also like for them to review closer collaboration with regard to broader Middle East and security issues.[23]

Reagan Vows to Maintain the American Military Presence in Beirut

The bombing of the Marine barracks in Beirut represented the boldest and most audacious act undertaken by radical forces to drive American troops from the war-torn capital of Lebanon. The bombing confronted Reagan with a vexing dilemma. If Reagan ordered the withdrawal of the Marines from Beirut, it would send a clear message to America's enemies in the Middle East that the United States could be driven from Lebanon through terrorist violence, severely undermining Washington's credibility in the region. However, if Reagan failed to order such action, then the Marines would be exposed to additional acts of terrorism.

Reagan quickly decided that the costs of an American military withdrawal from Beirut outweighed the benefits. A withdrawal could embolden Washington's enemies to follow the bombing of the Marine barracks in Beirut with a concerted and coordinated terrorist campaign to eliminate American influence from the Middle East. Such a development would have economically and strategically disastrous consequences for the United States, given the vital interests Washington has in the region. For Reagan, Lebanon served as the front line in America's battle to maintain its influence in the Middle East in the face of a determined drive by Washington's enemies to remove this nation's presence from the region.

In the days following the bombing of the Marine barracks in Beirut, Reagan used two occasions to publicly defend his decision to maintain the American military presence in the war-ravaged capital of Lebanon. Reagan did so the day following the bombing in public remarks at the White House and in a subsequent nationwide television address. Reagan's defense of his policy in Lebanon was based upon talking points the White House produced. In his talking points, Reagan would argue that

> Stability in the Middle East — and progress toward peace there — is vital to world peace and to the health of the international economy. No region of the world is more crucial to our well-being at home. The outcome [of the civil war] in Lebanon will affect the future of the Middle East. The contest there is between those who want to settle their differences peacefully and radicals who seek dominance through fear and hate.... At stake is the right of a small nation, Lebanon, to live from outside threat and domination. It is a test of the kind of world we want our children to live in.

In his talking points, Reagan was to have warned of the dire consequences which would allegedly accrue from an American military withdrawal from Beirut.

> If violence and intimidation succeed [in Lebanon], it will be a devastating blow to the peace process and Israel's quest for true security.... If America's cause is defeated by brute force, our role in the world is much weakened everywhere. Friends who rely on us will be disheartened. We will all be less secure and less free. If we are driven out of Lebanon, the radicals, the rejectionists [against the peace process], the violent would have won. The message will be sent that relying on the Soviet Union pays off because you can't rely on the United States. If we, as Americans, decide we do not want the role and influence of a great power, I shudder to think of the world of anarchy and danger that lies ahead.

Given the dire consequences which would allegedly accrue from an American military withdrawal from Beirut, Reagan would conclude by vowing that the Marines would remain in the battle-scarred capital of Lebanon until they had completed their mission of restoring political stability to the war-torn nation: "We will not turn away [from Lebanon]. There is cause for hope. There is an attainable goal, but to reach it we must be courageous and we must be steadfast."[24]

Reagan's first opportunity to use his talking points to publicly defend American policy in Lebanon came in remarks he delivered to regional editors and broadcasters in the State Dining Room on October 24, 1983. Reagan warned that an American military withdrawal from Beirut would have disastrous economic and strategic consequences for the United States in the Middle East.

> We must not allow international criminals and thugs such as these [involved in the bombing of the Marine barracks in Beirut] to undermine the peace in Lebanon....

If others feel confident that they can intimidate us and our allies in Lebanon, they will become more bold elsewhere. If Lebanon ends up under the tyranny of forces hostile to the West, not only will our strategic position in the Eastern Mediterranean be threatened, but also the stability of the entire Middle East including the vast resource areas of the Arabian Peninsula.

Given the disastrous consequences which would allegedly accrue from an American military withdrawal from Beirut, Reagan categorically and emphatically affirmed that he would not even consider such action: "The United States will not be intimidated by terrorists.... The option we cannot consider is withdrawing [the Marines from Beirut] while their mission still remains."[25]

Reagan Links American Policy in Lebanon to the Peace Process

In the days following the bombing of the Marine barracks in Beirut, the White House produced another set of talking points for Reagan which linked American policy in Lebanon to the peace process. Reagan would begin by reiterating his argument that the presence of the Marines in Beirut was vital to preserving American interests in the Middle East.

> Our efforts in the Middle East and the presence of our Marines and the forces of our allies in Lebanon stem from a shared recognition that the peace and stability of this region are necessary conditions if we are to protect the vital interests on which so much of the world depends.... Lebanon should be seen as a microcosm of what is at stake in this vital region ... because the opponents we face in Lebanon would, given the chance, jeopardize our vital interests as a whole. They promote war and terror instead of peace and security. They thrive on chaos and recognize that they will not have their way if stability returned [to Lebanon]. The events of the past, especially those of last Sunday [October 23, 1983], are clearly intended to test our resolve and staying power. I am afraid the assumption underlying those events is that the U.S. is a helpless giant shackled by the specter of another unpopular war [like Vietnam].

In order to demonstrate American resolve against radical forces determined to drive the Marines from Beirut, Reagan was to have reiterated his commitment to maintain the American military presence in the war-ravaged capital of Lebanon: "We will join our principal allies and friends in the Middle East in reassuring the Lebanese people of our rock-ribbed support against the enemies of peace and stability who thrive on violence."

In his talking points, Reagan would have emphasized that the restoration of political stability to Lebanon was critical to the success of the peace process. Reagan would have argued,

> We confront extremists and factions of many stripes working overtime to block progress in resolving Lebanon's nightmare as a way of stalling progress on the Palestinian issue and a lasting regional peace.... The assumption is that if we and our allies can be made to abandon our objectives in Lebanon, we will be deterred from pursuing the broader peace process.

Reagan would have noted that "a resolution of the Lebanon tragedy is the first priority on our Middle East agenda." However, Reagan would have also made it clear that the ultimate goal of American policy in the Middle East, once political stability was restored to Lebanon, was a comprehensive peace settlement in the region: "To underline our commitment to peace, let me take this opportunity to rededicate my administration to the initiative we announced on September 1, 1982, because the resolution of the Palestinian issue is at rock bottom the best hope for a just and lasting peace in the Middle East."[26]

Reagan's nationwide television address delivered from the Oval Office on October 27, 1983, provided the president an opportunity to use his talking points in linking American policy in Lebanon to the peace process. Reagan pointedly warned that an American military withdrawal from Beirut would deal a fatal blow to the peace process, as no comprehensive peace settlement in the Middle East was possible as long as Israel's northern Arab neighbor remained engulfed in chaos and turmoil. Alluding to the peace plan for the Middle East he had unveiled on September 1, 1982, Reagan noted, "A little over a year ago ... I proposed a peace plan for the Middle East.... Before the necessary negotiations could begin, it was essential to get all foreign forces out of Lebanon and end the fighting there."

In taking a page from his talking points, Reagan argued that the restoration of political stability to Lebanon must be linked to the broader goal of achieving a comprehensive peace settlement in the Middle East.

> Beyond ... Lebanon, let us remember that our main goal and purpose is to achieve a broader peace in all of the Middle East. The factions and bitterness that we see in Lebanon are just a microcosm of the difficulties spread across much of that region. A peace initiative for the entire Middle East ... still offers the best hope for bringing peace to the region.

In addition to allegedly dealing a fatal blow to the peace process in the Middle East, Reagan ominously warned that an American military withdrawal from Beirut would also enhance the strategic power of Washington's enemies in the Middle East, resulting in a spread of Soviet influence throughout the region, which would threaten the industrial world's access to the vast oil reserves of the Persian Gulf.

> Let me ask those who say we should get out of Lebanon: If we were to leave Lebanon now, what message would that send to those who foment terrorism and instability?...
>
> If we turn our backs on Lebanon now, what would be the future of Israel?...
>
> If terrorism and intimidation succeed, it'll be a devastating blow to the peace process and to Israel's search for genuine security. It won't just be Lebanon sentenced to a future of chaos. Can the United States, or the free world for that matter, stand by and see the Middle East incorporated into the Soviet bloc? What of Europe and Japan's dependence on Middle East oil for the energy to fuel their industries? The Middle East is ... vital to our national security and economic well-being.[27]

Reagan's warning of the disastrous economic and strategic consequences which would allegedly accrue from an American military withdrawal from Beirut was echoed by Shultz. On October 24, 1983, Shultz made separate appearances before the Senate Foreign Relations and House Foreign Affairs Committees, respectively, to defend American policy in Lebanon. In his opening statement, Shultz reiterated Reagan's position that an American military withdrawal from Beirut would deal a fatal blow to the peace process.

> The stakes in Lebanon are high. If Lebanon is forced to yield to the dictates of outsiders, we will be in no position to encourage others in the Middle East to take the necessary steps to bring peace to the region. If terrorists can drive us from Lebanon, we would show weakness at a time when resolve is imperative. If we were to abandon the central government [of Lebanon], we would only make more distant the day when Arabs and Israelis will be willing to negotiate the future of the West Bank, the Palestinian people, and Israeli security.[28]

Reagan Signs Two National Security Decision Directives on Lebanon

On October 18, 1983, Reagan met with members of the National Security Planning Group (NSPG), chaired by the president and composed of his senior foreign and national security advisers. The purpose of the meeting was to review American policy in the Middle East. McFarlane used talking points to prepare for the meeting. The talking points reveal that Reagan was to have begun the meeting by explaining, "This meeting is to pick up where we left off last Friday [October 14, 1983]. The draft strategy paper used last evening is a useful framework to discuss our next steps in Lebanon and more generally the Middle East." Reagan was then to have turned to Shultz and asked, "Secretary Shultz, would you lead the discussion on the recommended course of action and the next steps for decision?" Shultz would have responded by announcing, "Mr. President, I think we have enough here to prepare a decision directive for your signature. We will circulate a draft to principals this afternoon and have it ready for your signature tomorrow."[29]

On October 29, 1983, McFarlane sent a memorandum, marked "secret," to Shultz; Secretary of Defense Caspar W. Weinberger; William J. Casey, director of the CIA; and John W. Vessey, chairman of the Joint Chiefs of Staff. The purpose of the memorandum was to advise the four officials of the Reagan Administration on the status of the National Security Decision Directive (NSDD) Shultz referred to in the NSPG meeting held on October 18. On August 8, 2000, NARA de-classified the memorandum which informed the four officials that

> The President has again reviewed the State [Department] memorandum (Our strategy in Lebanon and the Middle East) of October 17, 1983, which was discussed at the NSPG [meeting] on October 18, 1983.... In light of the discussion at the October 18 NSPG and of subsequent developments, the President has approved the decisions forwarded in the attached National Security Directive [111].[30]

Most of NSDD 111, which Reagan signed on October 28, 1983, remains classified. The declassified portion of NSDD 111 reveals that Reagan had approved a new two-track policy in the Middle East. The first track called for advancing the peace process, consistent with Reagan's reaffirmation of his commitment to achieve a comprehensive peace settlement in the Middle East he made in the days following the bombing of the Marine barracks in Beirut.

> We need to reassert American leadership in the wide range of challenges we face in the Middle East. The initial success and approval which greeted my September 1, 1982, peace initiative was because it was bold, innovative, and challenged long-held assumptions about obstacles to resolving the Palestinian problem. We must regain the initiative by acting once more in a bold way, especially in the aftermath of the Beirut tragedies.

However, contrary to Reagan's claim that his peace plan won a receptive ear in the Middle East, the proposal was flatly rejected by both Israel and the radical Arab nations, led by Syria: Israel, because it called for a withdrawal of the Jewish state from occupied Arab territories; Arab radicals, because it rejected the establishment of an independent Palestinian state. Support for the Reagan Plan only came from the moderate Arab nations, led by Egypt and Saudi Arabia.[31]

In addition to a renewed American commitment to reinvigorate the moribund peace process, NSDD 111 ordered an expansion in the rules of engagement regarding the strategic heights overlooking the Beirut International Airport where the Marines were based. Reagan had already expanded those rules of engagement in September 1983 when Druze militiamen launched a military offensive against Lebanese Army units occupying Suq al Gharb, a mountain town which overlooked the Marine base at the airport. Fearing that the Marines would be dangerously exposed to hostile fire should Suq al Gharb fall to Druze militiamen, on September 11 Reagan granted Colonel Timothy Geraghty, commander of the Marines in Beirut, authority to order American naval forces off the coast of Lebanon to attack the Druze militiamen. On September 19 Geraghty issued the order, and American naval forces launched a barrage of fire against Druze positions around Suq al Gharb, enabling the embattled Lebanese Army to retain its positions in the mountain town.[32]

NSDD 111 granted the commander of the Marines in Beirut authority to order American military action to prevent hostile forces from overrunning any place along the strategic heights overlooking the war-torn capital of Lebanon, extending beyond Suq al Gharb.

> The rules of engagement governing use of U.S. ground, naval, and air support for the strategic high ground which controls the approaches to Beirut will be modified. The changes should allow support for the Lebanese Armed Forces [LAF] such as that currently authorized for Suq al Gharb, when, in the judgment of the U.S. ground commander, LAF positions controlling the strategic arteries in Beirut are in danger of being overrun by hostile forces.[33]

During December 1–2, 1983, the NSPG held two meetings, respectively, to review American policy in Lebanon. On December 2 Poindexter sent a memorandum, marked "top secret," to Shultz, Casey, and Vessey, and Deputy Secretary of Defense W. Paul Thayer. On August 8, 2000, NARA declassified the memorandum which informed the four officials of the Reagan Administration that "As a result of this afternoon's NSPG meeting, the attached draft NSDD [117] is forwarded for comment and/or concurrence. Please provide response by noon, December 3, 1983."[34]

On August 9, 2000, NARA declassified NSDD 117. On December 5, 1983, Reagan signed NSDD 117 which was entitled "Lebanon." In NSDD 117 Reagan announced:

> Pursuant to the December 1, 1983, NSPG meeting on this subject, the following decisions will govern the next steps in Lebanon.
> 1. The decisions directed in NSDD 111 bearing on our diplomatic and military measures for Lebanon are reaffirmed. This specifically includes measures to assure the rules of engagement provide for an effective self-defense against a range of foreseeable threats.
> 2. The U.S. contingent of the MNF supported by naval surface and tactical air forces will pursue a policy of vigorous self-defense against all

attacks from any hostile quarter. Responsive attacks will be used to destroy targets originating fire if this can be done with minimal collateral damage.

3. In the event that the above action cannot be carried out due to risk of collateral damage or lack of precise information on the source of fire, the destructive fire will be directed against discrete military targets in unpopulated areas which are organizationally associated with the firing units.

4. Moreover, the United States will insist that the government of Lebanon undertake a more aggressive security posture in and around Beirut against radical Lebanese and foreign elements which pose a security risk to the MNF.[35]

NSDD 117 authorized an expansion in the rules of engagement for American military forces in Lebanon beyond those promulgated in NSDD 111. The latter NSDD authorized American military forces to engage in offensive action only if the strategic heights overlooking Beirut were in danger of falling under the control of hostile combatants. By contrast, NSDD 117 authorized a policy of "vigorous self-defense" wherever they came under hostile fire, regardless of whether control of the strategic heights overlooking Beirut was at stake. On December 3, 1983, the first opportunity to implement the newly-expanded rules of engagement came when Syrian anti-aircraft batteries fired at American reconnaissance planes undertaking surveillance missions over the Bekka Valley. Reagan responded the following day by ordering the American bombing of Syrian military positions from where the fire had originated.[36]

Members of Congress Urge a Reassessment of American Policy in Lebanon

Reagan's determination to deepen American involvement in the Lebanese Civil War through a policy of "vigorous self-defense," in which the president authorized American military forces in Beirut to respond to hostile fire and provide tactical and operational support for the embattled Lebanese Army controlling the strategic heights overlooking the Beirut International Airport, set off alarm bells on Capitol Hill. On September 29, 1983, Congress passed Senate Joint Resolution 159 which authorized the Marines to remain in Beirut for an additional eighteen months.[37] On October 12 Reagan signed the resolution.[38] The Senate passed the resolution by a close margin of fifty-four to forty-six. The vote broke down almost exclusively along party lines, with fifty-two Republicans and two Democrats supporting the resolution, and forty-three Democrats and three Republicans opposing it.[39] By contrast, the House of Representatives passed the resolution by a resounding margin of 270 to 161. Though the vote on the resolution largely broke down along party lines, the legislation enjoyed a large measure of bipartisan support in the House, which was absent in the Senate, with 140 Republicans and 130 Democrats supporting the resolution, and 134 Democrats and twenty-seven Republicans opposing it.[40] However, in light of Reagan's new policy of "vigorous self-defense," there was growing sentiment in Congress that its members should reassess their support for the American military presence in Beirut which they had authorized through passage of Senate Joint Resolution 159.

Leading the drive in Congress to reassess American policy in Lebanon were Representatives Thomas J. Downey of New York, Charles E. Bennett of Florida, and Leon Panetta of California. On December 14, 1983, the three representatives circulated a letter to the other members of the House in which they announced:

> We invite you to join us in writing Speaker [of the House] Thomas O'Neill to urge that the issue of U.S. military involvement in Lebanon be placed at the top of the agenda of issues to be discussed during the second session [of the 98th Congress]. The most recent use of U.S. military force in the Lebanese conflict, including the bombing a week ago of Syrian positions along the Beirut-Damascus highway, marks a fundamental departure from the mission of U.S. forces authorized by Congress last September. American casualties during the last fourteen months of the "peacekeeping" mission now stand at 257 killed in action. With no end to the bloodshed in sight, we feel it is essential that the mission of our Marines be spelled out in no uncertain terms, or they be extracted altogether from what is quickly becoming an ever-expanding military involvement [in the Lebanese Civil War].
>
> Congress must, of course, play a role in that decision. And it is with such considerations in mind that we have drafted the attached letter to the Speaker urging an immediate review of our deepening military involvement in the Lebanese conflict.[41]

On December 21, 1983, the three representatives sent their letter to O'Neill in which they informed the speaker of the House:

> We are deeply disturbed by our deepening military involvement in the Lebanese conflict. Two hundred fifty-seven brave Americans have died in the fourteen months of the "peacekeeping" mission, and the challenge of the nation is to ensure that those lives were not lost in vain.
>
> Congress acknowledged the possibility of American casualties when it approved legislation (Senate Joint Resolution 159) authorizing for eighteen months continued U.S. participation in the Multinational Force deployed in Beirut. Yet the authorization provided for the limited commitment of U.S.

Marines solely for the purposes of ensuring continued operation of the Beirut International Airport and security of the nearby neighborhoods.

With the American bombing earlier this month of Syrian positions many miles from the Lebanese capital, we have reached a new threshold in what has become an ever-expanding U.S. military presence in Lebanon. The inevitable result of our shifting policy has been to transform the perception of our soldiers over the last few months from neutral peacekeepers to active participants in a civil conflict. This is not the mission approved by Congress, nor is there an indication that the American people have approved such a policy.

Our purpose for writing is to urge that the issue of the U.S. military involvement in the Lebanese conflict be placed at the top of the agenda of issues to be discussed during the second session of the 98th Congress. It is essential that Congress have the opportunity to review our commitment [to the MNF] before additional lives are lost, and we look to your leadership to ensure continued congressional participation in the development of U.S. policy toward Lebanon.[42]

The campaign by Downey, Bennett, and Panetta to involve Congress in a reassessment of American policy in Lebanon received critical support from Dante B. Fascell of Florida, chairman of the House Foreign Affairs Committee. On December 14, 1983, Fascell issued a statement vowing to lead Congress in a review of American policy in Lebanon.

In authorizing the continued presence of the U.S. Marines in Lebanon, the Congress clearly intended both the letter and spirit of that authorizing legislation to be strictly observed....

Congress will soon undertake a review of that commitment in light of recent events. As we assert congressional authority in this area, my personal goal will be to act within the cooperative decision-making structure provided by the War Powers Resolution. I do not seek confrontation or constitutional impasse; instead my only objective will be to promote the best national security interests of the United States.

Fascell made it clear that the purpose of Congress' review of American policy in Lebanon would be to consider whether to support an American military withdrawal from Beirut: "Congress will be directly and properly involved in deciding whether a continued U.S. peacekeeping role is necessary or justified." Fascell concluded his statement by vowing to use his authority as chairman of the House Foreign Affairs Committee in order to ensure that Congress would subject American policy in Lebanon to a complete and thorough review: "As ... Chairman of this committee, I am ready to lead that review effort."[43] As chairman, Fascell was among the most influential voices in Congress on American foreign policy. Accordingly, Fascell's vow to lead a review of American policy in Lebanon guaranteed that this issue would be at the top of the agenda on Capitol Hill once the second session of the 98th Congress commenced in January 1984.

For Reagan, any congressional reassessment of American policy in Lebanon could have resulted in legislative action requiring a withdrawal of the Marines from Beirut. To counter this possibility, the NSC produced talking points which members of Congress who supported Reagan's policy in Lebanon were to use in defending the continued American military presence in Beirut. On January 24, 1984, Teicher sent a memorandum to seven members of the NSC staff: "Attached are draft papers which explain what we are about in Lebanon and could be used by supportive Congressmen in answering [the concerns of their] constituents. Some of these materials could also be useful with the press."[44]

The NSC's talking points essentially repeated the dire consequences which would allegedly accrue from an American military withdrawal from Beirut which Reagan and Shultz had made in the days following the bombing of the Marine barracks in Beirut. The talking points addressed the following question which governed American policy in Lebanon in the weeks and months following the bombing: "What could happen if the MNF is withdrawn now?" The NSC answered this question by making the following points:

1. [The] current "entente" of moderate Arab countries, which is developing to counter Syrian actions [in Lebanon], could collapse.
2. Jordan will be less willing to enter the peace process because of fear of Syrian reaction.
3. Saudi Arabia and others would be unwilling to stand up to Syrian and Libyan objections to [the] re-entry of Egypt to the Arab world [as a result of Arab opposition to the Camp David peace treaty].
4. [Arab] Gulf states would doubt [the] U.S. commitment to their security and U.S. staying power [in the Middle East].
5. [An American military withdrawal from Beirut] would be perceived as [a] major Soviet victory which would enhance [the] Soviet status in the region.
6. [The] government of Lebanon would have less counterweight to [the] Syrian presence [in Lebanon] as it tried to sort out its problems and would most likely fall.
7. Political "reconciliation" [in Lebanon] would be on Syrian terms.
8. Without a chance to achieve political reconciliation on Lebanese (rather than Syrian) terms, Lebanon will remain internally unstable.

9. Instability in Lebanon threatens Israeli security and keeps alive the possibility of a Syrian-Israeli confrontation in Lebanon.⁴⁵

The NSC's defense of American policy in Lebanon fell upon deaf ears in Congress. By the time the second session of the 98th Congress opened in January 1984, there was increasing clamor among lawmakers to require an American military withdrawal from Beirut. This manifested itself in the circulation of a draft concurrent resolution in the House on February 1 which would have required "the prompt and orderly withdrawal of the United States Armed Forces participating in the Multinational Force in Lebanon." The resolution argued that such action was required because

> The situation in Lebanon is drifting out of control and the administration's policy regarding Lebanon is not working. The United States is reacting to events rather than implementing policies which are in the national interest of the United States.... The failure of the administration's policy has led to widespread concern among the American people that continued participation by United States Armed Forces is not in the national interest.⁴⁶

The State Department was determined to defeat any effort in Congress to require an American military withdrawal from Beirut. To this end, on February 1, 1984, the State Department prepared a response to the draft concurrent resolution being circulated in the House which would have required a withdrawal. Representing the department would be Undersecretary of State for Political Affairs Lawrence S. Eagleburger, who would issue an opening statement outlining the Reagan Administration's position on the resolution before members of the Foreign Affairs Committee, which would exercise jurisdiction over the legislation upon its introduction in the House. In his statement opposing the resolution, Eagleburger would have argued:

> Lebanon is a moderate country — indeed a democracy and long-time friend of the United States ... and is under assault for that very reason.
> If the forces of extremism are permitted to overthrow a moderate government ... what chances are there that other moderate Arab states will risk committing themselves to peace [with Israel]? If extremism takes over in Lebanon, it will strengthen the forces of extremism in the entire Middle East, and weaken and dishearten all those who believe in moderation and negotiation. The security of Israel is bound to be affected. To put it positively, if those who believe in peace succeed in Lebanon, it will strengthen the forces of peace in the entire region.⁴⁷

Opposing the State Department in urging the White House to defeat efforts in Congress to require an American military withdrawal from Beirut was Donald Rumsfeld, the president's special envoy to the Middle East. On February 1, 1984, Rumsfeld urged introduction of an alternative resolution to the one being considered in the House which would have required a withdrawal. Unlike the House resolution, Rumsfeld's proposed measure would encourage Reagan to consider a withdrawal of some, though by no means all, of the Marines from Beirut.

> The President is encouraged ... in consultation with the government of Lebanon and other nations presently participating in the MNF, to consider possible redeployment of some elements of U.S. Armed Forces authorized to participate in the MNF...to positions where their presence will demonstrate [the] U.S. commitment to a unified and independent Lebanon, and to the extent possible, reduce their exposure to hostilities.[48]

Reagan Signs NSDD 123

Eagleburger never had an opportunity to appear before members of Congress to oppose the concurrent resolution being circulated in the House which would have required an American military withdrawal from Beirut. This is because, as the resolution was being circulated, the NSC was laying the groundwork for Reagan to order such action on his own, consistent with Rumsfeld's recommendation. On February 1, 1984, McFarlane sent a memorandum, marked "top secret," to Shultz, Weinberger, Casey, Vessey, and David Stockman, director of the Office of Management and Budget. In his memorandum, McFarlane informed the four officials of the Reagan Administration, "The President has approved the attached National Security Decision Directive (NSDD 123). Knowledge of and access to this document must be restricted to the minimum number of people required to implement the actions directed."[49] The text of NSDD 123 was marked "top secret." On November 15, 2000, NARA declassified McFarlane's memorandum and most of the text of NSDD 123.

Signed by Reagan on February 1, 1984, NSDD 123 announced:

> At an NSC meeting held on January 26, 1984, the Chairman, Joint Chiefs of Staff presented a plan for modifications to the U.S. military role in Lebanon.
>
> The plan provides for possible actions the government of the United States could take to assist the government of Lebanon in responding to changing threats and military requirements. The GOL [government of Lebanon] faces three significant military problems: the need to increase the size and effectiveness of the LAF so that the GOL can extend its area of control; the need to deter or counter firing on Greater Beirut from Syrian-controlled areas; and the need to improve GOL capability to combat terrorism.
>
> In light of the JCS presentation and attendant analysis, the following actions, which strengthen our capability to carry out U.S. policy in Lebanon, are approved in principle.

1. Improve the LAF capability for counter-battery operations by repositioning the target acquisition radar presently in the country, possibly providing additional radar capability, improving the flow of targeting information to the LAF, providing counter-battery training, and providing more modern artillery ammunition.
2. To enhance the safety of MNF personnel, authority would be granted for U.S. naval forces to provide naval gunfire and air support against any units in Syrian-controlled territory in Lebanon firing into Greater Beirut as well as any unit conducting a hostile attack directly on MNF or U.S. personnel or facilities. Existing authorities for the conduct of self-defense are reaffirmed.
3. Provide counter-terrorism [and] counter-insurgency training to the LAF by deploying a company-size unit of Special Operations Forces to Lebanon to act as trainers.
4. Accelerate U.S. equipment deliveries to the LAF and provide increased training.

To assure readiness to implement actions listed above, the following should be undertaken immediately:

1. Ambassador Rumsfeld is authorized to consult promptly with the GOL on the concept outlined above. The objective is to encourage President Gemayel to request the type of reorientation described above from the U.S. and other MNF contributors. The results of this consultation should be reported and assessed. Possible modifications to this plan should be proposed, if necessary, prior to consultations with MNF contributors.
2. The Secretary of Defense and the Chairman, JCS, shall develop for the President's review, a proposed timetable for the phase down of USMNF military personnel ashore and a plan for the continuing U.S. military presence offshore, taking full account of political, as well as military, considerations. Implementation of these will be closely integrated into actions directed in the NSDD. In accordance with my suggestion on January 26, consideration should be given to quartering at least a portion of the residual force at the BIA [Beirut International Airport].[50]

Under NSDD 123, the United States would provide the Lebanese Army the capability to assume security over the war-torn nation through arms transfers and training. This would allow Reagan to achieve the ultimate objective of NSDD 123: the phased American military withdrawal from Beirut. By February 1, 1984, Reagan had come to the painful realization that the American military presence in Beirut had lost the support of Congress. Substantial opposition to this presence existed in Congress even before the bombing of the Marine barracks in the war-torn capital of Lebanon. As we have seen, Senate Joint Resolution 159, which authorized the Marines to remain in Beirut for eighteen months, was passed with a slim majority in the Senate. To be sure, substantial support for the resolution existed in the House; but in light of the bombing of the Marine barracks in Beirut, and

Reagan's decision to expand the rules of engagement for American military forces in Lebanon, it is safe to assume that support for the American military presence in Beirut had substantially dissipated in the House in the weeks and months following passage of Senate Joint Resolution 159. Indeed, it was only a matter of time before the passage of new legislation requiring an American military withdrawal from Beirut. The circulation of a concurrent resolution in the House on February 1, 1984, requiring a withdrawal represented the first step in passage of such legislation, which was imminent. Accordingly, Reagan was faced with the following two alternatives: either he could order a withdrawal or Congress would do so. To spare himself the humiliation of being forced by Congress to order a withdrawal, Reagan decided to do so on his own.

However, before NSDD 123 could be implemented, Beirut became engulfed in a new round of chaos and turmoil. On February 2, 1984, heavy and intense fighting erupted between the Lebanese Army and the Shiite Amal militia in West Beirut. Shiite members of the army refused to take part in its military offensive against their co-religionists of the Amal militia. On February 4 Moslem members of the Cabinet resigned in protest against the offensive, resulting in the immediate collapse of the government. With Shiites having defected from the army, the offensive collapsed, and West Beirut fell under the control of Amal and Druze militiamen on February 6.[51]

The crisis in Beirut created three new and politically devastating realities for the United States in Lebanon. First, with a Lebanese government existing in name only, Reagan's hopes of using the MNF to facilitate the restoration of the sovereignty of the Beirut regime throughout its territory were permanently dashed: Obviously this objective could not be attained since no functioning government existed. Second, with the Lebanese Army having disintegrated along sectarian lines, Reagan's plan to transfer security over the war-torn nation to its military, pursuant to NSDD 123, could obviously not be implemented. Third, the presence of anti–American Shiite and Druze militiamen in West Beirut, where the MNF was based, left the Marines dangerously exposed to additional acts of terrorism.

Reagan Orders the American Military Withdrawal from Beirut

With the political and strategic tide having suddenly and decidedly turned against the United States in Lebanon, Reagan had no alternative but to order an immediate American military withdrawal from Beirut. The primary mission of the MNF was to facilitate the restoration of the sovereignty of the Lebanese government throughout its territory, which obviously could not be achieved in the wake of the collapse of the regime in Beirut. The continued presence of the MNF in Beirut was sure to invite additional acts of terrorism against the Marines which would destroy what little support existed in Congress for the American military presence in the war-torn capital of Lebanon.

With the MNF in complete shambles, and the potential for another devastating terrorist attack against the Marines now ominously looming, on February 7, 1984, Reagan issued a statement in which he announced that he was ordering an American military withdrawal from Beirut.[52] The withdrawal of French, Italian, and British troops from Beirut quickly followed, bringing a quick end to the ill-fated mission of the MNF.[53] The American exit from Beirut created the worldwide impression, which was largely true, that the Marines had been driven from Lebanon through terrorist violence.

Reagan's decision to order the American military withdrawal from Beirut severely undermined his commitment to preserve American economic and strategic interests in the Middle East in the face of the chaos and turmoil which engulfed Lebanon. Reagan had repeatedly vowed that he would not order a withdrawal, warning that such action would have devastating consequences for American interests in the Middle East. In a complete and abrupt reversal, and even repudiation, of his previous position, Reagan was now ordering such action. In the wake of Reagan's about-face, he appeared to be irresolute, vacillating, uncertain, and even unreliable, in confronting the challenge of terrorist violence in Beirut. He repeatedly proclaimed his determination not to allow American policy in Lebanon to be influenced by the specter of terrorism; then in a repudiation of his position, he suddenly ordered an American military withdrawal from Beirut when the deteriorating security situation in the war-torn capital of Lebanon greatly heightened prospects for additional acts of terrorism against the Marines. Given the hopeless circumstances Reagan confronted in Beirut, one cannot argue with his correct decision to order the withdrawal. But the withdrawal itself represented a tacit admission by Reagan that his decision to send the Marines to Beirut in the first place was a mistake, and the president had failed to acknowledge his error until the devastating bombing of their barracks in the war-ravaged capital of Lebanon. When it came to Beirut, Reagan had completely lost credibility: His actions defied his words regarding the American military presence in the battle-scarred capital of Lebanon, and his mishandling of the entire Beirut fiasco would have grave implications for Washington's interests in the Middle East.

The loss of credibility Reagan suffered as a result of the Beirut fiasco came on the heels of his mishandling of his peace plan, wherein, with great fanfare, he had unveiled his proposal only to withdraw it in the face of Israeli objections. Reagan saw the MNF mission in Beirut as a means to salvage his peace plan, believing that Israel would feel more secure in entering into negotiations with its Arab neighbors once political stability was restored to Lebanon. With the failure of the mission, Reagan was now left with no options for resuscitating his peace plan.

Indeed, as we have seen, Reagan had repeatedly vowed to revive the moribund peace process in the days and weeks following the bombing of the Marine barracks in Beirut. However, Reagan's renewed commitment to the peace process was conditioned upon the restoration of political stability to Lebanon. Reagan reckoned that as long as Israel's northern neighbor remained engulfed in chaos and turmoil, the Jewish state could not be expected to make the political and territorial concessions required to achieve a just and lasting peace in the Middle East.

Reagan's decision to order the American military withdrawal from Beirut, in the midst of the continuing violence and instability besetting Lebanon, resulted in the president's final abandonment of his commitment to advance the peace process. With the MNF having completely failed to make any contribution to restoring political stability to Lebanon, Reagan concluded that he could not require Israel to make the political concessions required to achieve a just and lasting peace in the Middle East. Rather, Reagan was determined to support Israel's position that the Jewish state should not make any such concessions. With Reagan in complete agreement with Israel on the peace process, he reverted to his original policy, pursued prior to the Jewish state's invasion of Lebanon, of linking the interests of Washington in the Middle East closely and firmly to those of Tel Aviv.

Reagan Formalizes the Strategic Alliance Between the United States and Israel

The bombing of the American Marine barracks in Beirut persuaded Reagan that American strategic interests in the Middle East would be best served by strengthening, broadening, deepening, and enhancing the alliance the United States has enjoyed with Israel since its creation in 1948. The bombing served as a vivid reminder, if one was needed, of the fanatic determination of America's enemies in Lebanon to drive the Marines from Beirut. As we have seen, Reagan was convinced that such an outcome would deal a severe blow to American interests in the Middle East, and have serious repercussions for the ability of Washington to maintain its influence in the region. To forestall this outcome, Reagan decided to formalize the strategic alliance between the United States and Israel. Reagan intended to procure Israeli assistance in preserving American influence in Lebanon and the broader Middle East.

Israel would serve as a surrogate to protect American interests in the Middle East, beginning in the nation where the United States was confronting its stiffest challenge in the region — Lebanon. This was consistent with Reagan's long-time and firmly-held belief that Israel represented a strategic asset to the United States in the Middle East. In an article published in the August 15, 1979, edition of *The Washington Post*, Reagan attacked the Carter Administration for allegedly failing to recognize the strategic value of Israel to the United States.

> American policymakers downgrade Israel's geopolitical importance as a stabilizing force, as a deterrent to radical hegemony, and as a military offset to the Soviet Union. The fall of [the Shah of] Iran has increased Israel's value as perhaps the only remaining strategic asset in the region on which the United States can truly rely; other pro–Western states in the region, especially Saudi Arabia and the smaller [Persian] Gulf kingdoms are weak and vulnerable.[54]

In acknowledging Reagan's view that Israel represented a strategic asset to the United States in the Middle East, Lou Cannon notes:

> Reagan operated under the assumption that U.S. interests were linked to those of Israel.... While his views on most other subjects changed during his metamorphosis from liberal Democrat to conservative Republican, Reagan remained staunchly pro–Israel.... He came to regard Israel as a strategic bulwark against Soviet intervention in the Middle East.

In a position paper on American policy in the Middle East which he issued during the 1980 presidential campaign, Reagan declared, "The crucial element determining the success or failure of American policy [in the Middle East] is the fate of Israel."[55]

Reagan's strong and unswerving support for Israel was shared by members of the NSC staff. Following the bombing of the Marine barracks in Beirut, the NSC produced a document entitled "Rebuilding U.S.–Israel Relations." The purpose of the document was to urge Reagan to strengthen the strategic alliance between the United States and Israel. The document argued:

> The United States is at a critical juncture in the Middle East with its interests under serious threat in Lebanon and the Persian Gulf. Rebuilding the strategic alliance with Israel is a crucial factor in protecting these interests.

> Action needs to be taken now because the Soviet [military] build-up in Syria and Syria's policy in Lebanon pose a serious threat, not only to Israel, but also to U.S. power and prestige in the Eastern Mediterranean and our position of influence in the Middle East.

The NSC argued that the United States had failed to utilize Israel as a strategic bulwark against the threat the Soviet Union and its primary client state in the Middle East — Syria — allegedly posed to American interests in the region.

> The existence of this threat has not ... diminished the level of mistrust [of the United States] in Jerusalem because Israel finds itself excluded from military cooperation with the United States despite its ability to make a difference to the Soviet and Syrian calculus ... Israel and its friends in the United States find it difficult to understand the motivation behind the exclusion of Israel from the American defense concept.

In order to counter the threat that the Soviet Union and Syria allegedly posed to American interests in the Middle East, the NSC urged Reagan to strengthen the strategic alliance between the United States and Israel.

> A strategic understanding [between the United States and Israel] involving coordination against Syria and the Soviet Union and longer term military cooperation would serve our immediate needs in Lebanon and our overall interests in the Eastern Mediterranean. This understanding is already long overdue and has weakened our deterrent posture against Syria and the Soviet Union. Given the high profile of Soviet involvement in Syria, the need for such an understanding is urgent. Joint military exercises in the Eastern Mediterranean, military cooperation, and pre-positioning arrangements in Israel would go a long way toward restoring Israel's trust in U.S. policy [in the Middle East] at the same time as it served American interests. Given the clear threat that our Arab friends now face from Soviet-backed radicalism, their objections [to the Israeli-American alliance] can weigh less heavily in our calculus.

The NSC concluded its document by urging Reagan to quickly schedule a summit meeting with Prime Minister Yitzak Shamir in order to reach agreement on measures which would strengthen, broaden, deepen, and enhance the strategic alliance between the United States and Israel: "At the earliest opportunity the Prime Minister and Defense Minister [of Israel] should be invited to Washington for a detailed exchange of views designed to lay the basis for a cooperative approach to our common concerns."[56]

Reagan quickly acted upon the NSC's recommendations by scheduling a summit meeting with Shamir at the White House. Reagan affirmed his decision to formalize this alliance through NSDD 115 which he signed on November 26, 1983, two days before Shamir arrived in Washington to hold a two-day summit meeting with the president. In NSDD 115 Reagan declared:

> The forthcoming visit of Prime Minister Shamir affords us a unique opportunity to make progress on our Middle East agenda and to develop a more mature strategic relationship with the government of Israel. In order to put these discussions in a proper strategic context, we need to stress that, from the USG [United States government] perspective, the array of threats to our vital interests in the Eastern Mediterranean, the Middle East, and Southwest Asia posed by the Soviet Union, Syria, Libya, and the fundamentalist Islamic regime in Iran dictate that we enhance and deepen our security cooperation with Israel and the moderate Arab states.

Reagan made it clear that his commitment to strengthening the strategic alliance between the United States and Israel did not reflect any weakening in his commitment to the peace process: "The U.S. remains committed to the [peace] process ... as amplified and elaborated in my initiative of September 1, 1982." However, Reagan failed to explain how he could remain committed to his peace plan for the Middle East while strengthening America's strategic alliance with the very nation in the region which remained most adamantly opposed to his proposal — Israel. In truth, Reagan had one of two choices: either to pursue his peace plan by sacrificing American relations with Israel, or abandoning his proposal altogether in favor of strengthening the alliance between Washington and Tel Aviv. Reagan, of course, chose the latter option, and his stated commitment in NSDD 115 to pursue his peace plan represented an exercise in disingenuousness.

Reagan concluded by declaring, "In signing this [directive] I still believe that we must retain some plausibility and persuade Israel that our only hope for peace depends on not driving a wedge between ourselves and the moderate Arab states."[57] However, Reagan failed to acknowledge the fact that by strengthening, broadening, deepening, and enhancing the strategic alliance between the United States and Israel, Washington would be necessarily driving a wedge between itself and the moderate Arab nations, all of which, with the exception of Egypt, remained sworn enemies of the Jewish state. As we will see, this would have wide-ranging implications for Reagan's ability to mobilize the support of the moderate Arab nations for the United States in its bitter and acrimonious conflict with Libya which occurred in 1986.

Reagan officially announced his decision to formalize the strategic alliance between the United States and Israel at a joint news conference with Shamir on November 29, 1983, at the South Portico of the White House following the conclusion of their two-day summit meeting. With Shamir standing at his side, Reagan announced, "We have agreed to increase our cooperation in areas where our interests coincide, particularly in the political and military areas." Addressing the issue of Israeli-American military co-operation, Reagan declared:

> I am pleased to announce that we have agreed to establish a joint political-military group to examine ways in which we can enhance U.S.–Israeli co-operation. This group will give priority attention to the threat to our mutual interest posed by increased Soviet involvement in the Middle East. Among the specific areas to be considered are combined planning, joint exercises, and requirements for [the] pre-positioning of U.S. equipment in Israel.

In addition to enhanced Israeli-American military co-operation, Reagan announced that he and Shamir had reached agreement to involve the United States in a major effort to stimulate the development of the Israeli defense industry.

> We've agreed to take a number of other concrete steps aimed at bolstering Israel's economy and security. These include asking Congress for improved terms for our security assistance to Israel; using military assistance for development of the Lavi aircraft in the United States and for offshore procurement of Lavi components manufactured in Israel; permitting U.S. contractors to enter into contracts with the government of Israel, consistent with U.S. law, which would allow Israeli industry to participate in the production of weapons systems procured with foreign military sales credits; [and] offering to negotiate a free trade area with Israel.[58]

During his presidency, Reagan succeeded in forging a political consensus in Washington which conceived Israel as a strategic asset to the United States in the Middle East. As Bernard Reich aptly notes:

> In the 1980s Israel increasingly came to be viewed as a strategic asset and the only reliable ally of the United States in the Middle East by Ronald Reagan, other policymakers as well as Congressman, and other public officials. U.S. economic and military assistance had risen to $3 billion annually, all of it in grants, and was supplemented by millions more for special arrangements. Strategic co-operation became the catch-phrase among those who argued that Israel could be useful in supporting U.S. interests throughout the Middle East.[59]

Reagan Scuttles the Jordanian-Palestinian Peace Initiative

With Reagan having decided to shelve his peace plan in the face of Israeli objections, and his efforts to revive his proposal through the restoration of political stability in Lebanon having died in the rubble of the destruction of the Marine barracks in Beirut, the peace process came to an abrupt halt. To revive the moribund peace process, on February 11, 1985, King Hussein of Jordan and Yasser Arafat, chairman of the PLO, unveiled a peace initiative of their own. The initiative called for the establishment of a joint Jordanian-Palestinian delegation which would represent the Palestinians in peace talks with Israel. Those talks would take place through an international conference which representatives of Israel and its Arab neighbors would attend.[60]

However, no Middle East peace talks could be held until the United States and the PLO entered into a formal dialogue, for the obvious reason that both sides had vital roles to play in the peace process. In exchange for Israel's willingness to sign a second disengagement agreement with Egypt in 1975, Ford assured Tel Aviv that the United States would have no contacts with the PLO until the organization recognized the right of the Jewish state to exist and accepted United Nations Security Council Resolutions 242 and 338. Those resolutions called upon the negotiation of a comprehensive peace settlement in the Middle East in which Israel would withdraw from occupied Arab territories in exchange for acceptance by its Arab neighbors of the right of the Jewish state to exist within secure and recognized borders. The Foreign Aid Authorization Act of 1985 added a third condition the PLO would have to meet before the United States agreed to enter into a formal dialogue with the organization: that the group would have to renounce the use of terrorism.[61]

Consistent with his view that the PLO was a terrorist organization and his opposition to Palestinian statehood, Reagan was very reluctant to provide support for the Jordanian-Palestinian peace initiative. True, Reagan initially made a positive overture to Jordan and the PLO, authorizing Richard Murphy, assistant secretary of State for Near Eastern and South Asian Affairs, to visit Amman on August 9, 1985. The purpose of the visit was to enable Murphy to meet with members of a Jordanian-Palestinian delegation which Jordan and the PLO had designated to represent the Palestinians in future peace talks with Israel. However, Reagan ordered a cancellation of the meeting at the last minute.[62] Reagan's action came in response to Israeli objections to the meeting. In an interview with Madiha Rashid al-Madfai, a member of the American diplomatic team involved in the planning for the meeting candidly admitted, "What Jordan could see was a U.S. which could not, or would not, move without Israel's consent. Israel objected to the whole process."[63]

Israeli objections to Murphy's planned meeting with a delegation of Palestinians in Amman was part of a larger public relations campaign the leading member of its Washington lobby, AIPAC, launched on August 6,

1985, warning against any American contacts with the PLO.[64] Consistent with its status as Israel's primary representative in Washington, AIPAC constituted an important political constituency, and Reagan was determined to avoid offending the interest group on the sensitive issue of establishing American contacts with the PLO.[65] As al-Madfai aptly notes:

> It was only when the world press began speculating about the identity of the chosen Palestinians in the delegation that the Zionist lobby in Washington decided to voice publicly its objections to the intended meeting [between Murphy and members of the delegation] and apply such pressure on the administration that the latter began, as King Hussein put it in his address to the nation on February 19, 1986, "to justify, then defend, and finally retreat from its obligations [to enter into a dialogue with the PLO], as stated to Jordan."[66]

Despite the cancellation of Murphy's planned meeting with members of a joint Jordanian-Palestinian delegation in Amman, the Reagan Administration entered into indirect contacts with the PLO through the auspices of Jordan. The purpose of those contacts was to determine the basis upon which the United States and the PLO could enter into a formal dialogue which remained essential to the success of the Jordanian-Palestinian peace initiative. To this end, on January 27, 1986, Arafat informed the Reagan Administration that he was willing to accept American terms for the opening of a dialogue, but only if the United States recognized the right of the Palestinians to exercise self-determination, which was tantamount to the president's announcement of support for the establishment of a Palestinian state. This ran counter to the expression of opposition to Palestinian statehood the president had made in his nationwide television address on September 1, 1982, in which he unveiled his peace plan for the Middle East.

On February 5, 1986, the Reagan Administration informed Arafat that the White House would reaffirm existing American policy which recognized the legitimate rights of the Palestinians. But the administration made it clear that the White House would not recognize the right of the Palestinians to exercise self-determination. Israel remained flatly opposed to Palestinian statehood, and Reagan was determined that American policy on this issue remain consistent with that of the Jewish state. Nevertheless, the Reagan Administration conceded that representatives of the Palestinians would be free to pursue their demand for statehood in any peace talks they might enter into with Israel.

On February 6, 1986, Arafat responded by reaffirming that he would not accept American terms for the opening of a dialogue between the United States and the PLO unless the Reagan Administration recognized the right of the Palestinians to exercise self-determination, which the White House remained adamant in its refusal to do. The impasse between the United States and the PLO over the thorny issue of Palestinian statehood resulted in the collapse of the Jordanian-Palestinian peace initiative. On February 19 Hussein announced in a nationwide television address that he was abandoning the initiative.[67]

By the end of 1985 Reagan had linked the interests of the United States so closely to those of Israel that Washington was incapable of serving as an honest broker in the Arab-Israeli conflict, resulting in continuing stalemate in the peace process, and a severe erosion of American credibility in the Arab world.[68] Hussein, a key and longtime Arab ally of the United States, acknowledged this fact in an interview with *The New York Times* in March 1984 in which the king delivered an uncharacteristically blunt attack against Washington, charging, "The U.S. is not free to move [in its Middle East policy] except within the limits of what AIPAC, the Zionists, and the State of Israel determine for it."[69]

Dine Praises the Improvement in Israeli-American Relations

Reagan's decision to formalize the strategic alliance between the United States and Israel did not go unnoticed by AIPAC. Addressing the annual policy conference of AIPAC in Washington on April 6, 1986, Thomas A. Dine, executive director of the interest group, argued that Israeli-American relations were better during the Reagan Administration than they had been at any previous point in time since the creation of the Jewish state in 1948.

> This relationship today between the United States and Israel is excellent. This relationship has entered a revolutionary era. We are no longer talking about a transformation of that relationship; we are talking about a revolution. The old order in which Israel was regarded as a liability, a hindrance to America's relationship with the Arab world, [and] a loud and naughty child — that order has crumbled. In its place, a new relationship is being built, one in which Israel is treated as — and acts as — an ally, not just a friend, an asset, rather than a liability, a mature and capable partner, [and] not some vassal state.

Dine argued that Reagan's decision to formalize the strategic alliance between the United States and Israel during his summit meeting with Shamir in November 1983 represented the foundation for the substantial improvement in Israeli-American relations which had occurred during the president's tenure in office.

It is hard to believe that barely two years have passed since the American President and the Israeli Prime Minister announced that the two countries would embark on joint planning, joint exercises, and pre-positioning of military equipment in Israel. But at President Reagan's initiative and in pursuit of his vision, Israel is now being treated as an ally. What were mere words at the outset of Ronald Reagan's Presidency have now been translated into tangible actions undertaken by both countries in pursuit of their common interests as fighting democracies.

Dine argued that Reagan's decision to formalize the strategic alliance between the United States and Israel was vital to the interests of the Jewish state.

> This [strategic] relationship is vital to the future of Israel for several reasons. First, to have the United States standing by Israel in this way sends a strong deterrent signal to radical forces in the Arab world, and to the Soviet Union. It tells them that any thought of driving a wedge between the U.S. and Israel, about isolating Israel in order to destroy the Jewish state, is foreclosed.
>
> Second, strategic cooperation is improving Israel's access to the most advanced American technologies, and these will contribute significantly to Israel's defense.
>
> Third, the President has said that the U.S. will consider the use of Israeli facilities to stockpile U.S. defense items for joint use in preparation for a possible emergency in the region. Pre-positioning will strengthen the ability of U.S. forces to maintain security there [in the Middle East], while also providing Israel with additional stockpile to draw upon in a crisis.
>
> Fourth, the U.S. is stepping up dramatically its own purchases of goods and services from Israeli firms. This too helps to reduce the burden of Israel's defense by increasing production runs and reducing unit cost of defense items.

Dine argued that the strategic alliance between the United States and Israel was so strong and unshakable that it was unlikely to be reversed in the future. Dine illustrated his point by quoting to his audience the remarks of Secretary of State George Shultz.

> Let me ... share with you what Secretary of State George Shultz recently explained. He said the point of strategic cooperation is, and I quote, "To build institutional arrangements so that eight years from now, if there is a Secretary of State who is not positive about Israel, he will not be able to overcome the bureaucratic relationship between Israel and the U.S. that we [in the Reagan Administration] have established." Think about that. For a Secretary of State to feel that way — think about how far we have come [in improving Israeli-American relations].
>
> And on the question of defending Israel, the Secretary of State forecasted, "Eight years from now discussions about Israel's security will be different. They will be about the highest state-of-the-art weapons technology and how

Israel is taking advantage of that technology. That is how we are going to secure Israel."

Dine concluded his remarks on the strategic alliance between Washington and Tel Aviv by reiterating that Israeli-American relations had blossomed beyond belief during the Reagan Administration, and this represented a revolutionary development in opening a new chapter in those ties: "We are in the middle of a revolution in the area of strategic cooperation, and this President and this Secretary of State are going to leave a legacy that will be important to Israel's security for decades to come."

In addition to strategic cooperation, Dine argued that diplomatic relations between the United States and Israel had dramatically improved during the Reagan presidency.

> We also see a revolution [in Israeli-American relations] in the diplomatic sphere. The State Department used to define success in the peace process in terms of how much pressure the U.S. was bringing to bear on Israel to make concessions [to its Arab neighbors]. Now Israel is treated as a partner in the peace process. Cooperation on the strategic level is complimented by coordination on the diplomatic level. The United States now only moves in the peace process after the closest consultations with the government of Israel. Trust ... has been established in the diplomatic discourse between the United States and Israel.

Dine argued that the revolutionary development in Israeli-American relations he claimed had occurred was the result of the fact that a powerful pro–Israel constituency in the federal bureaucracy had emerged, ensuring that the strategic alliance between Washington and Tel Aviv would endure in perpetuity.

> We are in the midst of a revolution which is raising U.S.–Israel relations to new heights. In the process a whole new constituency of support for Israel is being built in precisely the area we are weakest — among government officials in the State, Defense, and Treasury Departments, in the CIA, in science, trade, agriculture, and other agencies. These are the people responsible for proposing policy and for implementing it. In a crisis these anonymous officials will play a vital role. And they are learning through valuable personal experience, the value of the Israel to the United States. In other words, we are talking not only about a revolution in the relationship between the two states, but also the attitudes of people responsible for that relationship. That is what we mean when we talk about sinking down roots that will secure the tree of U.S.–Israeli relations from future storms.[70]

Dine's central argument — that Israeli-American relations had undergone a significant improvement during the Reagan Administration — is undoubtedly correct: Whether that improvement represented a revolution in Israeli-American relations — as Dine argued — is questionable. The United States and Israel have historically enjoyed very strong and close relations since the creation of the Jewish state in 1948; that was as true before Reagan entered the White House as it was during his presidency. However, in formalizing the strategic alliance between the United States and Israel, as well as drawing Washington closer to Tel Aviv in a number of other ways, Reagan had engineered a shift in American policy in the Middle East more strongly in favor of the Jewish state than had been the case under his predecessors — certainly with respect to those presidents who had served in office during the 1970s.

Nixon, Ford, and Carter had committed themselves to an American policy in the Middle East which, at least in appearance, though not substance, was evenhanded. Reagan saw no need to even create the appearance of pursuing an evenhanded American policy in the Middle East. Rather, Reagan was explicit in declaring his strong and unequivocal support for Israel, and his decision to formalize the strategic alliance between the United States and Israel and abandon any pretense that Washington served as an honest broker in the peace process was consistent with his pro–Israel proclivities. Reagan's pursuit of a pro–Israel policy in the Middle East did not come without costs: It weakened the credibility of the United States in the Arab world, and emboldened radical forces in the Middle East, led by Qaddafi, to direct, sponsor, and instigate terrorist attacks against American interests. The practical effect of this policy was to set the stage for military confrontation between the United States and Libya, and in the ensuing conflict, moderate Arab nations would have no alternative but to throw their support behind Qaddafi, a sworn enemy of the Jewish state, rather than the pro–Israel president residing in the White House.

With Qaddafi assured of the support of a united Arab world, the renegade leader of Libya calculated that the benefits of mounting an international terrorist campaign against American interests exceeded the costs. Indeed, Qaddafi was assured that his regime had a reasonable chance of surviving its confrontation with the United States, as Reagan was highly unlikely to take military action to remove the mercurial leader of Libya from power as long as he had the support of the moderate Arab nations allied with Washington. Since Qaddafi could legitimately claim victory in any future conflict with the United States as long as his regime survived the confrontation, the irrepressible leader of Libya had every incentive to launch an international terrorist campaign against American interests. With the strategic calculus in the Middle East having swung in favor of the forces of Arab radicalism, led by Qaddafi, as result of Reagan's close and enthusiastic embrace of Israel, the rogue leader of Libya had the political opening he needed to mount an international terrorist campaign against American interests, setting the stage for the momentous conflict between Washington and Tripoli which erupted in the opening months of 1986.

Conclusion

During the first five years of his presidency, Reagan pursued a policy in the Middle East based upon strong and unequivocal support for Israel which left little room for the United States to pursue an effective strategy to jumpstart the stalled peace process in the Middle East. Reagan began his presidency by branding the PLO as a terrorist organization and all but sanctioning Israeli settlement activity in the occupied Arab territories, positions which deprived the United States of credibility as an honest broker in establishing a just and lasting peace in the Middle East. The peace process floundered accordingly.

Reagan attempted to breathe new life into the flagging peace process when he attempted to exploit the opportunities for peace in the Middle East created by Israel's successful expulsion of members of the PLO from Beirut and South Lebanon. Reagan did so by unveiling his peace plan for the Middle East. But Reagan shelved his plan in response to Israeli objections to his call for the withdrawal of the Jewish state from occupied Arab territories. Reagan then proceeded to revive his moribund peace plan by establishing the MNF in Beirut in an effort to restore political stability to Lebanon. Reagan hoped that a peaceful and stable Lebanon would give Israel the security the Jewish state needed in order to make the political and territorial concessions required to achieve a just and lasting peace in the Middle East. However, Reagan's efforts to pursue the road to peace in the Middle East through Lebanon was dealt a fatal blow with the bombing of the American Marine barracks in Beirut, the resurgence of street fighting in the war-ravaged capital, and the collapse of the Lebanese government, which ultimately resulted in the president's decision to order the American military withdrawal from the battle-scarred city.

After the bombing of the Marine barracks in Beirut, Reagan reverted to pursuing a policy in the Middle East, based upon open and unabashed support for Israel, abandoning any pretense that the United States would serve as an honest broker in the peace process. Reagan formalized the strategic alliance between the United States and Israel in 1983, and scuttled a peace initiative Jordan and the PLO pursued two years later designed to jump-start the stalled peace process. By the end of 1985, Reagan had tied the interests of the United States so closely to those of Israel that Washington suffered a severe erosion of credibility in the Arab world. Within this unfavorable political environment Reagan had inadvertently created for the United States in the Middle East, Qaddafi emerged as Washington's primary enemy in the Arab world. Qaddafi was determined to challenge American interests in the Middle East by waging an international terrorist campaign directed against Western European targets frequented by Americans. Qaddafi unveiled this campaign on December 27, 1985, when Libyan-sponsored Palestinian terrorists launched a devastating automatic weapons and grenade attack against the international airports in Rome and Vienna, respectively.

It is safe to assume that Qaddafi fully recognized that his own embrace of international terrorism would inevitably provoke a military confrontation between the United States and Libya. Given the asymmetry of military power between the United States and Libya, Qaddafi also recognized that his regime's only hope of surviving such a confrontation lay in rallying the Arab world to his side. Reagan's decision to formalize the strategic alliance between the United States and Israel and abandon any pretense that Washington would serve as an honest broker in the peace process provided Qaddafi the opportunity to gain the sympathy, and even respect, of the moderate Arab regimes, which would have otherwise been predisposed to oppose the radical leader of Libya. Indeed, when given a choice between Reagan and Qaddafi, which the American bombing of Libya presented them with, the leaders of the moderate Arab nations opted for their fellow Arab head of state, a sworn enemy of Israel, rather than the pro–Israel president of the United States.

As we have seen, Reagan's decision to formalize the alliance between the United States and Israel was based upon his longtime and firmly-held view that the Jewish state represented a strategic asset to Washington in the Middle East. However, this view turned out to be a monumental strategic misconception. By strengthening, broadening, deepening, and enhancing this alliance, Reagan drove a wedge between the United States and the moderate Arab nations. This substantially weakened Reagan's hand in pursuing his war against Qaddafi, as he was deprived of the requisite support in the Arab world needed in order to prevail in this conflict.

Reagan hoped to win his war against Qaddafi by making a persuasive case that the renegade leader of Libya was an enthusiastic sponsor, exponent, and instigator of international terrorism. By branding Qaddafi as an international rogue and menace, Reagan intended to isolate the revolutionary firebrand of Libya from the rest of the world community, and mobilize the requisite global support he would need to ultimately pursue regime change in Tripoli should he have deemed such action to be necessary. However, Qaddafi's isolation from the rest of the international community could not be achieved without the support of the moderate Arab nations. Unfortunately for Reagan, such support was not forthcoming because the moderate Arab regimes found the president's open and unabashed embrace of Israel to be more unpalatable than Qaddafi's equally open and unabashed embrace of international terrorism. Contrary to Reagan's deeply-held assumption, Israel turned out to be a strategic liability, rather than asset, for the United States in the Middle East: The alliance between Washington and Tel Aviv deprived the president of the support he would need among the moderate Arab nations in order to successfully confront arguably the greatest international crisis of his presidency: the threat posed to this nation by Qaddafi's open and enthusiastic embrace and sponsorship of global terrorism as the centerpiece of Libya's drive to challenge American interests in the region.

CHAPTER TWO

The Reagan Administration Unsuccessfully Attempts to Isolate Libya

> *European governments ... began ruling out diplomatic and economic sanctions [against Libya] as soon as U.S. officials publicly called for such measures.*[1]
>
> — Brian L. Davis, author

On December 27, 1985, relations between Washington and Tripoli suffered a profound, calamitous, and irreversible deterioration when Libyan-sponsored Palestinian terrorists, in a well coordinated pair of deadly assaults, attacked the international airports at Rome and Vienna. Why would Libya have any reason to involve itself in the attacks? The answer to this question lies in the fact that the entire ideological edifice of the Qaddafi regime during the 1970s and 1980s rested upon its commitment to Arab nationalism. For Qaddafi, the Palestinian cause was central to the Libyan leader's own determination to the lead the Arab nationalist movement, such as it existed during that time. As Ronald Bruce St. John notes,

> In Qaddafi's mind, Palestine was an integral part of the Arab nation; and the latter could never be truly free and united until Palestine was completely liberated. The enemy was Zionism, together with Western colonialist and imperialist powers, especially the United States, responsible for visiting indignity upon the Arab people. Qaddafi's prolonged advocacy of the use of force against Israel later contributed to a bitter feud with ... Arafat.[2]

St. John's observations concerning Qaddafi's emotional attachment to the Palestinian cause is supported by Brian L. Davis, who notes, "No passion in Qaddafi is greater than his hatred for the State of Israel, and the

Palestinian cause is for him so surpassingly righteous that it serves ... as a rationalization for terrorism."³ Given his radical anti-American and anti-Israeli views, Qaddafi saw the Rome and Vienna attacks, which were directed against targets of those two nations, as a legitimate military operation designed to strike a blow against the "forces of Zionism and American imperialism." Indeed, on December 29, 1985, Libya's state news agency hailed the attacks as "heroic operations."⁴ During the three and a half months following the attacks, the Reagan Administration launched a campaign to build worldwide support for isolating Libya from the rest of the international community. To prevail in this effort, the administration went to extraordinary lengths to build a credible case designed to demonstrate that Qaddafi represented an international rogue and menace who was pursuing a global terrorist campaign which began after angry protesters sacked and burned the American Embassy in Tripoli with the acquiescence of their renegade leader on December 2, 1979.

But in point of fact, until the Rome and Vienna attacks, most Libyan-sponsored acts of international terrorism involved the assassinations or attempted murders of Libyan exiles living in exile. On May 6, 1981, Secretary of State Alexander M. Haig, Jr., responded to these acts of terrorism by ordering the closure of the Libyan People's Bureau in Washington and the expulsion of its twenty-seven-member diplomatic staff from the United States.⁵ But this was essentially the extent of the Reagan Administration's response to Tripoli's policy of directing assassinations against Libyan dissidents living in exile.

However, on November 23, 1985, three Libyan-sponsored Palestinian terrorists hijacked an Egypt Air airliner, forcing the airplane to land in Malta, where Egyptian commandos stormed the aircraft, and in the ensuing melee sixty passengers were killed, resulting in the bloodiest hijacking until 9–11. The terrorists were members of Fatah — The Revolutionary Council (FRC) — a renegade Palestinian organization, led by Sabri Banna, commonly known as Abu Nidal, who rejected the PLO's prohibition against terrorist attacks outside of Israel and the occupied Arab territories. In 1985 Abu Nidal had taken refuge in Tripoli following his expulsion from Iraq.⁶

The Egypt Air hijacking signaled that the Qaddafi regime had moved beyond the assassinations of Libyan dissidents living in exile to a more threatening and dangerous form of international terrorism involving random attacks against civilian targets of Tripoli's most ardent enemies — in the case of Egypt because of the peace treaty Cairo and Tel Aviv signed in 1979. And yet the Reagan Administration failed to respond to the hijacking despite the fact that the Palestinian terrorists had shot three Americans and dumped them onto the runway where miraculously two had survived. The most likely reason for the administration's lack of response was the fact that the bloodbath and carnage associated with the hijacking was due, not to the murderous behavior of the Palestinian terrorists, but to Egypt's ill-advised decision to storm the hijacked airliner.

One month following the Egypt Air hijacking, Libyan-sponsored Palestinian terrorists linked to the FRC struck again — this time at the international airports in Rome and Vienna, respectively. And unlike in the case of the hijacking, the Reagan Administration did take this latest act of international terrorism seriously because it was specifically directed against two American targets — the TWA and Pan Am ticket counters at the Rome airport — and involved an international facility frequented by Americans. And unlike in the case of the hijacking, where the death toll was caused by a firefight between Egyptian commandos and Palestinian terrorists, the murders at the international airports in Rome and Vienna were deliberately caused by the attackers, and not the unintentional consequence of a gun battle. Beyond even the hijacking, the Rome and Vienna attacks signaled that the Qaddafi regime had moved to the deadliest and most menacing phase of its international terrorist campaign, involving random assaults against foreign targets designed to indiscriminately kill as many innocent individuals as possible. It was only with this more heinous and threatening form of international terrorism, which the Qaddafi regime inaugurated with the Rome and Vienna attacks, that the administration finally took serious notice of the threat Libya posed to the world community.

To be sure, the Reagan Administration was not completely oblivious to the threat posed by Libyan-sponsored international terrorism prior to the Rome and Vienna attacks. On March 9, 1982, Reagan imposed an embargo both against the American importation of Libyan oil and the export of American goods and services to Libya possessing military applications, and oil and gas technology not readily available from non–American suppliers. The embargo was in response to credible evidence the Reagan Administration claimed existed that the Qaddafi regime had sent assassination squads to the United States to murder unnamed officials of the federal government and to launch terrorist attacks against American facilities both at home and abroad.[7]

Addressing the annual convention of the American Bar Association in Washington on July 8, 1985, Reagan condemned Qaddafi for his "outrages against civilized conduct."[8] On July 29 Reagan backed up his words against Qaddafi with practical action: The president signed a finding on Libya authorizing the conducting of planned American covert action designed to instigate the overthrow of the renegade leader of Libya.[9] Administered by the NSC, the covert action was code named Operation Flower.[10] Whether Operation Flower was ever implemented is unknown, as the documents pertaining to the covert action remain classified.

But it was not until the Rome and Vienna attacks that the Reagan Administration actually engaged in a concerted and coordinated campaign designed to isolate Libya from the rest of the international community. Prior to the attacks, the administration was intent upon confronting Libyan-sponsored international terrorism through a combination of limited economic sanctions and presidential rebukes. This was consistent with the fact that the administration really did not consider Libyan-sponsored international terrorism to represent a threat to the world community, as long as it was confined largely to the assassinations and attempted murders of Libyan dissidents living in exile. It was only when Libya dramatically expanded the scope of its international terrorist campaign with the Rome and Vienna attacks that the administration finally decided to consider Tripoli a serious threat to the global community, and launch its all-out campaign intended to demonize Qaddafi and isolate his regime from the rest of the world.

Palestinians Launch Terrorist Attacks in Rome and Vienna

On the morning of December 27, 1985, four Palestinian terrorists, using machine guns and hand grenades, launched an attack at the ticket counters of the El Al, TWA, and Pan Am airlines and nearby snack bar at Leonardo de Vinci International Airport in Rome. Sixteen civilians, including five Americans, were killed and over seventy others were wounded in the attack. Italian security personnel killed three of the Palestinian terrorists and captured the fourth. Almost simultaneously, three Palestinian terrorists, also using machine guns and grenades, launched an attack against travelers waiting at the departure gate to board an Israeli El Al airliner bound for Tel Aviv at Schwechat International Airport in Vienna. Four of the travelers were killed and over forty wounded in the attack. Austrian police killed one of the Palestinian terrorist and captured the remaining two after a brief car chase.

Shortly following the Rome and Vienna attacks, a radio station in Malaga, Spain, received a phone call from an individual claiming that the assaults were carried out by the FRC. The three surviving Palestinian terrorists admitted to being members of the FRC. Italian and Austrian investigators found a Libyan link to the Rome and Vienna attacks when they traced the passports carried by the Palestinian terrorists to a batch which Libyan authorities had confiscated from Tunisian guest workers who had been expelled from Libya in 1985.[11]

The White House wasted no time in attempting to determine the identity of those responsible for the Rome and Vienna attacks. On December 28, 1985, the White House Situation Room was set up to monitor all intelligence information arriving in Washington on the attacks. Those in attendance included members of the Joint Chiefs of Staff (JCS). After sifting through the intelligence reports, members of the JCS sent a document, marked "top secret," to officials administering eight military command centers throughout the United States. On May 30, 2001, NARA declassified most of the document which began by reporting on what was then known about the Rome and Vienna attacks.

> At approximately 0900 hours, 27 Dec 85, terrorists threw grenades and opened fire with automatic weapons simultaneously at the El Al check counters in the Vienna and Rome International Airports. The attack in Rome killed or wounded at least twenty AMCITS [American citizens]. Intelligence sources have linked the attacks to the Abu Nidal organization with Libyan support. The USG [United States Government] has publicly stated that, once positive identification of those responsible is made, appropriate retaliatory action will be taken.

Members of the JCS were unanimous in their belief that the only appropriate retaliatory action Reagan should order in response to the Rome and Vienna attacks was American air strikes against Libya: "[The United States should] conduct a retaliatory tactical air strike against the Libyan General Intelligence Institute and be prepared to conduct a more comprehensive strike against the Libyan intelligence, security, or governmental apparatus." In preparation for these anticipated air strikes, members of the JCS requested that military officials at the eight command centers, who received the 'top secret" document from the White House Situation Room, "nominate options which, optimally, would maximize target damage, have the least collateral damage [against Libyan civilians], and the lowest possible risk to U.S. forces [launching the air strikes against Libya].

Members of the JCS emphasized, "The primary target for attack is the Libyan General Intelligence Institute. However, [the Libyan] civilian population will not be attacked. Air defense installations which threaten the attacking, supporting, reconnaissance, and SAR [search and rescue] forces may also be attacked. Attack aircraft will attempt to minimize collateral damage."

Members of the JCS warned that American air strikes against Libya could provoke "heightened terrorist activities" against American interests. Accordingly, they requested the officials of the eight military command centers who received the "top secret" document from the White House Situation Room to prepare contingency plans for American military action to destroy the military capabilities of Libya: "Should the situation deteriorate further [following military action against Libya], more comprehensive action may be required. [We] request you develop [contingency plans] specifically designed to neutralize Libyan power projection capability including their tactical air forces, air defense forces, and sea power. [The] commanders' estimate [of the resources required to achieve this objective] should include recommended actions for protection of [the] strike force."[12]

Following the issuance of its "top secret" document, the White House Situation Room distributed a note, marked "confidential," to members of the president's staff providing an update on the Rome and Vienna attacks:

> [The] State [Department] confirmed that five Americans have died as a result of yesterday's attack at Rome's airport.
> State also reports twelve Americans are being treated in [the] hospital and seven to eight Americans have been treated and released.
> According to State, there were no Americans among the victims of the Vienna airport attack.[13]

As the White House Situation Room was apprising members of Reagan's staff concerning the latest developments in the Rome and Vienna attacks, the State Department prepared a document entitled "Terrorism: Theme Paper" for Robert B. Oakley, its director of counterterrorism, to use in his remarks to the media regarding the deadly assaults. In the document, Oakley was to have laid blame for the attacks squarely upon the shoulders of the notorious and shadowy Palestinian terrorist group headed by Abu Nidal.

> The attacks in the Rome and Vienna airports were deliberately intended to indiscriminately kill innocent people. Their motive was murder, pure and simple.
> The prime suspect for the attacks is the Abu Nidal group which is the most dangerous of the Middle Eastern terrorist organizations. The indiscriminate attack, the choice of targets, preliminary evidence, and method of operation point to Abu Nidal, a renegade Palestinian group.
> Abu Nidal's group are vicious criminals and should be treated as such. These are murderers who go out of their way to target civilians and have attacked and killed many Arabs as well as Israelis, Americans, and Europeans.

In identifying the states which sponsored the Abu Nidal terrorist group, Oakley was to have pointed the finger squarely at Libya: "Abu Nidal has enjoyed the support of several countries this year; Syria and now primarily Libya."

Oakley was to have noted that in 1982 Reagan imposed limited economic sanctions against Libya. However, the sanctions failed to persuade Qaddafi to abandon his involvement in international terrorism due to the fact that the nations of Western Europe had failed to follow America's lead in imposing punitive economic measures of their own against Libya.

> For years we have been leading an effort to exert economic and political pressures on countries supporting terrorism. We have imposed economic sanctions against Libya, for example, such as cutting off the sale of militarily useful aircraft and spare parts.
> Unfortunately, these efforts to make Libya and other countries supporting terrorism think twice and end their support have not been as effective as they should be because other countries, including Western Europe, have been unwilling to take similar steps. One reason they cite is fear that their companies will lose business.

The State Department prepared Oakley for two questions he was likely to face from the media: first, was the Reagan Administration preparing for a retaliatory response to the Rome and Vienna attacks? and second, was planning for such action being taken in coordination with Israel? Oakley was to have responded to the first question with the remarks: "The U.S. government has maintained a wide variety of options to deal with and try to deter terrorism. These include potential use of military or police assets as we consider appropriate. We are not going to speculate at this point as to what we might do in individual cases."

Oakley was to have responded to the second question involving Israel with the following remarks: "All states have an obligation to protect their citizens and thus share a common interest in working to eradicate terrorism. Specific responses are a matter for each government, however, and we are not coordinating with anyone regarding how we might react to attacks against our citizens."[14]

On December 30, 1985, Donald R. Fortier, deputy assistant to the president for national security affairs, sent a memorandum marked "secret/sensitive" to Reagan. On April 23, 2001, NARA declassified most of the memorandum and its attachment. In his memorandum Fortier informed Reagan, "I am attaching a copy of the most recent information available on those we believe responsible for the El Al attacks [in Rome and Vienna]. As you can see, the weight of the evidence is shifting increasingly toward Abu Nidal." Fortier informed Reagan that the NSC was in the process of recommending the appropriate retaliatory measures the president should order in response to the Rome and Vienna attacks.

> We are developing a coordinated set of options for you to consider. These range from expanded economic controls (e.g. American citizens now in Libya are helping to lift 80 percent of Qaddafi's oil) to military strikes against the terrorist infrastructure in Libya. We will complete our work on the options tomorrow and then circulate the paper to NSPG [National Security Planning Group] principals. Once you and the other principals have had a chance to reflect on the paper, we will seek to set up a secure conference call to discuss further action you may wish to take.

Fortier concluded his memorandum by recommending that the Reagan Administration avoid speculation as to whether American military action against Libya was actively being considered by the White House.

> I am urging press spokesman at [the] State [Department] and elsewhere not to speculate openly about military strikes against Libya. We do not want to restrict your choices [in retaliating against Libya] or raise expectations we are unable to satisfy. At the same time, if a strike seems warranted, we want to avoid openly telegraphing the punch.[15]

Attached to Fortier's memorandum was a document the NSC had prepared entitled "Responsibility for El Al Attacks." The document reiterated the consensus which had been forged within the Reagan Administration in the days following the Rome and Vienna attacks that responsibility for the deadly assaults lay squarely on the shoulders of the notorious and shadowy Palestinian terrorist group headed by Abu Nidal.

> Evidence continues to mount that Abu Nidal was responsible for the attacks at the Vienna and Rome airports.
> During interrogation, the two surviving terrorists in Vienna independently stated that they were members of and sponsored in their attack by the Abu Nidal group.
> The terrorist hospitalized in Rome has identified himself as a member of Abu Nidal.
> The modus operandi of the coordinated attacks matches that of previous attacks by Abu Nidal operatives in Western Europe in recent years. The attackers used automatic weapons and grenades and were intent on causing indiscriminate casualties.

The NSC also confirmed the consensus the Reagan Administration had forged that Libya represented the primary state sponsor of the Abu Nidal Palestinian terrorist group: "Libyan involvement with Abu Nidal has grown in the last few months, and Tripoli's foreknowledge of the attacks in Rome and Vienna seems likely." Fortier's document noted that Libya had applauded the Rome and Vienna attacks as justifiable retaliation for the Sabra and Shatila massacres: "The Libyan news agency on 29 December heralded the attacks as 'heroic operations executed by the sons of the martyrs of the Sabra and Shatila [refugee] camps.'"

The NSC alleged that the Rome and Vienna attacks were the result of an alliance Qaddafi and Abu Nidal had forged in the months preceding the deadly assaults and that as a result of this entente future terrorist acts by the renegade Palestinian leader were inevitable.

> In recent months Abu Nidal has shown signs of being closely aligned with Qaddafi. We believe that the attacks in Vienna and Rome, together with the Egypt Air hijacking, may be the result of this evolving relationship.
> In the spring of 1985 Abu Nidal and Qaddafi apparently reached general agreement on the need to concentrate on targeting moderate Arab states, Israel, and the U.S. This coincided with Libyan announcement of a 'Pan Arab Command' to unify dissident groups to conduct attacks against these same targets.
> Libyan support toward the Abu Nidal organization reportedly has grown this year.

The NSC concluded by expressing doubts that Qaddafi could assert control over the renegade Palestinian terrorist group headed by Abu Nidal, making the organization an especially loose cannon which could launch explosive attacks at any time of its choosing regardless of the sentiments of states which sponsored the group: "The Abu Nidal group's track record of successful terrorist operations probably is appealing to Qaddafi. Increased funding by Libya is unlikely to win Qaddafi real leverage over the group which was not wholly responsive to Syrian direction."[16]

Reagan Imposes an Economic Embargo Against Libya

Despite the recommendations of members of the JCS that Reagan order American air strikes against Libya in retaliation for the Rome and Vienna attacks, the president failed to take this option. Rather, Reagan chose the more benign and moderate retaliatory option of imposing an American economic embargo against Libya instead. At first blush, this choice seems odd: Reagan had issued a clear and unambiguous statement regarding American policy toward international terrorism from the very outset of his presidency. Addressing a welcome ceremony held on January 27, 1981, on the South Lawn of the White House in honor of the fifty-three Americans who were taken hostage at the United States Embassy in Tehran, and held in captivity for 444 days before they were freed by Iran thirty-three minutes after he was sworn into office a week earlier, Reagan declared, "Let terrorists be aware that when the rules of international behavior are violated, our policy will be swift and effective retribution."[17] The Rome and Vienna attacks certainly provided Reagan an opportunity to implement his policy of "swift and effective retribution," whether justified or not, but the president chose not to do so.

Accordingly, we are left with a perplexing question: Why did Reagan fail to order American military action against Libya in retaliation for the Rome and Vienna attacks? A definitive answer to this question must await declassification of all presidential records pertaining to the events leading to the American bombing of Libya on April 14, 1986. However, the evidence currently available at the Reagan Library suggests that the president chose economic sanctions as an alternative to military action in response to Libyan complicity in the Rome and Vienna attacks for two reasons: First, he had reason to believe that economic sanctions would persuade Qaddafi to abandon his involvement in international terrorism; and second, the White House feared that American military action against Libya carried too many risks to American interests.

Leading the effort in the White House to persuade Reagan that economic sanctions, not American military action, represented a more appropriate retaliatory response to Libyan complicity in the Rome and Vienna attacks was Elaine L. Morton, a policy analyst for the Crisis Management Center of the NSC. On December 28, 1985, Morton prepared a document entitled "Non-Military Alternatives" which was distributed to the White House staff. In the document, Morton argued, "The United States still possesses considerable economic leverage over Libya, particularly during a time when the oil market has caused Libyan financial reserves to drop to new lows and when popular discontent is rising in response to economic privation."

Morton noted that in 1982 Reagan imposed economic sanctions against Libya. However, the sanctions were still restrictive; 1,500 American citizens were employed in Libya. Americans were responsible for 80 percent of Libyan oil production. The United States exported $400 million in goods and services annually to Libya to support its ambitious economic development program which was financed through oil exports to Western Europe.

Morton noted that under the International Emergency Economic Powers Act (IEEPA) Reagan had the authority to prohibit all trade with Libya and ban all American citizens and permanent legal residents from residing in the revolutionary Arab nation. This would obviously have the potential to inflict substantial damage upon the Libyan economy, given the critical role the United States and its citizens played in the operation of Tripoli's oil industry and the industrial development of the revolutionary Arab nation. In making the case for economic sanctions as an alternative to American military action in retaliation for Libyan complicity in the Rome and Vienna attacks, Morton noted that

> [The] State [Department] is currently assessing the advisability of utilizing [the] IEEPA with respect to Libya. There are two major advantages of this approach. First, in contrast to military options, the impact of economic sanctions is easier to control and unforeseen consequences less likely to arise. Second, the language required in using [the] IEEPA — declaration of an economic emergency threatening the foreign policy and national security interests of the US — is tailor-made for making a strong point about the dangers of state-supported terrorism.[18]

Morton essentially made the case for economic sanctions as the appropriate retaliatory response to Libyan complicity in the Rome and Vienna attacks based upon the following argument: Libya was heavily dependent upon the United States as a source of goods and services critical to its economic development. Accordingly, sanctions would have a devastating impact upon the Libyan economy, and therefore, they could be used to persuade Qaddafi that he must abandon his involvement in international terrorism. The United States exerted substantial economic leverage against Libya which Washington could use to persuade Qaddafi to change his behavior. Moreover, economic sanctions carried none of the risks inherent in American military action against Libya which threatened a dangerous escalation in tensions between Washington and Tripoli.

Morton's case for economic sanctions received critical support from the CIA which produced a document on December 30, 1985, containing its own assessment of Libyan dependence upon the United States and Western Europe. The document was prepared for use by members of the Crisis Pre-Planning Group (CPPG), an interagency task force the White House established following the Rome and Vienna attacks to monitor the growing crisis between Washington and Tripoli. On December 28 members of the CPPG held their first meeting to consider the attacks.

On December 31, 1985, Rodney B. McDaniel, special assistant to the president and executive secretary of the NSC, sent a memorandum marked "secret/sensitive" to Fortier. Attached to McDaniel's memorandum was another document the CIA had produced. On April 23, 2001, NARA partially declassified both memorandums. But the memorandum which the CIA produced on December 30, 1985, remains mostly classified, with only one page, entitled "U.S. and Western Economic Involvement in Libya," having been made public. In his memorandum, McDaniel recommended to Fortier, "That you sign the memorandum ... forwarding the CIA assessments to the CPPG participants attending the meeting on December 28."[19]

In that portion of its memorandum Fortier transmitted to members of the CPPG which is declassified, the CIA noted:

> The Libyan economy is almost entirely dependent on the oil sector which accounts for over 90 percent of Libyan export revenues. In addition, Qaddafi is engaged in major industrial and construction projects that have both practical and political value for him domestically. Libya is heavily import-dependent: for food, as well as for industrial goods and technical skills needed to keep the economy going.
>
> The U.S. and other OECD [Organization for Economic Development] countries are heavily involved [in the Libyan economy]. The OECD accounts for 75 percent of Libyan trade, 70 percent of Libyan food imports, and 25 percent of Libyan arms imports.

The CIA noted that the United States and its citizens still played a critical role in the Libyan economy, despite Reagan's imposition of sanctions against Tripoli.

> Even under the terms of our current economic sanctions, the U.S. is Libya's third largest trading partner with annual exports of $304 million (mostly heavy industrial and construction equipment). A ball park estimate of engineer and other service contracts adds another $200 million.
>
> U.S. citizens working in Libya provide highly technical skills in the oil and construction sectors. Despite our passport restrictions and the President's request for voluntary withdrawal [from Libya], approximately 1,000 to 1,500 Americans have remained [in] or returned [to Libya]. From 700 to 1,200 would leave if forced to under [the] IEEPA.

The CIA noted that Western Europe had even more extensive economic relations with oil-rich Libya than the United States did.

> Almost $8 billion of Libyan oil exports go to Western Europe annually. Major importers are Italy ($2.7 billion) and the FRG [Federal Republic of Germany] ($2.2 billion). Italy, the FRG, Japan, the U.K. [United Kingdom], and France are all major exporters to Libya, predominantly in electric and heavy industrial goods and equipment. Italy ($1.7 billion) and the FRG ($800 million) have the highest export totals. Unlike the others, Italy is heavily involved in supplying arms [to Libya].
>
> Libya is dependent on foreign workers for most of its highly skilled jobs. Italy has 17,000 workers there, [and] the U.K. 8,500, mostly in the oil sector. Canadians are also there in significant numbers and have made up much of the gap caused by the drawdown of the Americans [from Libya] in 1981.[20]

The "secret" CIA document Fortier transmitted to members of the CPPG left no doubt that American economic sanctions would have a potentially crippling effect upon Tripoli, given the critical role the United States played in the Libyan economy. But the document also made it clear that Western Europe played an even greater role in the Libyan economy than

United States did. Given the extensive economic relations they enjoyed with oil-rich Libya, it was unlikely that the major industrial nations of Western Europe would join the United States in imposing sanctions of their own against Libya. And without Western European participation in the establishment of a comprehensive international economic sanctions regime against Libya, it was doubtful that an American economic embargo against Tripoli alone would have its desired effect of persuading Qaddafi to abandon his involvement in international terrorism. Qaddafi could easily replace the trade with the United States Libya stood to lose from American economic sanctions with the import of additional goods and services from Western Europe.

Morton was correct in her argument that American economic sanctions had a good chance to persuade Qaddafi to change his international behavior — but only if the nations of Western Europe imposed sanctions of their own. And as the State Department made clear in the talking points Oakley used in conveying the Reagan Administration's response to the Rome and Vienna attacks, the nations of Western Europe were unlikely to sacrifice the extensive and lucrative economic relations they enjoyed with oil-rich Libya in order to join the United States in its campaign to isolate Tripoli from the rest of the international community.

The Reagan Administration Opts for the Imposition of American Economic Sanctions Against Libya

During the first week of January 1986 the Reagan Administration forged a consensus that economic sanctions represented the most appropriate retaliatory response to Libyan involvement in the Rome and Vienna attacks. Accordingly, the NSC produced a draft executive order for Reagan's signature which imposed an American economic embargo against Libya. Accompanying the executive order were letters Reagan would send to O'Neill and Vice President George Bush, acting in his capacity as president of the Senate, informing the two leaders of his decision to impose the embargo. On January 7, 1986, Howard J. Teicher, director of Near East and South Asia affairs for the NSC, sent a memorandum, marked "secret," along with the executive order and letters, to William F. Martin, director of international economic affairs for the NSC, informing him, "Attached ... for your signature is a memorandum to David Chew [White House staff secretary and deputy assistant to the president] providing him with NSC concurrence without change on: the executive order, the report to Congress, [and] a transmittal letter to Congress ... [Stephen I.] Danzansky [special assistant to the president and senior director for international affairs], [James R.] Stark [director of political-military affairs for the NSC], [Paul B.] Thompson [deputy executive secretary and staff legal counsel for the NSC], and Morton concur." Teicher concluded his memorandum to Martin by recommending, "That you sign the memo."[21] Martin quickly signed and sent the memorandum, marked "secret," to Chew. Attached to that document was a memorandum Martin also sent to Chew informing him, "The NSC has reviewed the executive order ... and recommends its approval without change. The NSC also concurs in the report to Congress [and] the transmittal letter."[22]

Upon receiving the approval of the NSC, Reagan issued Executive Order 12543 in which the president proclaimed, "I ... find that the policies and actions of the government of Libya constitute an unusual and extraordinary threat to the national security and foreign policy of the United States and hereby declare a national emergency to deal with that threat." To confront this threat, the executive order prohibited all trade, commercial transactions, and transportation between the United States and Libya, and forbade all individuals residing in this nation from traveling to the revolutionary Arab state.[23]

Hours following his imposition of a trade, transportation, and travel embargo against Libya, Reagan held a news conference in the East Room of the White House. Reagan used the occasion to announce his decision to impose the embargo. Reagan used talking points the NSC produced in order to prepare him for the opening remarks he delivered at his news conference in which he announced his decision. On January 7, 1986, Martin sent a memorandum to Speakes informing the White House deputy press secretary, "Attached are ... talking points regarding Libya prepared by the NSC for the President's use in his press conference this evening."[24]

In his talking points, Reagan was to have condemned Qaddafi for his involvement in international terrorism.

1. Qaddafi's role [in international terrorism] is well-known.
2. Qaddafi has already exported terrorism to the U.S., killing and wounding opponents of his regime.

In announcing his decision to impose an American economic embargo against Libya, Reagan was to have explained the punitive measures he was taking against Tripoli in retaliation for its involvement in international terrorism.

By invoking [the] Emergency Economic Powers Act, [I]

1. Banned direct important and export trade.
2. Banned all service contracts.
3. Banned travel to Libya, other than what may be required for ... journalism.

Reagan was to have appealed to the other nations of the world to join the United States in taking steps to isolate Libya from the rest of the international community.

1. Cooperation of our allies and other friends is critical to exact [a] cost on Qaddafi by isolating Libya politically and economically.
2. [The] U.S. will consult with allies and other friends to encourage cooperation in imposing economic and political sanctions [against Libya]. Depending on the effects of these steps, we may decide to pursue additional options.
3. Europe has borne the brunt of Qaddafi's latest outrages. European leaders surely recognize that the public sentiment for firm action against those who support terror is growing. For example, airport workers have gone on strike to protest this situation [acts of international terrorism against airports in Western Europe].
4. In our consultations, the U.S. will make it clear our position that allies will discourage, to the maximum extent possible, their nations from replacing departing U.S. business and personnel.
5. Many Arab leaders have suffered from the scourge of terrorism. Arab leaders are aware of Qaddafi's uncivilized behavior. He is a threat to them as well.

Reagan's talking points called for him to conclude the opening remarks of his news conference by issuing an oblique, but unmistakable, warning that he would order American military action against Libya unless Qaddafi abandoned his involvement in international terrorism.

1. [The] U.S. continues to reserve the right to act in an appropriate manner in self-defense.
2. All available measures remain under consideration to bring terrorists to justice.
3. If Qaddafi continues his involvement in international terrorism, I will consider other measures [against Libya].[25]

During his news conference, Reagan adhered closely to the talking points the NSC had prepared. Reagan opened his news conference by issuing a statement, which was also produced by the NSC, in which he charged that the Vienna and Rome attacks were only the latest in a long string of acts of international terrorism Qaddafi had directed, sponsored, and instigated.

On December 27 terrorists attacked the Rome and Vienna international airports.... These murderers could not carry out their crimes without sanctuary and support provided by regimes such as Colonel Qaddafi's in Libya. Qaddafi's longstanding involvement in terrorism is well documented, and there's irrefutable evidence of his role in these attacks. The Rome and Vienna murders are only the latest in a series of brutal terrorist acts committed with Qaddafi's backing. Qaddafi and other Libyan officials have publicly admitted that the Libyan government has abetted and supported the notorious Abu Nidal terrorist group which was directly responsible for the Rome and Vienna attacks. Qaddafi called them heroic actions, and I call them criminal outrages by an outlaw regime.

Reagan appealed to the other nations to join the United States in taking steps to isolate Libya from the rest of the international community. Reagan directed his appeal especially to the nations of Western Europe which maintained extensive economic ties with oil-rich Libya. Reagan noted that the United States was making economic sacrifices in severing its ties to Libya. Reagan implored the international community not to allow economic self-interest to abrogate the moral responsibility the nations of the world had to isolate Libya in light of Qaddafi's reckless and open embrace of international terrorism.

> We've urged repeatedly that the world community act decisively and in concert to exact from Qaddafi a high price for his support and encouragement of terrorism. The United States has already taken a series of steps to curtail most direct trade between our two countries, while encouraging our friends to do likewise. Terrorists and those who harbor them must be denied sympathy, safe haven, and support. In light of this latest evidence of Libya's growing role in international terrorism, it is clear that steps taken so far have not been sufficient. Tougher, more comprehensive measures [against Libya] are required by the international community.

In announcing his decision to impose an economic embargo against Libya, Reagan noted,

> I've taken measures to end virtually all direct economic activities between the United States or U.S. nationals and Libya. These measures ... impose a total ban on direct import and export trade with Libya.... They prohibit commercial contracts and other transactions with Libya, including travel-related activities other than those needed for journalism.
>
> We've taken these steps after much reflection and full awareness of the economic consequences which the United States stands to incur as a result. Civilized nations cannot continue to tolerate in the name of material gain and self-interest the murder of innocents. Qaddafi deserves to be treated as a pariah in the world community. We call on friends in Western Europe and elsewhere to join us in isolating him. Americans will not understand other nations moving into Libya to take commercial advantage of our departure. We will consult with all our key allies to pursue the goal of broader cooperation.

Reagan noted that, following the Rome and Vienna attacks, Prime Minister Bettino Craxi of Italy had urged the international community to identify "those states that guarantee terrorists protection and the possibility to arm and organize themselves to carry out bloody raids." In responding to Craxi's remarks, Reagan noted that "Qaddafi's Libya is such a nation, and we call upon other nations to join us in denying it the normal economic and diplomatic privileges of the civilized world." Reagan concluded the opening remarks delivered at his news conference by issuing his oblique, but unmistakable, warning that he would order American military action if the economic embargo he was imposing failed to persuade Qaddafi to abandon his involvement in international terrorism: "If these actions do not end Qaddafi's terrorism, I promise you that further steps will be taken [against Libya]."[26]

In his letters to O'Neill and Bush, Reagan reiterated his appeal to the rest of the international community to join the United States in taking steps to isolate Libya.

> The United States reaffirms its call to Libya and all nations supporting terrorism to turn away from that policy. The United States also calls upon other nations to join us in isolating the terrorists and their supporters. We must demonstrate by firm political and economic sanctions that the international community considers such actions intolerable [and] that states that engage in such actions cannot expect to be accepted members of the international community.
>
> Failure to call Libya to account for its policy places the civilized world at the mercy of terrorism. This has necessitated the steps I have taken today. The terrible tragedies of Vienna and Rome demonstrate that no nation can be immune [from international terrorism, and] that each nation must bear its fair share of the vital effort against the politics of terror. I call upon every nation to do so now.[27]

The fact that Reagan rejected the recommendation of members of the JSC for retaliatory American air strikes against Libya in response to the Rome and Vienna attacks did not mean that the president had foreclosed future use of the military option in confronting the threat posed by Libyan-sponsored international terrorism. Rather, Reagan was persuaded to give economic sanctions a chance to work; if they failed to convince Qaddafi to abandon his involvement in international terrorism, the president could always opt for the use of American military force against Libya. As Reagan wrote in his diary hours before his news conference on January 7, 1986, in which he announced that he was imposing an American economic embargo against Libya,

> I finally came down on the side of an executive order bringing Americans and American business home from Libya and canceling relations — trade, etc. with them.... If Mr. Qaddafi does not push another terrorist attack, okay we've

been successful with our implied threat. If, on the other hand, he mistakes this for weakness and does loose another one [terrorist attack], we will have [Libyan] targets in mind and respond with a h — l of a punch.[28]

The Reagan Administration Attempts to Elicit Western European Support for Isolating Libya

The Reagan Administration fully recognized that its campaign to isolate Libya from the rest of the international community could not succeed without Western European support. In the wake of Reagan's imposition of the American economic embargo against Libya, Tripoli was almost completely dependent upon Western Europe as a source of goods and services. This gave the nations of Western Europe substantial economic leverage they could use to persuade Qaddafi to abandon his involvement in international terrorism. The Reagan Administration was determined to persuade the nations of Western Europe to use this leverage to convince Qaddafi to change his behavior. To this end, following Reagan's imposition of the American economic embargo against Libya, the United States Information Agency (USIA), in a document marked "confidential," and declassified by NARA on May 3, 1999, unveiled a "public diplomacy strategy" designed to "convince influential Europeans that":

1. Terrorism is a scourge that aims over time to take advantage of our open, tolerant societies to disrupt and destroy the fabric of Western political and social life.
2. Determined and cooperative international resistance to all those who are encouraging, funding, and training terrorists ... is essential to European as well as Western stability (Libya is a clear example of a state against which determined action must be brought to bear).
3. The U.S. will conduct its own resistance to this threat in a rational and measured way; we are not going to overreact, however. We reserve the right to keep our options open and will take whatever steps are needed to combat the overall terrorist threat.
4. At the same time, we recognize that there are a measured range of options which each country will consider for itself; in confronting the Libyan threat, for example, there are a variety of steps that can be taken involving trade measures, servicing and maintenance of Libyan aircraft and vessels, controls on individuals traveling on Libyan passports, etc. We are looking, however, for action, not merely statements of intent.

The USIA stressed:

A public diplomacy strategy focused on Europe should:
1. Define terrorism as a scourge being waged against the West and its values by ruthless opponents.

2. Define Libyan terrorism as a cold-blooded instrument of Libya's national policy directed against Libyan dissidents, other Arab states; in effect anyone opposed to Qaddafi, rather than as an expression of pan–Arab solidarity.
3. Document Libyan involvement over the years in terrorist actions, including those outside Europe as well as in Europe.
4. De-mythologize Qaddafi both as a man and leader.

The USIA document noted that among "common European perceptions" of American policy toward Libya was, "The U.S. talks tough but will not take military action against Libya because [the] military cost [to the United States] is too high; the European allies will not support us; [there would be] adverse reaction [against such action] in the Islamic world; [and because of] fear of [Libya] unleashing a terrorist wave in the U.S." The USIA suggested that the Reagan Administration should respond to Western European skepticism regarding American resolve to use military force against Libya by informing the nations of the region, "The President is clearing the decks and sending notice to Europe as well as to Libya that the U.S. recognizes the nature of the terrorist threat as an extremely serious one and will take whatever action that becomes necessary to combat it."

American policy toward Libya remained based upon the Reagan Administration's commitment to elicit Western European participation in the imposition of a credible and effective international sanctions regime against the revolutionary Arab nation designed to persuade Qaddafi to abandon his involvement in international terrorism. However, the nations of Western Europe remained adamant in their refusal to join such a regime because, according to the administration, they believed, "Economic sanctions will not work because they have not worked in the past." The USIA suggested that the American rejoinder to this argument should be, "Economic sanctions are an appropriate means at this time to signal U.S. resolve [against Libya]."[29]

The USIA document shows that eliciting Western European participation in the development of a credible and effective international sanctions regime against Libya remained the linchpin of the Reagan Administration's strategy to isolate Tripoli from the rest of the world community. The administration was determined to demonstrate that, if the nations of Western Europe failed to join the United States in imposing economic sanctions of their own against Libya, then Reagan was prepared to order American military action against Tripoli. The hope was that the nations of Western Europe would seek to avert such action by imposing economic sanctions against Libya.

Given Libya's dependence upon Western Europe as a source of goods and services, especially in the wake of the American economic embargo, the loss of trade from this region would deal a devastating blow to the Qaddafi regime, imperiling its survival. Qaddafi would have no alternative but to abandon his involvement in international terrorism if he faced the threat of Western European economic sanctions. However, as we will see, despite intense American pressure, the nations of Western Europe remained adamant in their determination to retain their extensive economic relations with oil-rich Libya. In the end, the American bombing of Libya was as much a response to the Reagan Administration's frustration with Western European coddling of Qaddafi as it was the president's determination to remove Tripoli as the primary source of international terrorism.

Broomfield Expresses Support for Reagan's Policy Toward Libya

Reagan's call for the international community to join the United States in taking steps to isolate Libya received critical support from Representative William S. Broomfield of Michigan, the ranking Republican member of the House Foreign Affairs Committee. On January 6, 1986, Broomfield sent a letter to Reagan informing the president, "I share your concern about the recent tragic terrorist incidents in Rome and Vienna and Libya's active support for terrorism around the world." Broomfield expressed his support for Reagan's strategy for confronting the threat posed by Libyan-sponsored terrorism.

> As you know, fighting the complex issue of terrorism is a formidable problem that defies simple solutions. While the military option is a legitimate one, a broad range of economic pressures should be brought to bear on Libya. This can include military, political, and economic pressures which will serve to up the price of terrorism for Colonel Qaddafi. I believe it is important to work in concert with our allies to make the costs of terrorism for Qaddafi higher than any benefits that Mr. Qaddafi can possibly derive from engaging in and supporting terrorism.

Broomfield expressed agreement with Reagan that the focus of the president's efforts to isolate Libya must be directed toward eliciting Western European participation in this endeavor.

> In taking punitive measures against Libya, our government should enlist wide international support against that country. I realize that many of our European allies are reluctant to join our country in bringing certain kinds of pressures on Libya. We must, however, do everything that we can to convince

them that positive action must be brought to bear on supporters of terrorism. With the increase in terrorism in recent years, many nations around the world have taken a more realistic attitude toward the problem in order to more effectively combat this growing international menace.

Broomfield concluded his letter by expressing to Reagan, "I commend you for your strong stand against terrorism."[30]

Broomfield's letter is significant insofar as he served as the ranking Republican member on the House Foreign Affairs Committee. Members of the committee represented the primary experts on foreign policy in the House of Representatives, who constituted an important source of influence in Congress with respect to international affairs. Accordingly, Broomfield's letter most likely reflected the consensus within the committee, and the wider Congress, regarding how Reagan should confront the growing threat posed by Libyan-sponsored international terrorism. The letter suggested that Congress supported Reagan's decision to opt for the imposition of economic sanctions as an alternative to the use of American military force in persuading Qaddafi to abandon his involvement in international terrorism.

However, Broomfield's letter also reflected the joint consensus between the Reagan Administration and Congress that American economic sanctions alone would fail to have their desired effect. Rather, only the establishment of a credible and effective international economic sanctions regime, involving Western European participation, would inflict the necessary punishment required to persuade Qaddafi to change his behavior. By the time Reagan imposed the American economic embargo against Libya, both his administration and Congress had reached a consensus that the next step in the president's war against Qaddafi must be a concerted effort to elicit Western European participation in the sanctions regime which would persuade the renegade leader in Tripoli to join the community of civilized nations in renouncing his support for international terrorism. In the following weeks that is precisely where the administration's campaign to isolate Libya from the rest of the international community was directed.

The Reagan Administration Releases a Dossier Outlining Its Case Against Qaddafi

Economic sanctions represented only one element of a two-pronged strategy the Reagan Administration pursued in its efforts to isolate Libya from the rest of the international community. The other leg of that strategy was the development of a dossier designed to portray Qaddafi to the international community in dark and sinister terms, arguing that the rogue leader of Libya was a dangerous and unstable megalomaniac who represented a threat and menace to the rest of the world. The Reagan Administration's ability to isolate Libya from the rest of the international community was ultimately dependent upon the White House's success in persuading the nations of the world to accept this dark and sinister view of Qaddafi. If the international community embraced the administration's portrayal of Qaddafi as a dangerous and menacing figure on the world stage, then the White House strategy of isolating Libya from the rest of the world would succeed. However, if the administration failed in this effort, and the world community continued to scoff at the notion that Qaddafi truly represented a global menace, the United States would have to proceed alone in its efforts to persuade the renegade leader of Libya to abandon his involvement in international terrorism.

Accordingly, the Reagan Administration's ability to successfully achieve its objective of isolating Libya was dependent upon its development of a credible dossier which would persuade the international community that Qaddafi posed a grave threat to the nations of the world. If the administration were able to successfully make its case against Qaddafi in the court of world opinion then the renegade leader of Libya would have no choice but to end his support of international terrorism. This would be the only option available to Qaddafi if he hoped to escape the stigma of being branded an international pariah and subjecting his regime to isolation from the rest of the world.

Unless the Reagan Administration could effectively isolate Libya from the rest of the world, the only option left for Reagan to persuade Qaddafi to change his behavior was American military action against Tripoli. Reagan was determined to avoid such action, hoping instead that the imposition of a comprehensive economic sanctions regime could serve to convince Qaddafi to join the community of civilized nations in renouncing his support for international terrorism.

Reagan's announcement that he was imposing an economic embargo against Libya was coupled by the State Department's release of the administration's dossier outlining the American case against Qaddafi before the court of international opinion. Released in January 1986, the dossier was entitled "Libya Under Qaddafi: A Pattern of Aggression." The title essentially told the story the Reagan Administration wanted the international community to know: that Qaddafi represented a dangerous and menacing figure on the global stage, bent upon pursuing a reign of terror against the nations of the world designed to serve his own megalomaniacal purposes. The purpose was to portray Qaddafi as an international rogue and outlaw operating completely outside the bounds of civilized behavior. The hope was for the international community to accept this dark and menacing portrayal of Qaddafi in order that the rest of the world could join the United States in isolating the revolutionary firebrand of Libya as the only credible and effective means to bring his reign of terror against the nations of the globe to a final end.

The State Department opened its dossier outlining the Reagan Administration's case against Qaddafi by stridently and unequivocally denouncing the rogue leader of Libya as an international menace and outlaw.

> He fancies himself a leader and agent of historic forces that will reorder Third World priorities to his taste. His vision provides both a motive and rationale for providing military and financial aid to radical regimes, and for undermining moderate governments by creating or supporting subversive groups and abetting terrorists. Qaddafi's aggressive policies increasingly have focused on undermining U.S. and other Western interests in the Third World, as he sees these as the main barrier to his radical and expansionist goals.... He is particularly hostile to Israel and the United States. His tactics include a mixture of threats and material support for terrorism, offers of cooperation, economic incentives and intimidation, and outright military aggression.

The State Department noted that Qaddafi used international terrorism as his chief instrument to expand his influence throughout the Third World.

> Qaddafi has used terrorism as one of the primary instruments of his foreign policy and supports radical groups that use terrorist tactics. Tripoli operates numerous training sites for foreign dissident groups that provide instruction on the use of explosive devices, hijacking, assassination, and various commando and guerilla techniques. It also provides terrorist training outside Libya, and abuses diplomatic privilege by storing arms and explosives at its diplomatic establishments.

The State Department noted that Libyan foreign policy was based upon Qaddafi's commitment to the subversion of moderate Arab regimes.

> Qaddafi ... targets moderate Arab governments for their refusal to continue the military struggle against Israel and for their links to the West. There is evidence of Libyan-backed assassination plots against President [Hosni] Mubarak of Egypt. For example, those arrested after last November's attempted attack on Libyan exiles in Egypt stated Qaddafi's target list included Mubarak. We believe that Qaddafi has added Jordan's King Hussein and Iraq's Saddam Hussein to his hit list because of restored ties to Cairo and Washington, respectively.

The State Department argued that Qaddafi was committed to emerging as the dominant leader of the Arab world by subverting moderate regimes, and that the mercurial ruler of Libya had directed much of his efforts in this regard to destabilizing the Egyptian government in retaliation for having signed the Camp David peace treaty with Israel in 1979.

> Qaddafi's foremost ambition is to dominate and unite the Arab world. He frequently compares himself to Garibaldi and Bismark, and has justified the use of violence and terrorism against moderate regimes as necessary to achieve Arab unity.
>
> Egypt, because of its peace treaty with Israel, is a special target. Libyan agents have been active in Egypt since the 1970s, and Qaddafi has offered support to various opponents of the Egyptian government. In October 1981, immediately after President Sadat was assassinated, Qaddafi called on Egyptians to overthrow their government; within a week, at the Cairo International Airport, two bombs exploded that had been concealed in luggage uploaded from a flight originating in Tripoli.
>
> More recently, Qaddafi has sought to embarrass the government of President Mubarak and undermine the Egyptian economy. In July 1984 a Libyan ship commanded by a senior Libyan naval commando laid mines in the Red Sea and the Gulf of Suez that damaged eighteen merchant ships. In May 1985 the Egyptians thwarted a plot by radical Palestinians, backed by Libya, to destroy the U.S. Embassy in Cairo with a truck bomb. Last summer, Qaddafi expelled over 10,000 Egyptian workers in Libya — confiscating their savings and most of their belongings — in what was in part an effort to place a greater burden on the strained Egyptian economy. Also during 1985, Cairo captured several teams of Libyan-supported Egyptian dissidents who reported that their plan was to destabilize the Mubarak government through sabotage and inciting civil unrest.

In addition to his efforts to destabilize the Egyptian government, the State Department noted that Qaddafi was committed to undermining the peace process by marginalizing Arafat's leadership over the PLO because of the chairman's commitment to a negotiated peace settlement with Israel, and enhancing the stature of Palestinian radical organizations committed to the destruction of the Jewish state.

> Libya is staunchly opposed to the Middle East peace process and Qaddafi is doing all he can to subvert it.... Qaddafi has been especially eager to undermine the influence of PLO ... Chairman Yasser Arafat because Qaddafi perceives him as too willing to consider a negotiated settlement with Israel. As a result, Qaddafi has thrown his support to radical Palestinian groups — including the Fatah Revolutionary Council led by Abu Nidal — that advocate continued war against Israel. Since 1981, Qaddafi has shipped these groups items as prosaic as uniforms and as powerful as tanks and BM-21 multiple rocket launchers. In 1984 Libyan troops participated in the Syrian-backed assault on Arafat's forces in northern Lebanon.

In addition to undermining the peace process, the State Department argued that the primary means Qaddafi had chosen to enhance his influence in the Arab world was through the establishment of strong ties to radical Palestinian terrorist groups.

> Longstanding Libyan support for radical Palestinian groups is growing. Qaddafi has provided safe haven, money, and arms to these groups.... Training for Palestinians and other radicals frequently takes place at several locations in Libya. These anti–Arafat Palestinians are widely engaged in terrorist activity in Israel and the occupied territories.

The State Department devoted particular focus to the most disturbing aspect of Qaddafi's growing ties with radical Palestinian terrorist groups: the Libyan leader's alliance with Abu Nidal.

> Libya provided passports to the Abu Nidal members responsible for the attack at the El Al counter in Vienna. The Abu Nidal group is particularly appealing to Qaddafi because of its track record of successful terrorist operations. Abu Nidal's targeting of moderate Palestinians and moderate Arab leaders is consistent with Libya's antipathy toward participants in the peace process. According to Libyan press reports, Abu Nidal met with Qaddafi in Libya at least twice in 1985.... In addition, Libya has provided sanctuary, training assistance, and financial support to the Abu Nidal organization and there are reliable press and other reports that its headquarters has been moved to Libya.

The State Department noted that Qaddafi's ties to Abu Nidal were particularly disturbing given the fact that the rogue Palestinian leader's organization represented arguably the most dangerous and effective terrorist group in the world.

> The Abu Nidal group is among the most dangerous of the Middle Eastern terrorist organizations. It is probably the best organized and most effective of the radical Palestinian terrorist groups, carefully planning its operations and keeping its information tightly compartmentalized.
> The group has repeatedly demonstrated its ability to operate in any country it chooses. It has staged attacks in over twenty locations on three continents, and operates throughout the Middle East.
> Abu Nidal has conducted over sixty terrorist attacks during the last eight years — at least thirty of them since the beginning of 1984. Two-thirds of the group's nearly twenty attacks this year have taken place in Western Europe, as innocent bystanders increasingly have become casualties of the group's assaults.

The State Department noted that the Abu Nidal organization arose in opposition to Arafat's prohibition against Palestinian acts of terrorism outside of Israel and the occupied Arab territories. The organization was originally based in Iraq, and the transfer of its operations to Libya had ominous implications as Abu Nidal was guaranteed the operational freedom in Tripoli which the renegade Palestinian leader lacked during his previous years of refuge in Baghdad.

> The [Abu Nidal] group was formed in 1974 after Arafat instituted a ban on PLO involvement with terrorism outside Israel and the occupied territories. Abu Nidal's views gained favor with the Iraqi regime which helped him create the organization.
>
> Beginning in the early 1980s, Baghdad suppressed activities of the Abu Nidal group out of Iraq. Elements of the group then moved to Damascus. Since early 1984 Libya began to provide increased support to the group, and Abu Nidal himself and many of the group's operations may have been moved there within the last twelve months.

The State Department warned that, after concentrating on no particular part of the world, the geographical focus of Abu Nidal's international terrorist campaign had shifted to Western Europe, and that the rebel Palestinian leader's alliance with Qaddafi was certain to enhance his capacity to launch terrorist attacks in the region.

> Even before the recent attacks in the Vienna and Rome airports, Abu Nidal had begun to concentrate his field of operations in Western Europe. Although his targets have been the usual enemies — for example, British, Israeli, moderate Arab — he has become very indiscriminate about injuring bystanders.... The pattern of concentrating his efforts in Europe has coincided with the strengthening of his links to Libya. The likelihood of Libyan financing, safe haven, and logistic assistance should be very helpful to his future international terrorist operations.

In addition to his support for radical Palestinian terrorist groups, Qaddafi represented a staunch backer of the Islamic revolutionary regime of Iran. The State Department noted that "Qaddafi has allied himself with Iran in its war against Iraq, and has provided Tehran with T-55 tanks, antitank and antiaircraft artillery, and even Scud rockets."

The State Department concluded its dossier outlining the Reagan Administration's case against Qaddafi by reiterating its argument that the rogue leader of Libya was an international menace and outlaw who operated completely outside the norms of civilized behavior and posed a grave threat to the world community.

> Qaddafi's subversion is not limited to those countries that are direct objects of his ambitions. The international community as a whole suffers from Qaddafi's disrespect for international norms of behavior and accepted practice. Qaddafi has abused diplomatic privilege for terrorist purposes, reneged on international agreements, and blatantly used terrorist violence against political opponents. In addition, Qaddafi's support of terrorism ... helps legitimize terrorism as an acceptable political activity.[31]

The State Department Produces a List of Terrorist Acts Involving Libya

Accompanying the State Department's dossier outlining the Reagan Administration's case against Qaddafi was a specific, detailed, and exhaustive list of terrorist acts involving Libya. The first major terrorist act on the list was the sacking and burning of the American Embassy by Libyan mobs on December 2, 1979. The list proceeded to document fifty-one additional terrorist acts ending with the Rome and Vienna attacks on December 27, 1985. The list showed that from the end of 1979 through the conclusion of 1983 there were twenty-five terrorist acts involving Libya, averaging six a year. From the beginning of 1984 through the end of 1985 there were twenty-seven terrorist acts, averaging thirteen a year.[32]

The Rome and Vienna attacks signaled a significant change in the tactics Libya used in pursuing its international terrorist campaign. Prior to those attacks, Libyan terrorist tactics mostly involved the assassination or attempted murder of Libyan dissidents living in exile, primarily in Western Europe, and to a lesser extent in the United States. The Rome and Vienna attacks represented a sharp departure from the Qaddafi regime's focus on assassinating Libyan dissidents living in exile: Rather, they represented random and indiscriminate assaults against innocent individuals designed to kill as many people as possible, with Tripoli's terrorist operations now centered squarely in Western Europe. The attacks were the result of an alliance forged between Qaddafi and Abu Nidal in 1985. By providing sanctuary and financial assistance to Abu Nidal and his murderous organization, Libya granted the rogue Palestinian leader the capability to pursue his ultimate aim of transforming Western Europe into a major theater of terrorist operations for his group.

Fundamental to the Reagan Administration's case that Qaddafi represented an international rogue and menace was the White House's claim that the renegade leader of Libya had forged an alliance with the notorious Palestinian terrorist Abu Nidal. And the existence of this alliance was confirmed by none other than Abu Nidal. In 1985 the West German newspaper *Der Spiegel* published an interview with Abu Nidal which was conducted with the radical Palestinian leader in Tripoli. In the interview, Abu Nidal declared that he and Qaddafi were "linked by a deep and strong friendship." Abu Nidal praised Qaddafi, proclaiming, "He is of great help to us."[33]

Qaddafi's decision to forge an alliance with Abu Nidal, and provide the resources the rogue Palestinian leader required to launch the Rome and Vienna attacks, could very well have been in response to Reagan's actions to formalize the strategic alliance between the United States and Israel, and thwart the Jordanian-Palestinian peace initiative launched in 1985. With those actions, American credibility in the Arab world had sunk to a low point. Qaddafi was intent upon exploiting that loss of credibility in order to emerge as Washington's leading enemy in the Middle East.

By providing critical support for the Rome and Vienna attacks which involved assaults against two specific American targets — the TWA and Pan Am ticket counters at the international airports in Rome — Qaddafi inaugurated his campaign to challenge American power in the Middle East. Given the extremely limited military capabilities of Libya, Qaddafi was reduced to using international terrorism as the only weapon in his arsenal to combat the United States. While there was no prospect that Libyan-sponsored international terrorism could prove effective in achieving Qaddafi's aim of eliminating American influence from the Middle East, his tactics would prove sufficiently disruptive to enable the revolutionary firebrand of Libya to pose a threat to the world community, let alone the United States.

Accordingly, Qaddafi had every reason to expect an American retaliatory response to his sponsorship of international terrorism. Qaddafi also had every reason to believe that, in the inevitable military confrontation between the United States and Libya which was sure to come, the moderate Arab leaders would support their fellow Arab head of state in Tripoli, a sworn enemy of Israel, rather than the pro–Israel president residing in the White House. Armed with the critical support of the moderate Arab nations, the Qaddafi government was guaranteed to survive its military confrontation with the United States, as Washington would never pursue regime change in Libya without the support of America's allies in the Arab world. Qaddafi turned out to be a brilliant political strategist who recognized that the moderate Arab nations ultimately found Reagan's enthusiastic and unabashed embrace of Israel to be even more distasteful than the Libyan leader's equally enthusiastic and unabashed embrace of international terrorism. With Reagan's hand against Qaddafi severely weakened by his strong and unswerving support for Israel, Qaddafi felt free to pursue his international terrorist campaign directed against American interests, recognizing that he had an excellent chance of surviving his inevitable military confrontation with the United States.

The Reagan Administration Fails to Elicit International Support for Isolating Libya from the Rest of the World

Reagan's appeal to the international community, especially the nations of Western Europe, to join the United States in establishing a comprehensive global economic sanctions regime against Libya fell upon deaf ears. The other industrial nations were willing to impose only token punitive measures against Libya, which would have no discernable effect upon the economy of the revolutionary Arab nation. The fact that the United States would have to act alone in its efforts to isolate Libya from the rest of the international community, without any discernable support from the rest of the world, became evident on January 28, 1986, when Murphy appeared before the Subcommittee on Europe and the Middle East of the House Foreign Affairs Committee. Murphy began his remarks before the committee by issuing a statement on recent developments in the Middle East. Coming only three weeks following Reagan's announcement that he was imposing an American economic embargo against Libya, Murphy devoted much of his remarks to the growing crisis between Washington and Tripoli.

Murphy began his statement on Libya by expressing the Reagan Administration's argument:

> The Qaddafi regime has a long record of overt and covert aggression against its neighbors and support for international terrorism. Following the December 27 attacks on the Rome and Vienna airports by the Abu Nidal group and the clear evidence of Libyan involvement, the President decided to take rigorous, but measured and focused, steps to underscore our opposition to Qaddafi's policies in support of terrorism and induce Qaddafi to change his policies. President Reagan banned direct trade with Libya on January 7.

Murphy made it clear that the American economic embargo against Libya was designed to convey three clear messages to Qaddafi.

> First, the United States made the unambiguous statement that we will not do business with a person who has placed himself far outside the boundaries of civilized conduct.
>
> Second, the measures announced by President Reagan made the point that Qaddafi's continued support for terrorism carries a cost for Libya. Last year the United States was Libya's third largest export partner. American companies lifted almost half of Libya's oil production. We do not contend that our measures, taken by themselves, will do irreparable harm to Qaddafi. However, they will over the short term, cause important dislocations in the Libyan economy.

The third message the American economic embargo was designed to convey was the most ominous: that Reagan was prepared to order American military action against Libya if Qaddafi failed to abandon his involvement in international terrorism.

> Third, the steps we have taken to date are not the most severe actions that could be levied against Qaddafi. In light of the heinous nature of terrorist acts,

these are modest measures. If Libyan aid to terrorists continues, however, the United States has the option of imposing a range of more severe actions [against Libya].

Despite his oblique warning of the possibility of American military action against Libya, Murphy expressed the Reagan Administration's publicly stated hope that such a move could be avoided, and that the president's decision to impose an American economic embargo against Libya would represent his final response to Qaddafi's involvement in international terrorism: "The steps we have taken may not be our final response [to Qaddafi's involvement in international terrorism], but we sincerely hope that additional actions will not be necessary."

Murphy noted that "Deputy Secretary [of State John C.] Whitehead just returned from a visit to nine allied capitals where he conveyed our deep concern at the threat that terrorism represents in the world." The purpose of the Whitehead mission was to persuade the nations of Western Europe to join the United States in imposing diplomatic and economic sanctions against Libya. Murphy said that while the Reagan Administration was not requesting that the nations of Western Europe completely sever diplomatic and economic relations with Libya, the United States did expect its Atlantic allies to adopt limited measures against Tripoli: "We do not expect our allies to duplicate our actions, but rather, to examine additional measures appropriate to each individual case." However, contrary to Murphy's claims, Whitehead did indeed seek specific Western European measures during his visit to the region, which included a reduction in the importation of Libyan oil, the imposition of an arms embargo against Tripoli, the issuance of an official statement condemning Libyan sponsorship of international terrorism, and the closure of Libyan People's Bureaus throughout the area, which the United States claimed served as bases for fomenting international terrorism. However, Whitehead came home empty-handed: The deputy secretary of state failed to persuade the governments of any of the nine industrial nations he visited to take such action.

To be sure, during a meeting held in Brussels on January 27, 1986, the foreign ministers of the European Community (EC) agreed to impose an arms embargo against Libya and suspend the issuance of additional credits to Tripoli. But the foreign ministers rejected American appeals that they impose diplomatic and economic sanctions against Libya. France, Italy, Spain, and Greece rejected a British proposal to condemn Libyan sponsorship of international terrorism and reduce Western European imports of Libyan oil.[34] Moreover, the arms embargo the EC imposed upon Libya was itself a token punitive measure, as the Soviet Union, not Western Europe, represented Tripoli's primary source of military weaponry, and Moscow could easily replace the hardware the revolutionary Arab nation stood to lose from the Western European arms embargo.[35] Echoing the oblique warning Murphy delivered in his testimony to members of the House Foreign Affairs Committee, Whitehead, in remarks delivered to reporters upon his return to Washington on January 27, ominously noted that Reagan "reserved the right to come back to the military option in case the non-military, peaceful measures [against Libya] failed to work."[36] While the Whitehead mission proved to be a dismal failure, insofar as it succeeded in garnering only token Western European punitive measures against Libya, Murphy attempted to put a positive, albeit deceptive, spin on the deputy secretary of state's trip: "While the Deputy Secretary found occasional differences over tactics [against Libya] among our allies, we are encouraged by the broad commitment to close, effective action in the fight against terrorism."

Murphy noted that Qaddafi's strategy against the United States was based upon his efforts to rally support for Libya throughout the rest of the Arab world by wrapping himself around the mantle of the Palestinian cause. Accordingly, Murphy implied that a critical element in the Reagan Administration's campaign to politically marginalize Qaddafi within the Arab world was to reinvigorate the moribund peace process in order that the renegade leader of Libya would be deprived of the opportunity to exploit the Palestinian problem for his own political advantage.

> Qaddafi has responded to our actions [against Libya] by [issuing] threats and [engaging in] posturing, including the promise to train any Arab who wishes to become a terrorist in support of the Palestinian cause. He relishes his role as chief defender of that cause. Our efforts and those of our Arab friends to pursue the path of a just and durable negotiated [peace] settlement [in the Middle East] are abhorrent to him. We will prove him wrong.[37]

A major question Murphy did not answer is why the Reagan Administration had failed to persuade the nations of Western Europe to impose diplomatic and economic sanctions against Libya. Such sanctions were vital to the administration's campaign to establish a credible and effective regime which could result in the isolation of Libya from the rest of the international community. The most likely answer is that the nations of Western Europe believed that Qaddafi's international terrorist campaign was the result of the political instability which has long plagued the Middle East. At the heart of this instability was the continuing and intractable conflict between Israel and the Arab world. The nations of Western Europe believed that Qaddafi's appeal and influence within the Arab world, such as it existed during the 1980s, could best be defused by a renewed effort to advance the peace process, and not through the imposition of punitive measures against Libya, as the Reagan Administration advocated. As St. John aptly notes,

> Many EC governments ... felt that the overall American approach to terrorism in general, and Libya in particular, was in error; they believed that it only addressed the symptoms of the disease, which they saw as the Palestinian question. The governments of France, Greece, and Italy in particular supported the Palestinian cause to a greater degree than the United States, emphasizing the issue was largely a political one to be resolved through negotiation. In this milieu, the use of force, or even the threat to use force, produced dismay across the European political spectrum where it was felt that force would not address the issue [of international terrorism] in a positive way and could result in an increase in the level of terrorism. Finally, a belief that the anti-terrorist policies of the Reagan Administration were fatally flawed only reinforced the longstanding determination of many European governments to pursue a foreign policy autonomous from the United States.[38]

While a fundamental difference of opinion between the two sides of the Atlantic over Middle East diplomacy was certainly a factor in Western European resistance to the imposition of diplomatic and economic sanctions against Libya, the nations of the region had a more practical reason to resist such measures: They had extensive economic relations with oil-rich Libya and were reluctant to sacrifice those lucrative ties, even to advance the cause of combating Libyan-sponsored international terrorism. As Davis aptly notes, "The reason generally considered most important in [Western European] rejection of sanctions [is that] Libya was the sixteenth leading buyer of EC exports.... The pattern of placing economic interests ahead of combating terrorism was nothing new for Europeans."

Davis notes that much of Libyan imports of Western European goods and services were financed through credits the nations of the region had issued to Tripoli. The imposition of Western European economic sanctions was almost certain to provoke Libya into reneging on its commitment to repay its debt: "The Qaddafi regime had accumulated ... arrears for [Western European] work and they wanted to make sure to collect [their Libyan debt]."[39] In 1986 Libyan debt to Tripoli's leading Western European trade partner — Italy — amounted to $800 million.[40]

Conclusion

The Rome and Vienna attacks represent a critical turning point in the events leading up to the American bombing of Libya. The attacks represent a significant change in the tactics Qaddafi used in pursuing his international terrorist campaign: from a focus on the assassination and attempted murder of Libyan dissidents living in exile, to pursuing terrorist attacks against unsuspecting sites designed to indiscriminately kill as many innocent individuals as possible.

The Rome and Vienna attacks were the result of an alliance forged between Qaddafi and Abu Nidal in 1985. By providing Abu Nidal and his murderous organization with sanctuary and financial assistance, Qaddafi granted the rogue Palestinian leader the capability to pursue his objective of transforming Western Europe into a major theater of terrorist operations for his group. The combination of Libyan financial resources and Abu Nidal's organizational capabilities ensured that the range, scope, and extent of Qaddafi's international terrorist campaign, especially directed against American targets in Western Europe, would broaden, deepen, and expand.

The Reagan Administration was determined to respond to the grave threat Qaddafi posed to the international community by eliciting worldwide participation in the establishment of an international economic sanctions regime against Libya. Critical to the success of this effort was the administration's determination to persuade the nations of Western Europe to join the United States in imposing economic sanctions of their own against Libya. This would ensure that a credible and effective international economic sanctions regime against Libya could be imposed. Given Libya's dependence upon the United States and Western Europe as a source of goods and services, such a regime would have a devastating effect upon Tripoli, causing severe economic dislocations which were sure to threaten the survival of the Qaddafi government. Accordingly, Qaddafi would have no alternative but to abandon his involvement in international terrorism had such a regime been established.

At his news conference on January 7, 1986, Reagan announced that he was imposing an American economic embargo against Libya, and he appealed to the international community, especially the nations of Western Europe, to join the United States in establishing sanctions of their own against the revolutionary Arab nation. However, the nations of Western Europe refused to do so. They did not perceive Qaddafi as a sufficient threat to justify severing the extensive economic relations they enjoyed with oil-rich Libya. Without Western European participation, American economic sanctions, taken alone, would have almost no effect upon Libya: Western Europe could easily replace the goods and services Tripoli stood to lose from the United States. As Stanik aptly notes, "Reagan's strategy had failed to induce Qaddafi to renounce terrorism and subversion because America's European allies had given the policy little support.... They feared Libyan reprisals and wanted to avoid any action that might threaten their lucrative commercial relationships with Libya."[41]

The failure of the Reagan Administration to persuade the nations of Western Europe to join the United States in imposing economic sanctions of their own against Libya left the president no alternative but to exercise the military option if he were to have any hope of persuading Qaddafi to abandon his involvement in international terrorism. On January 28, 1986, Murphy appeared before the House Foreign Affairs Committee and reported that Whitehead had returned home empty-handed from his trip to Western Europe where the deputy secretary of state had failed in his effort to persuade the nations of the region to follow America's lead in imposing economic sanctions of their own against Libya. Without Western European participation, the American economic embargo, taken alone, was guaranteed to fail to inflict the economic punishment upon Libya required to provide Qaddafi an incentive to cut his ties to international terrorism. The failure of the Whitehead mission ensured that a military showdown between the United States and Libya was inevitable, unavoidable, and only a matter of time.

CHAPTER THREE

Heading Toward a Military Showdown

There were numerous attempts politically, economically, and militarily by the United States to provoke a confrontation with Libya.[1]
— R.A. Davidson III, retired officer, United States Army

Despite the failure of the Whitehead mission in January 1986, the Reagan Administration was determined to press ahead in its efforts to isolate Libya from the rest of the international community. However, the administration's strategy for doing so involved the conducting of risky and provocative American air and naval exercises in the Gulf of Sidra, described as routine military maneuvers, in March 1986. This demonstration of American military power only succeeded in inexorably moving the United States and Libya toward confrontation.

This was not the first time the United States had undertaken such maneuvers. During 1973 to 1979, the United States conducted three such exercises; they were designed to challenge Qaddafi's declaration issued on October 11, 1973, asserting Libyan sovereignty over the Gulf of Sidra. Qaddafi's declaration contravened Article 7 of the 1958 Geneva Convention on Territorial Sea and Contiguous Zone under which the Gulf of Sidra was recognized to be in international waters.[2]

The first American air and naval exercises in the Gulf of Sidra conducted during the Reagan presidency occurred August 18–19, 1981. The exercises resulted in the downing of two Libyan warplanes which had crossed paths with American military aircraft in the gulf.[3] The United States conducted a subsequent round of exercises in the Gulf of Sidra in 1984.[4]

The American air and naval exercises conducted in the Gulf of Sidra in March 1986 were not designed to challenge Qaddafi's assertion of Libyan sovereignty over the waterway, as had been the case with all previous such maneuvers. Rather, coming during a period of heightened tensions between the United States and Libya, the exercises were actually designed to further the Reagan Administration's strategy of persuading the nations of Western Europe to join Washington in imposing diplomatic and economic sanctions of their own against Tripoli. The exercises were intended to serve notice upon Western Europe that Reagan was fully prepared to order American military action against Libya if Qaddafi failed to abandon his involvement in international terrorism. The nations of Western Europe were determined to avert such action; they retained extensive economic relations with oil-rich Libya and had every reason to fear that an American military operation against Tripoli would threaten the lucrative commercial ties they enjoyed with the Qaddafi regime.

The Reagan Administration hoped that the nations of Western Europe would respond to the looming specter of military confrontation between the United States and Libya by joining Washington in imposing diplomatic and economic sanctions of their own against Tripoli. In the aftermath of Reagan's imposition of an American economic embargo, Libya was almost completely dependent upon Western Europe as a source of goods and services. Accordingly, Western European economic sanctions would deal a crippling and devastating blow to the Libyan economy, and imperil the very survival of the Qaddafi regime. Qaddafi would have no alternative but to abandon his involvement in international terrorism if such sanctions were imposed. The Reagan Administration's policy toward Libya essentially rested upon convincing the nations of Western Europe that, without action on their own to persuade Qaddafi to change his behavior, an American military operation against Libya was imminent. The hope was that the nations of Western Europe would act on their own to avert this prospect by imposing diplomatic and economic sanctions against Libya designed to compel Qaddafi to join the community of civilized nations in renouncing his support for international terrorism.

Reagan Orders the Conducting of American Air and Naval Exercises Off the Coast of Libya

During January 7–8, 1986, Reagan signed two documents designed to confront the threat posed by Libyan-sponsored international terrorism. The first document, signed on January 7, was, of course, the executive order imposing an American economic embargo against Libya. The second document, signed the following day, was an NSDD which remains classified.[5] However, the annex to the NSDD entitled "Acting Against Libyan Support for International Terrorism," marked "top secret," has been partially declassified.

On January 7, 1986, Howard J. Teicher, director of Near East and South Asia affairs for the NSC, sent a memorandum, marked "confidential," to John M. Poindexter, assistant to the president for national security affairs, informing him, "Attached ... for your signature is a cover memo distributing the annex to the NSSD on a restricted basis." Teicher recommended that Poindexter sign the memorandum, marked "top secret."[6] The memorandum, which was sent to Shultz; Secretary of Defense Caspar W. Weinberger; William J. Casey, director of the CIA; and William J. Crowe, Jr., chairman of the JCS, informed the four officials of the Reagan Administration, "The President has signed the attached National Security Decision Directive (NSDD) Annex."[7] The annex declared:

> In support of stated objectives of [the] NSDD ... this annex directs additional military measures and intelligence actions.
>
> Near-term military deployments shall signal U.S. resolve, reduce the potential risk to American citizens in Libya, heighten the readiness of U.S. forces to conduct military action, and create uncertainty regarding U.S. intentions [toward Libya]. To accomplish this mission:
> 1. A second carrier battle group shall proceed as soon as possible to the Central Mediterranean Sea.
> 2. These forces shall conduct operations in international waters, to include the Gulf of Sidra, which demonstrate U.S. resolve and capability [against Libya].
> 3. The Secretary of Defense should submit a plan for these operations for review and approval by January 9, 1986.
>
> Our long-terms goals in Libya remain unchanged.[8]

Weinberger Urges Reagan to Press Ahead with the American Campaign to Isolate Libya

As we have seen, the annex to the NSDD Reagan signed on January 8, 1986, directed Weinberger to submit a plan to the president for conducting American air and naval exercises off the coast of Libya the following day. However, for unknown reasons, Weinberger failed to submit the plan until February 10. The plan was contained in a memorandum, marked "top secret," Weinberger sent to Reagan. On May 30, 2001, NARA declassified most of the memorandum.

Weinberger began his memorandum by outlining the Reagan Administration's efforts to isolate Libya from the rest of the international community. To this end, Weinberger informed Reagan:

> U.S. policy toward Libya is aimed at convincing Qaddafi we will not tolerate his support for terrorism. We have taken unilateral measures to isolate him and to create costs [to Libya] for continuing his policies [in support of international terrorism]. Basically, our measures sharply reduce economic ties with Libya and will ultimately sever them. Also, virtually all Americans will leave Libya and not travel there in the future.

Weinberger assured Reagan that the United States would not act alone in its campaign to isolate Libya from the rest of the international community, but would instead continue its efforts to elicit support from the other industrial nations to join Washington in imposing economic sanctions of their own against Tripoli: "We are encouraging other friendly nations to join us in seeking peaceful means, [both] economic and political, to make it clear to Qaddafi that he must pay a high price for his policies [in support of international terrorism]. Deputy Secretary of State Whitehead's recent travel to Canada and Europe spearheaded the diplomatic effort."

Weinberger warned Reagan that Qaddafi was actively engaged in a campaign to rally support within Libya and the wider Arab world in favor of his opposition to American policy in the Middle East. Weinberger noted that the American economic embargo, combined with air and naval exercises the United States conducted in the Tripoli Flight Information Region (FIR) during January 26–30, 1986, had placed Qaddafi on the defensive.[9] Weinberger's assessment was that Qaddafi's efforts to mobilize domestic support within Libya for his cause was failing, largely due to the economic pressures the beleaguered leader in Tripoli confronted as a result of the sharp drop in international oil prices which adversely affected the Libyan economy.

> As a result of our political-economic measures against Libya and naval operations within the Tripoli FIR in late January, Qaddafi has been under considerable pressure internally. His attempts to rally public opinion [in Libya in support of his cause] have been met more with apathy than enthusiasm. Owing partially to the fortuitous drop in oil prices, concern is high among the business and professional classes that the Libyan economy is heading toward collapse. Some Libyan students have been arrested on suspicion of espionage.

However, despite his domestic failures at home, Weinberger warned Reagan that Qaddafi was making headway in his campaign to rally the wider Arab world to support his cause.

> Qaddafi has succeeded in rallying Arab political support for his position, but not to the point [that Arab nations were] considering "counter-sanctions"

against the U.S. A number of Arab friends [to the United States] have complained that the press play surrounding our actions [against Libya] has built Qaddafi up to the point where they, as brother Arabs, feel compelled to support him even though, privately, they hope our actions will succeed in moderating his behavior or precipitate internal [political] changes in Libya.

Weinberger warned Reagan that Qaddafi was prepared to instigate additional terrorist attacks against American interests should the president ultimately decide to order American military action against Libya: "Qaddafi has ... in the past week sponsored a conference of 'Arab revolutionary forces' which reportedly agreed to create hit groups to attack US interests in the event of a U.S. attack against Libya." However, despite the risks American military action against Libya carried, Weinberger believed that the United States should undertake naval and air exercises off the coast of Libya, consistent with the annex to the NSDD Reagan signed on January 8, 1986. Such a provocative act by the United States against Libya, coming as tensions between the two nations had substantially escalated in the wake of the Rome and Vienna attacks, carried the risk of provoking a military confrontation between the two enemies in the Mediterranean Sea. The United States had already conducted one such exercise in the Tripoli FIR in January 1986. Weinberger believed that, despite the risks they carried, further exercises would serve American interests in three ways: First, they would serve as a clear warning to Qaddafi that American military action was imminent unless he abandoned his involvement in international terrorism; second, they would force Tripoli to devote military resources to its defense against the provocative American air and naval exercises which would be conducted off the coast of Libya, thereby placing further strains on the already deteriorating Libyan economy; and third, they would encourage the nations of Western Europe to impose diplomatic and economic sanctions of their own against Libya, once the United States made it clear, through its air and naval maneuvers in the Mediterranean, that Washington was prepared to take military action against Tripoli if Qaddafi failed to abandon his involvement in international terrorism.

Coming in the wake of the American economic embargo, the imposition of Western European economic sanctions was certain to deal a devastating blow to Libya, given its dependence upon the nations of the region as a source of goods and services, and imperil the survival of the Qaddafi regime. Qaddafi would have no alternative but to abandon his involvement in international terrorism in the face of those sanctions. Accordingly, inducing the nations of Western Europe to impose economic sanctions against Libya represented the foundation of the Reagan Administration's strategy to persuade

Qaddafi to change his behavior; and the White House hoped that a show of American military force off the coast of Libya would finally persuade America's Atlantic allies to join Washington in its campaign to isolate Tripoli from the rest of the international community.

Consistent with the annex to the NSDD Reagan signed on January 8, 1986, Weinberger strongly urged the president to approve two American air and naval exercises which would be held in international waters off the coast of Libya Weinberger apprised the president of the benefits to American interests the secretary of defense believed that the military maneuvers would bring.

> Libyan air and naval units continued a high level of patrolling for several days following our naval operations in the Tripoli FIR, but have now returned to a normal status. The high alert placed severe strains on Libyan [naval] equipment and operators. Further such operations will, I believe, help keep Qaddafi off guard and uncertain as well as assist in our efforts to develop firmer support from the European governments for political and economic measures against Libya.

Weinberger informed Reagan, "A selected working group under OSD [Office of Secretary of Defense] leadership met [on] 5 February to consider near-term and surface naval operations within the Tripoli FIR and the Gulf of Sidra before the anticipated arrival of the USS America in the Central Mediterranean on or about 23 March." Based upon the deliberations of the working group, Weinberger recommended that Reagan approve two American air and naval exercises in international waters off the coast of Libya, the first consisting of air and surface naval forces to be conducted in the Tripoli FIR during February 12–15, 1986, and the second composed of three aircraft carrier task forces, to be undertaken in the Gulf of Sidra during March 23–31. Weinberger informed Reagan that, should the president grant approval for the recommended American air and naval exercises off the coast of Libya, then he should assure members of Congress that the military maneuvers were not intended to initiate any hostilities between Washington and Tripoli. Specifically, Weinberger addressed the issue of the War Powers Act which requires the president to notify Congress whenever he deploys American military forces in an area where hostilities are imminent. Weinberger argued that the American air and naval exercises off the coast of Libya carried no such dangers of hostilities, and that there was no anticipation that Reagan needed to invoke the War Powers Act once the exercises commenced.

> Upon your approval of resumed [air and naval] operations in the Tripoli FIR during February 12–15, we will initiate a public NOI [notice of intent] and the Department of State will inform friendly and allied states of our intention to conduct routine air and naval operations in this area during these dates.

Since our operations will not exceed those we conducted in January, and will be conducted in an area which even Libya recognizes as international waters, there is no expectation of "imminent hostilities" and no War Powers [Act] question arises. We should nonetheless consider informing key congressional leaders of our anticipated actions.

Weinberger stressed that the Reagan Administration must present the exercises as routine maneuvers, and not as an act of provocation against Tripoli, even though the secretary of defense had made it clear to the president that such a move was clearly designed as a hostile measure against the Qaddafi regime.

While Qaddafi will try to mobilize [the support of] the media to portray himself as the underdog and innocent victim [of American aggression], hostile press play [against the air and naval exercises] should be somewhat reduced from January, since such an operation will be considered less newsworthy. We would plan to take the line that these are routine operations in international waters (without amplification) and to continue back-grounding [you] on Qaddafi's subversion against his neighbors and support for terrorism.

Weinberger concluded his memorandum by assuring Reagan, "The select working group will continue to develop options and recommendations as Qaddafi reacts to these pressures. The JCS is developing other measures to assist this effort. I will provide you with periodic updates."[10]

The White House Remains Suspicious of Western European Intentions Toward Libya

As Weinberger's memorandum illustrates, the primary purpose of the American air and naval exercises he recommended that Reagan approve was to impress upon the nations of Western Europe that the president was poised to order military action against Libya if Qaddafi failed to abandon his involvement in international terrorism. Given the extensive economic relations the nations of Western Europe enjoyed in oil-rich Libya, any such action would undermine the interests of America's Atlantic allies. The hope in Washington was that the nations of Western Europe would respond to this imminent prospect by joining the United States in imposing economic sanctions against Libya. In the absence of economic relations with the United States and Western Europe, the Libyan economy would collapse, leaving Qaddafi no alternative but to change his behavior.

The reason the Reagan Administration was determined to go to such extraordinary lengths to demonstrate American resolve against Libya is that the White House distrusted the nations of Western Europe. The White House remained convinced that the nations of Western Europe, far from seeking to punish Libya for its involvement in international terrorism, would ultimately take advantage of the termination of American economic relations with Libya by replacing the goods and services Tripoli stood to lose from the United States.

White House suspicions of Western European intentions toward Libya were not unfounded. Following Reagan's imposition of the American economic embargo against Libya, Qaddafi mounted a lobbying campaign designed to entice the nations of Western Europe not to follow Washington's lead in imposing economic sanctions of their own. The NSC closely monitored this campaign, and in January 1986 produced a document on Qaddafi's progress in this regard entitled "Libyan Tactics Toward Western Europe." In the document, the NSC reported:

> Qaddafi summoned ambassadors from seven Western European countries on January 9, and according to press accounts of that meeting, Qaddafi thanked them for their refusal to support the [American] economic sanctions, and emphasized European interests in Libya, which he claimed included $13 billion in contracts, with 230 European companies working in Libya, hiring 40,000 Western Europeans. Qaddafi mentioned that Libya planned to spend $36 billion more in the next five years, and suggested in subsequent press statements that involvement in these projects would depend on the position taken by various [Western European] governments toward U.S. sanctions.

The NSC reported that Libya was attempting to entice the nations of Western Europe to subvert the American economic embargo against Tripoli with promises of expanded trade if they refused to join the United States in imposing sanctions of their own.

> [The] Tripoli press has continued with the conciliatory line [of Qaddafi] as well, stressing European refusal to adopt U.S. sanctions. Tripoli television reports that at one meeting of the Basic People's Congress (equivalent to provincial legislative bodies), the members adopted a measure to "reconsider our relations with certain countries of Western Europe which declare their rejection of ... Reagan," implying a campaign of additional trade relations with those Europeans who held the line against sanctions.

In addition to promising expanded trade with those nations of Western Europe which refused to follow the American lead in imposing economic sanctions against Libya, the NSC reported that Qaddafi had threatened terrorist violence against any government of the region which took such action.

> We have learned that Qaddafi may initiate new terrorist activities in those Western European countries that support U.S. sanctions.

In his press conference last week with Western, Arab, and other international press, Qaddafi publicly took a confrontational line and said, "I will shoulder the responsibility of liberating the Mediterranean from the U.S. presence henceforth. I will ally myself with all peace movements in Europe — with the Greens and the Bader movements — to destroy U.S. bases in Europe and in the Mediterranean."[11]

The White House feared that, through a combination of economic enticements and threat of terrorist violence, Qaddafi had succeeded in persuading the nations of Western Europe to subvert the American economic embargo. This belief was made clear during a meeting of the members of the CPPG held on February 13, 1986. On February 12 Rodney B. McDaniel, special assistant to the president and executive secretary of the NSC, sent a memorandum, marked "secret/sensitive," to his counterparts in the State, Treasury, and Defense Departments, the CIA, and JCS, as well as to Donald P. Gregg, assistant to the vice president for national security affairs. On May 30, 2000, NARA declassified the memorandum which announced, "The CPPG will convene on Thursday, February 13, 1986 at 3:30 p.m. in Room 208, Cordell Hall Conference Room. An agenda and list of participants are attached."[12] NARA declassified both the list of participants who attended the CPPG meeting, marked "secret/sensitive" on May 30, 2000, and most of the agenda of the conference, marked "secret," on April 23, 2001. Attendees of the meeting included five members of the NSC staff— Fortier, McDaniel, Teicher, Morton, and Ronald C. St. Martin — Undersecretary of State for Political Affairs Michael H. Armacost; Undersecretary of Defense for Policy Fred C. Ikle; Assistant Secretary of Defense for International Security Affairs Richard L. Armitage; Robert M. Gates, deputy director of the CIA; Robert M. Kimmitt, general counsel to the Treasury Department; and John H. Moellering, assistant to the chairman of the Joint Chiefs of Staff.[13] A major item on the agenda of the meeting was to provide its attendees the opportunity to assess "the effect of [American economic] sanctions" against Libya. State Department representatives who attended the meeting were to have addressed the issue of the "current status of allied cooperation" with the United States in its campaign to impose an international economic sanctions regime against Libya, and "prospects for further measures" to achieve this objective. Treasury Department representatives who attended the meeting were to have addressed the following three issues: "[the] status of compliance with [the] withdrawal order by U.S. firms [to sever their ties with Libya]," "undercutting [of the embargo] by [the] European allies," and "follow-on efforts to the Whitehead trip," which, as we saw in the previous chapter, was designed to persuade the nations of Western Europe to join the

United States in imposing economic sanctions of their own against Libya. Ikle and Armitage were to have presented their assessment of "the status of current U.S. [military] operations in the Central Mediterranean [and] prospects for planning for further operations"—the latter point representing a reference to the air and naval maneuvers the United States was preparing to conduct in the Gulf of Sidra in March.[14]

On February 12, 1986, St. Martin sent a memorandum, marked "secret/sensitive," to Fortier informing the deputy White House national security adviser, "Attached are talking points on Libya for your use at the CPPG [meeting] in Room 208 [on] Thursday, February 13, 1986."[15] Marked "secret/sensitive," the talking points Fortier received from St. Martin were mostly declassified by NARA on April 23, 2001. In his talking points, Fortier was to have begun the CPPG meeting on Libya by informing its attendees, "We have worked out the implementing mechanism for the January 7 economic sanctions [against Libya].... It would be valuable at this juncture to assess the effectiveness of the measures we have already taken, and begin to turn our attention to what needs to be done." Fortier was to have asked Gates the following question: "Bob, may I ask you to give us an intelligence update? I'm especially interested in the effect that the economic sanctions have had on the Libyan economy, and how long we can expect these effects to continue."

After listening to Gates' intelligence assessment, Fortier was then to have turned to Armacost and asked, "Mike, could you please bring us up to date on the current status of allied cooperation [in the sanctions] and prospects for further measures we can undertake as a follow-on to the Whitehead trip [to Western Europe]?" Fortier was also to have asked Kimmitt the following question: "Bob, could you please give us a report on the status of compliance by U.S. firms both with the January 7 withdrawal order [from Libya] and with implementing regulations issued last week [to enforce the sanctions]?" After receiving an assessment on the status of the American economic embargo against Libya, Fortier was to have asked representatives from the State and Treasury Departments and the CIA who attended the meeting "to comment on the extent to which the intended effect of the sanctions is being undercut by our European allies or other countries?"

Turning to the American air and naval exercises the United States was then conducting in the Tripoli FIR, Fortier was to have asked Ikle and Armitage the following question: "Fred, could I ask you and Rich to comment on the status of current operations in the Central Mediterranean?" Addressing the exercises the United States planned to conduct in the Gulf of Sidra in March, Fortier was to have asked Ikle, Armitage, and Moellering the following questions:

Has agreement been reached on the timing and modalities of a show of force within the area [of the Gulf of Sidra] claimed by Libya? Are there any problems we should anticipate now? For example, what are our obligations to inform Mediterranean states and regional states in advance [of the exercises]? With the [Capitol] Hill, should we informally fulfill the requirements of the War Powers Resolution by consulting key members [of Congress], as we did [during the exercises held] in August 1981?

Fortier's talking points concluded by noting that the Reagan Administration would develop contingency plans for American military action against Libya should Tripoli attempt to use force to challenge the American air and naval exercises scheduled to be conducted in March 1986: "DOD [Department of Defense] and JCS, with State [Department] and NSC concurrence, [are] to prepare an integrated strategy for the crossing [of the Gulf of Sidra], and responses to possible Libyan counter-measures [against the exercises]." [16] The talking points Fortier used to prepare himself for the CPPG meeting clearly reveal two facts: First, that the White House was concerned about the possibility that the American economic embargo might be undermined by either companies operating under the jurisdiction of the United States or the governments of Western Europe; and second, that the Reagan Administration was determined to press ahead with the American air and naval exercises in the Gulf of Sidra planned for March 1986, despite the risk and provocative nature of the military maneuvers.

On February 13, 1986, St. Martin and Morton sent a memorandum, marked "secret/sensitive," to Poindexter in which they summarized the results of the CPPG meeting held the previous day. On April 23, 2001, NARA partially declassified the memorandum, which reported, "The CPPG met today to review the effect of measures already undertaken against Libya and to consider preparations for further steps." St. Martin and Morton noted that representatives of the State and Treasury Departments attended the CPPG meeting, and reported that they were closely monitoring Western European economic activity in Libya in order to ensure that America's Atlantic allies did not undermine the American economic embargo against Tripoli. Specifically, the departments were determined to ensure that the nations of Western Europe did not replace the American goods and services Libya stood to lose from the embargo. Such action would render the embargo completely ineffective, ensuring the failure of the Reagan Administration's efforts to use economic sanctions to persuade Qaddafi to abandon his involvement in international terrorism. St. Martin and Morton noted that, during his trip to Western Europe, Whitehead had received certain unspecified commitments from the nations of the region regarding their pledge not to undermine the American economic embargo against Libya. The State and Treasury Departments were determined to ensure that the nations of Western Europe abided by those commitments.

> [The] State and Treasury [Departments] reported on their efforts to establish a baseline of European economic activity in Libya so that we can ... identify instances of undercutting with respect to our sanctions and ... identify areas in which it would be productive to request that they cease activity otherwise helpful to the Libyans. Once the baseline is established (on a country-by-country basis) we will be able to use diplomatic demarches to contrast, if necessary, what was promised John Whitehead and what is happening in fact. We will also be positioned to exert bilateral pressure in order to force cancellation of undesired [Western European] activities [in Libya].

St. Martin and Morton reported that the Reagan Administration was actively considering pursuing prosecutions of Americans who might defy the trade and travel embargo against Libya Reagan had imposed.

> Treasury is beginning to move from the "interpretative" to the "enforcement" phase of the E.O. [executive order imposing the embargo], and is considering selective referrals to [the] Justice [Department] (in instances of non-compliance), so that the word will get out that we mean business. Those who deliberately defy the travel ban would be allowed to come back into the U.S. in a way that denies them a media opportunity (e.g., arrest at entry), but does subject them to investigation and prosecution afterward.

In addition to ensuring enforcement of the American economic embargo among companies operating under the jurisdiction of the United States, St. Martin and Morton announced the formation of a Libya Task Force which would assume responsibility for monitoring any Western European effort to gain financial advantage by replacing the American goods and services Libya lost from the sanctions: "The Libya Task Force will produce a country-by-country list of the extent of [Western European] undercutting [of the sanctions]." Turning to the American air and naval exercises then being conducted in the Tripoli FIR, and the subsequent ones in the Gulf of Sidra planned for March 1986, St. Martin and Morton assured Poindexter that the Reagan Administration was laying the groundwork for conducting the latter military maneuvers: "Except for a brief update on the current exercises in the Central Mediterranean, discussion of military measures [against Libya] was deferred until a second CPPG [meeting] to be scheduled next week. At that time, the Freedom of Navigation exercise scheduled for late March will be discussed, along with necessary supplementary measures with the public, the Congress, and states in the region."[17]

By March 1986, the Reagan Administration became even more convinced that some nations of Western Europe were acting to subvert the American economic embargo against Libya by replacing the goods and services Tripoli had lost through the sanctions. Moreover, the administration was even more alarmed that some American companies were refusing to abide by the embargo, and continuing to pursue their trade relations with Libya. To this end, on March 10, 1986, Secretary of the Treasury James A. Baker III sent a memorandum to William Von Raab, commissioner of the U.S. Customs Service, which stressed the importance the Reagan Administration attached to strict enforcement of the American economic embargo against Libya.

> Now that the Libya sanctions are firmly in place, I want to be sure that we place a high priority on enforcing them. Attached to this memorandum are letters I have sent to Attorney General [Edwin] Meese and Secretary [of Commerce Malcolm] Baldridge asking them to give [the] Customs [Service] complete assistance in enforcing the sanctions. I know I can count on Customs for full and effective enforcement.[18]

In his letter to Meese, dated March 10, 1986, Baker informed the attorney general:

> I greatly appreciate the assistance you and the Department of Justice have provided in implementing the economic sanctions the President recently ordered against Libya. This letter requests continued support as we move into the enforcement phase.
>
> [The] Treasury [Department] is marshaling its resources to enforce the Libya sanctions. I have instructed the Commissioner of Customs, whose organization is primarily responsible, to give this matter high priority. For us to enforce the sanctions effectively, however, we will need Justice's assistance in the development of cases that result from enforcement efforts. I have instructed Doug Mulholland, my Special Assistant for National Security, to see that relevant information developed by the intelligence community is shared with the Department of Justice, especially the Federal Bureau of Investigation and the Office of Intelligence Policy and Review. After Justice has reviewed this material, we and Customs would appreciate being informed of the actions you believe are warranted.
>
> I know you share the President's commitment to effective Libya sanctions. Please convey my thanks to your staff for its continued support.[19]

In his letter to Baldridge, also dated March 10, 1986, Baker informed the Secretary of Commerce:

> Now that the economic sanctions President Reagan ordered against the government of Libya are in place, we are moving into a period when effective enforcement of the sanctions is paramount. I want to be sure at this critical time that we are making full use of our resources to enforce the sanctions, and I look forward to the assistance of the Department of Commerce in our effort.
>
> The Customs Service is primarily responsible for enforcement of the Libya

sanctions, and I have instructed the Commissioner to give this matter a high priority. In the course of its enforcement of the Export Administration Act, the Department of Commerce may become aware of information that may be helpful in enforcing the sanctions, and I would like to stress the importance of sharing such intelligence with Customs. In addition, I have asked Doug Mulholland, my Special Assistant for National Security, to ensure that relevant information developed by the intelligence community is shared with appropriate government agencies, including the Department of Commerce Intelligence Liaison.

I know you share the President's commitment to effective Libya sanctions. I ask that you emphasize the importance of our enforcement efforts to the people upon whose good work we depend for the success of them.[20]

The Treasury Department's concerns over the subversion of the American economic embargo by both some American companies as well as nations of Western Europe were relayed to the NSC. On March 17, 1986, Sherrie M. Cooksey, executive secretary of the Treasury Department, sent a memorandum to McDaniel informing her counterpart in the NSC:

The Department of Treasury is troubled by continuing reports of evasion of the President's executive order on Libya as well as back-filling by some European and other friendly-nation companies. We will take all necessary and appropriate enforcement actions in the United States within our powers. We have also called to the attention of other agencies the need to marshal U.S. government resources to enforce our sanctions.[21]

The internal memorandums within the Reagan Administration over the issue of enforcement of the American economic embargo clearly show two things: First, the administration placed a high priority on ensuring strict enforcement of the sanctions by all companies operating under the jurisdiction of the United States; and second, the administration deeply distrusted the nations of Western Europe, and believed that they might undermine the American embargo against Libya in order to serve their own economic interests. Accordingly, the administration was determined to closely monitor Western European economic activity in Libya in order to ensure that this did not occur. More importantly, the administration was determined to forge ahead with American air and naval exercises off the coast of Libya in order to demonstrate to the nations of Western Europe that unless they took economic measures of their own against Tripoli, Reagan was fully prepared to order military action against the Qaddafi regime if its renegade leader failed to abandon his involvement in international terrorism.

The Reagan Administration Prepares for a Military Showdown Between the United States and Libya

Reagan quickly approved the two American air and naval exercises off the coast of Libya Weinberger had recommended.[22] The more extensive of the two exercises was the second one involving three carrier battle groups scheduled to be conducted in the Gulf of Sidra in late March 1986. In the two weeks prior to the exercises, the Reagan Administration held extensive deliberations in order to consider the possibility that the maneuvers could provoke a military confrontation between American and Libyan forces in the Gulf of Sidra.

On March 7, 1986, Teicher and James R. Stark, director of political-military affairs for the NSC, sent a memorandum, marked "top secret," to Fortier. On June 21, 2000, NARA declassified most of the memorandum which informed Fortier, "Attached ... is a memorandum for your signature forwarding to CPPG attendees the agenda.... The CPPG is scheduled [to meet on] Monday, March 10, 5 p.m. in the White House Situation Room."

In their memorandum, Stark and Teicher made it clear to Fortier that the JCS had already drawn up a list of Libyan targets which American air and naval forces in the Gulf of Sidra would attack should they confront an assault from Libya. Stark and Teicher wanted Fortier's recommendations regarding Reagan's approval of contingency plans for American military action against Libya, should such a move become necessary.

> The purpose of the CPPG [meeting] is to review our currently planned military options for dealing with Libya and their possible consequences for a presidential decision next week. Specific areas you will want to raise questions are:
> 1. Will an FON [Freedom of Navigation] operation and limited [military] retaliation [against Libya] actually strengthen Qaddafi, and increase international criticism of the United States?
> 2. Are the JCS-recommended targets [for military action against Libya] the right ones?
> 3. How far down the chain of command should we place responsibility for the timing of the FON operation, and the launching of a possible response strike? Under what circumstances should another NSPG [meeting] be required? Are we satisfied with the rules of engagement?

Stark and Teicher warned that, should Reagan order American military action against Libya in response to any clashes between the two nations which might occur in the Gulf of Sidra, there was a possibility that such hostilities could trigger international terrorist attacks against American interests. In that event, Reagan would have no alternative but to broaden the scope of American military action against Libya. Stark and Teicher requested Fortier's recommendations on additional Libyan targets which the United States should attack in case tensions between the two nations further escalated: "We need to consider possible 'third-echelon' responses [to the threat from Libya]: How the U.S. would react to further Libyan military or terrorist attacks subsequent to the initial FON [Libyan] strike [and American] counter-strike. Should these include economic and political, as well as military, targets?"

Stark and Teicher had a number of other questions for Fortier which included the following: "What should the U.S. public affairs response be if Libya does not react to the FON challenge? What will we say if there is hostile Libyan reaction [to the FON exercise] and U.S. military counter-strikes? What happens if U.S. forces are lost or seriously damaged?"

Stark and Teicher concluded their memorandum by recommending to Fortier, "That you sign the memo ... forwarding the CPPG agenda." [23] Marked "top secret," the memorandum Stark and Teicher sent to Fortier for his signature was declassified by NARA on December 16, 1998. In his memorandum, sent to Armacost, Armitage, Gates, Moellering, Stark, and Teicher, Fortier informed the six officials of the Reagan Administration, "There will be a CPPG meeting in the White House Situation Room at 5 p.m., Monday, March 10, 1986. Attached [is] the agenda ... for your review.[24] Marked "top secret," most of the agenda was declassified by NARA on June 21, 2000. The agenda included "military options" Reagan should consider ordering if Libya attempted to use military force to challenge the American air and naval exercises in the Gulf of Sidra scheduled for late March, which were to be presented by representatives of the Defense Department and JCS who attended the meeting, including "[American] readiness to conduct FON operations," and "[a] proposed response to a Libyan attack," focusing on "initial targets" and "follow-on targets." State Department representatives who attended the meeting were to have presented a "diplomatic assessment" of "evolving European attitudes toward U.S. sanctions, and possible next steps" the Reagan Administration should pursue in its campaign to persuade America's Atlantic allies to join the United States in imposing economic sanctions of their own against Libya.[25]

Following the CPPG meeting on March 10, 1986, Stark sent a memorandum, marked "top secret," to Poindexter. On June 21, 2000, NARA declassified the memorandum which informed Poindexter:

> Attached ... is a memo from Rod McDaniel to Fred Ryan [director of presidential appointments and scheduling] proposing an NSPG [meeting] either for Thursday or Friday, March 13 or 14. At a CPPG [meeting] this afternoon

Three. Heading Toward a Military Showdown   99

it was decided that an NSPG [meeting] needs to be convened as soon as possible to approve plans for the upcoming FON operation in the Gulf of Sidra (March 23–29) and possible responses should Libya initiate hostilities.

Secretary Weinberger and Admiral Crowe are leaving for Europe Sunday, March 16, and Secretary Shultz is leaving March 19 or 20. Because of the key roles of all three, the NSPG [meeting] has to be held prior to their departure.

Jonathan Miller [deputy executive secretary for coordination for the NSC] and Howard Teicher concur [with this decision].

Stark concluded his memorandum by recommending to Poindexter, "That you authorize Rod McDaniel to sign the presidential schedule proposal [for an NSPG meeting] to Fred Ryan."[26]

Pursuant to Stark's request, McDaniel sent a memorandum to Ryan recommending that a one-hour NPPG meeting be scheduled for either March 13 or 14. McDaniel noted that Poindexter had recommended the meeting. Participants in the meeting would include, in addition to Reagan, Bush, Shultz, Weinberger, Poindexter, and Crowe, Casey, Meese, and Donald T. Regan, chief of staff to the president. The purpose of the meeting would be "to review U.S. policy on Libya." In requesting the meeting, McDaniel noted, "The President has met with the NPPG on this issue."

McDaniel informed Ryan that it was urgent that an NPPG meeting be held in the next three to four days because of the potential that American air and naval exercises in the Gulf of Sidra could provoke a military confrontation between American and Libyan forces in the Mediterranean. The NSPG needed to draw up a contingency plan for responding to any Libyan military attack against American forces participating in the exercises. Consistent with the view expressed by Stark, this needed to be done before the departure to Europe during the middle of March of three critical participants who would have to attend the scheduled NSPG meeting—Shultz, Weinberger, and Crowe: "The United States has important military exercises tentatively scheduled in the Mediterranean which could impact on U.S. policy toward Libya. Decisions on these operations need to be reached this week while the Secretaries of State and Defense and the CJCS [chairman of the Joint Chiefs of Staff] are still in Washington." McDaniel informed Ryan that Poindexter had recommended the NSPG meeting.[27]

Ryan approved McDaniel's request that an NSPG meeting be quickly scheduled. On March 12, 1986, Stark and Teicher sent a memorandum, marked "top secret," to Poindexter. On December 16, 1998, NARA declassified the memorandum, which informed Poindexter, "Attached ... is a memo for Rod McDaniel's signature announcing the NSPG meeting scheduled for Friday [March 14] on Libya." Stark and Teicher requested to Poindexter,

"That you authorize Rod McDaniel to sign the memo."[28] Poindexter quickly granted authorization to McDaniel to sign and send the memorandum, marked "top secret," to Gregg and the executive secretaries of the State, Defense, and Justice Departments, as well as the JCS and CIA. On June 21, 2000, NARA declassified the memorandum which announced, "There will be a restricted, principals' only meeting of the National Security Planning Group at 11 a.m. Friday, March 14, 1986, in the White House Situation Room. The meeting will review U.S. military operations against Libya."[29]

Attached to the memorandum Stark and Teicher sent to Poindexter was an agenda, marked "top secret," for the meeting of members of the NSPG which occurred on March 14, 1986. On June 21, 2000, NARA declassified the agenda, which focused on "military options" Weinberger and Crowe were to have recommended that Reagan consider in "response to [a possible] Libyan attack [against the] Freedom of Navigation operation" the United States was planning to conduct in late March. The options included either a "limited [American military] strike" against Libya, or an "expanded response."[30]

Following its meeting on March 10, 1986, the CPPG requested that the Defense Department draw up contingency plans for American military action against Libya in the event of that American air and naval forces in the Gulf of Sidra came under Libyan attack. The purpose of the NPPG meeting on March 14 would be to review those plans. On March 13 Weinberger sent a memorandum, marked "secret/sensitive," to Poindexter. Stamped upon the memorandum was a notification from NARA declaring that "upon removal of attachment, this document becomes unclassified." On December 16, 1998, NARA removed the attachment, which consisted of a Defense Department document containing the contingency plans for American military action against Libya the CPPG had requested, resulting in automatic declassification of the memorandum.

The Defense Department's memorandum was designed to formulate a White House strategy for addressing the potential for air and naval clashes between American and Libyan forces the American military maneuvers in the Gulf of Sidra threatened to provoke. In his memorandum, Weinberger informed Poindexter, "The 10 March CPPG [meeting] requested the Department of Defense to provide the attached paper for consideration at Friday's CPPG [meeting scheduled for March 14]. At the NSPG meeting I hope that we would review the plan, and consider possible other responses [to the threat of a Libyan-American military confrontation]."[31]

Most of the Defense Department document, marked "secret/sensitive," remains classified. However, one revealing portion of the document has been declassified. It shows that Weinberger's thoughts had radically changed during February to March 1986 regarding whether Reagan should be prepared to invoke the War Powers Act in anticipation of clashes between American and Libyan military forces once the United States conducted its scheduled air and naval exercises in the Gulf of Sidra. As we have seen, in February Weinberger believed that Qaddafi would respond to the exercises by confining himself to launching propaganda attacks against the United States, using the military maneuvers as an opportunity to portray Libya as a victim of "American aggression." However, upon further reflection in March, Weinberger came to share the White House view, as expressed by Stark and Teicher, that the exercises carried a high potential for provoking clashes between American and Libyan military forces in the Gulf of Sidra. Accordingly, the Defense Department document Weinberger sent to Poindexter urged that Reagan be prepared to invoke the War Powers Act upon commencement of the maneuvers: "Since there is a strong risk that Libya will react militarily when we cross the closure line [into the Gulf of Sidra], there is a possibility that the War Powers Act would apply. Because of that, and because of the need for prudent management of the [Capitol] Hill relationship, we recommend that we informally tell the Hill leadership just prior to the challenge across the closure line."[32]

On March 12, 1986, Crowe sent a memorandum, marked "top secret," to Weinberger. On May 30, 2001, NARA partially declassified the memorandum which confirmed the White House plan to conduct American air and naval exercises in the Gulf of Sidra: "During the period 23–29 March, EUCOM [European Command] will conduct a deliberate Freedom of Navigation [FON] challenge [against Libya] in the Gulf of Sidra, using both air and surface [naval] elements. This FON challenge will involve elements of three carrier battle groups.... EUCOM will issue a Notice of Intent twenty-four hours prior to commencing operations in the Tripoli FIR." However, Crowe warned Weinberger that the scheduled American air and naval exercises in the Gulf of Sidra carried a high risk that they would provoke clashes between American and Libyan military forces there: "There is a high probability that significant penetration [of the Gulf of Sidra] will generate hostile action [from Libya]."[33]

By the middle of March 1986 a strong consensus developed within the Reagan Administration that the planned American air and naval exercises in the Gulf of Sidra were likely to provoke a military confrontation between American and Libyan forces, and that contingency plans needed to be drawn up to confront this imminent threat. To this end, the Reagan Administration promulgated the Peacetime Rules of Engagement (PROE), which authorized on-scene commanders to respond militarily to any action perceived to threaten the security of American forces.[34] Since the administration believed that it was probable that Libya would attempt to use military force to challenge the scheduled American air and naval exercises in the Gulf of Sidra, the PROE essentially transformed these "routine" military maneuvers into outright hostile operations targeted against Tripoli. American commanders could interpret Libyan military maneuvers in the Gulf of Sidra conducted during the period of the scheduled exercises, however benign and inconsequential they might be, as a threat to American forces, requiring a retaliatory response. While the Reagan Administration publicly described the exercises as merely "routine" maneuvers, they were in fact military operations designed to provoke hostilities between the Washington and Tripoli, with the PROE providing commanders wide latitude to order an attack against any Libyan unit deemed to pose a threat to American forces which entered the Gulf of Sidra.

American and Libyan Military Forces Clash in the Gulf of Sidra

On March 23, 1986, American air and naval forces began their planned exercises in the Gulf of Sidra. Consistent with the Reagan Administration's fears, American and Libyan military forces engaged in a series of clashes during March 24–25. Not surprisingly, American forces demonstrated overwhelming military superiority against their Libyan opponents. During the clashes, American aircraft destroyed two Libyan missile boats and attacked and disabled Qaddafi's primary anti-aircraft missile battery based in Sirte on coast of the Gulf of Sidra.[35]

The clashes provoked an immediate congressional response, which came from Fascell. On March 24, 1986, Fascell sent a letter to Reagan, in which the congressman informed the president, "Your recent decision involving deployment off the coast of Libya has been a matter of great concern to me. That concern was heightened this morning by reports that an American aircraft was fired on by a Libyan missile." Given the outbreak of clashes between American and Libyan military forces, Fascell made it clear that Reagan had no alternative but to invoke the War Powers Act: "I write you in the context of my oversight responsibilities for full implementation of the War Powers Resolution. As the original House sponsor of that legislation, I have an abiding determination to assure full compliance with the law."

Fascell assured Reagan that he agreed with the president's assessment that Qaddafi represented an international menace: "Like you, I recognize that the actions of Libyan leader Qaddafi are contemptible in every respect. His repeated support for terrorism and his direct aggression against neighboring states merit the world's harshest condemnation." However, Fascell made it clear that Qaddafi's reckless behavior did not absolve Reagan from the responsibility the president had to abide by the War Powers Act.

> In pursuing policies intended to offset Mr. Qaddafi's actions, I am sure you would agree that we must respect and abide by our laws and constitutional procedures. In that connection, I believe your administration's actions in the Gulf of Sidra have failed to adequately satisfy the requirements of the War Powers Resolution.
>
> As demonstrated by today's reported attack, these deployments [of American forces in the Gulf of Sidra] constituted from the outset a situation where imminent involvement in hostilities was a distinct possibility, clearly indicated by the circumstances even prior to today's development.
>
> Under the circumstances, prior consultation with Congress was required under the War Powers Act.

In light of the clashes, Fascell urged Reagan to invoke the War Powers Act: "In view of these circumstances, I respectfully urge you to comply fully with provisions of the War Powers Resolution before the situation evolves further."[36]

Fascell's letter made it clear that the Reagan Administration had failed to involve members of Congress in the president's decision to conduct air and naval exercises in the Gulf of Sidra. As Fascell aptly noted, given the rising tensions between the United States and Libya in the wake of the Rome and Vienna attacks, the exercises were almost certain to provoke Libyan-American military confrontation in the Gulf of Sidra, a fact the administration fully acknowledged, albeit privately, rather than publicly, as we have seen. The administration was so painfully aware of the likelihood of such a confrontation that preparation for the exercises was coupled with contingency plans for a retaliatory response to a Libyan attack against American air and naval forces operating in the Gulf of Sidra which the White House fully expected. Those plans, as manifested in the issuance of the PROE, authorized on-scene military commanders to order an attack against any Libyan unit deemed to represent a threat to American forces in the Gulf of Sidra. Given the probability that Libya would attempt to challenge the American air and naval exercises, the PROE made a military confrontation between Washington and Tripoli in the Gulf of Sidra all but inevitable.

Given the high likelihood of a military confrontation between American and Libyan forces in the Gulf of Sidra, the Defense Department urged that Reagan must be prepared to invoke the War Powers Act, and involve the leaders of Congress in his decision to order American air and naval exercises off the Libyan coast, as we have seen. However, Fascell's letter makes it clear that Reagan ignored the department's recommendations and decided to forge ahead with the exercises without any congressional involvement in this action. The contempt Reagan showed for congressional authority in his decision to order the exercises triggered Fascell to send his letter to the president appealing for invocation of the War Powers Act, and involvement of Congress in the military confrontation between American and Libyan forces in the Gulf of Sidra the maneuvers provoked. Fascell's recommendations mirror those made by the Defense Department which Reagan chose to ignore.

The Reagan Administration Attempts to Address the Concerns of Members of Congress Over American Policy Toward Libya

Fascell's letter represents a clear and persuasive indicator of the growing unease and disenchantment in Congress over American policy toward Libya, especially the Reagan Administration's failure to involve lawmakers in the president's decision to order American air and naval exercises in the Gulf of Sidra. Accordingly, the administration had no alternative but to address Fascell's criticism in some manner. The White House strategy to address those concerns was contained in two memorandums which were sent to Poindexter: the first, from Nicholas Platt, executive secretary of the State Department, on March 25, 1986; and the second from Stark the following day.

In his memorandum, Platt informed Poindexter:

> The Departments of State and Defense have worked with other relevant agencies, including [the] Justice [Department], in developing papers related to the activities of U.S. forces in the Gulf of Sidra. [The] White House Counsel has led a series of discussions that has brought about substantial agreement that a report should be immediately filed with Congress describing the activities involved [in the Gulf of Sidra], and that some appropriate official should respond to the letter of March 24, 1986, of [House Foreign Affairs Committee] Chairman Fascell. To that end, the following documents are enclosed:
> 1. A transmittal memo from [the] State and Defense [Departments], accompanying the report to Congress on the activities involved [in the Gulf of Sidra].
> 2. A draft letter responding to Chairman Fascell.[37]

The memorandum from the State and Defense Departments Platt referred to was written by Whitehead, acting on behalf of Shultz, and Weinberger, respectively, which they sent to Reagan on March 26, 1986. In their memorandum, Weinberger and Whitehead informed Reagan:

> Attached for your signature is a report to Congress on the recent actions taken in self-defense by the U.S. Navy in the Gulf of Sidra. This report is submitted to keep Congress informed on these important developments. Further consultation with and/or reporting to Congress may be appropriate in the future, depending upon how circumstances develop.

Weinberger and Whitehead concluded their memorandum by recommending to Reagan "that you sign the proposed report and transmit it to Congress."[38]

Stark sent Platt's memorandum and its attachments to Poindexter. Accompanying those documents were two memorandums, dated March 26, 1986, and marked "secret." On June 21, 2000, NARA declassified the two memorandums: the first from Stark to Poindexter, and the second from the White House national security adviser to Reagan. In the first memorandum, Stark informed Poindexter:

> This memorandum forwards ... a memorandum from [the] State [Department]. Attached ... is a memorandum to the President recommending that he sign letters to the Speaker of the House ... and President pro tempore of the Senate ... on recent actions in the Gulf of Sidra. The report describes the Libyan attacks and U.S. responses without any reference to the War Powers Resolution. Wider distribution of the letters to other key members [of Congress] will be made informally.
>
> [This memorandum] also forwards a draft White House response to a letter from Chairman Fascell. This section is being handled separately and a letter will be sent to Fascell over [Assistant to the President for Legislative Affairs] Will Ball's signature.
>
> Jock Covey [a member of the Near East and South Asia Affairs Directorate of the NSC] and Ron Sable [special assistant to the president and director for legislative affairs of the NSC] concur [with this decision].

Stark concluded his memorandum by recommending to Poindexter "that you sign the memo to the President." Pursuant to Stark's recommendation, Poindexter initialed the line next to the word "Approve," and sent the memorandum to Reagan.[39]

In his memorandum, Poindexter informed Reagan that the central issue facing the president was, "Whether to sign [the] letters to the Speaker of the House and the President pro tempore of the Senate ... describing recent actions taken in self-defense by the U.S. Navy in the Gulf of Sidra." In making the decision, Poindexter pointed out to Reagan:

> Secretary Weinberger and Acting Secretary [of State] Whitehead recommend that, in order to keep Congress fully informed on the Libyan attacks and our response, you send Congress letters explaining these events.... Although U.S. operations in the Gulf of Sidra were part of routinely scheduled exercises

without any firm expectation of hostile Libyan action, there were in fact numerous instances in which U.S. forces were involved in hostile situations. It would, therefore, be prudent to report on the incidents in the Gulf, consistent with our desire to keep Congress fully informed. Will Ball and Fred Fielding [counsel to the president] concur with the letters.

Poindexter's claim made in his memorandum to Reagan that the administration had no "firm expectation of hostile Libyan action" against American air and naval forces engaged in exercises in the Gulf of Sidra could not have been further from the truth. As we have seen, such action was widely anticipated among Reagan's national security policy advisers during the planning for the exercises, and the Defense Department, upon the CPPG's request, drew up contingency plans for an American retaliatory response to a Libyan challenge to the military maneuvers which the White House fully expected.

Poindexter concluded his memorandum to Reagan by recommending "that you sign the letters." Reagan marked his initials "RR" on the line under the word "OK" and sent signed copies of the identical letters to O'Neill and Senate President pro tem Strom Thurmond of South Carolina on March 26, 1986.[40] In his letters, Reagan provided a detailed account of the clashes between American and Libyan military forces which had occurred in the Gulf of Sidra. Reagan also vowed that the American air and naval exercises in the Gulf of Sidra would continue, despite these clashes, and that the United States would take appropriate retaliatory military action should Libya fail to cease its attacks.

> U.S. forces will continue with their current exercises. We will not be deterred by Libyan attacks or threats from exercising our rights on and over the high seas under international law. If Libyan attacks do not cease we will continue to take measures necessary in the exercise of our right of self-defense to protect our forces.

In a subtle rebuke of Fascell's argument that his actions in the Gulf of Sidra violated the spirit, if not letter, of the War Powers Act, and represented a subversion of congressional war-making powers, Reagan asserted that he had full right to order the American military operations underway in the Gulf of Sidra, absent the approval of lawmakers, pursuant to his authority as commander in chief: "The deployment of these United States armed forces and the measures taken by them in self-defense during this incident were undertaken pursuant to my authority under the Constitution, including my authority as Commander-in-Chief of the U.S. Armed Forces."[41] In his letters to O'Neill and Thurmond, Reagan made it clear that he would not bow to his critics in Congress, led by Fascell, who demanded that the president involve lawmakers in all current and future military actions he might order against Libya.

If Congress had any doubts that Reagan was not about to cede any authority to lawmakers over current and future American military action against Libya he might order, they were laid to rest in the letter Ball sent to Fascell on March 25, 1986. This was in response to the letter Fascell had sent to Reagan the previous day. In his letter, Ball informed Fascell that "I hasten to respond to your letter of yesterday to the President to put quickly to rest the misconception you may have of the actions we have taken in the Gulf of Sidra." Ball reiterated the Reagan Administration's position that the United States had the full right to conduct air and naval exercises in the Gulf of Sidra.

> Our maneuvers in the Gulf have long been planned as part of the global freedom of navigation program by which the U.S. preserves its rights to use international waters and airspace. Similarly, prior operations did not provoke a [Libyan] response. We obviously cannot be deterred from exercising our rights by Qaddafi's legally baseless claims or by his threats [against the United States].

Ball expressed the Reagan Administration's flat rejection of Fascell's claims that the American military operations in the Gulf of Sidra violated the spirit, if not letter, of the War Powers Act.

> We disagree with your claim that our "actions in the Gulf of Sidra have failed to adequately satisfy the requirements of the War Powers Resolution." Nor do we believe that the resolution was intended to require consultation before conducting naval maneuvers in international waters or airspace. We considered this question carefully and concluded that conducting the operations did not place U.S. forces into hostilities or into a situation in which imminent hostilities were clearly indicated by the circumstances. Contrary to your letter's suggestion, it is not enough under the statute that the operations [in the Gulf of Sidra] create "a distinct possibility" of hostilities. After Libya attacked our forces, we notified congressional leaders.

Ball concluded his letter by reaffirming that the United States was exercising its freedom of navigation rights in the Gulf of Sidra: "Our actions have been known to all, including Qaddafi himself. The very purpose of the present operation has been to exercise our rights openly and unambiguously."[42]

In their memorandum to Reagan, Weinberger and Whitehead argued that the administration had to respond to its critics in Congress, led by Fascell, who argued that, in ordering military operations in the Gulf of Sidra without any congressional authority, the president was subverting the war-making powers of lawmakers and violating the spirit, if not letter, of the

War Powers Act. But the administration's response, as expressed in the letters Reagan and Ball sent to leaders of Congress, was to vow that the president would reserve his right to take military action against Libya, both then and in the future, without consulting with, let alone seeking approval from, lawmakers. It was this open contempt for congressional authority in the conduct of foreign and national security policy which would ultimately lead to the Reagan Administration's embroilment in the Iran-Contra scandal; indeed, Poindexter and his colleague on the NSC staff, Oliver L. North, were conducting the Iran-Contra diversion at the very time that the White House staff was seeking to marginalize congressional authority in the conduct of American policy toward Libya in March 1986.

Qaddafi Emerges Triumphant from the Gulf of Sidra Incident

As we have seen, Weinberger had expressed the concern that the American air and naval exercises conducted off the coast of Libya during the first three months of 1986 could allow Qaddafi to portray himself as a victim of American aggression, enabling him to garner sympathy, and even support, from the rest of the Arab world in his confrontation with the United States. Weinberger's concerns turned out to be correct. The foreign ministers of the Arab League responded to the clashes between American and Libyan military forces in the Gulf of Sidra by "condemning the American aggression against Libya" and called upon the rest of the Arab world to help Libya "repulse this aggression."[43] The Arab League's condemnation against the United States for the Libyan-American military confrontation in the Gulf of Sidra represented a strategic victory for Qaddafi in his confrontation with Washington. It meant that he was virtually assured that the rest of the Arab world would come to his side in future hostilities between Washington and Tripoli, even in the case of an American retaliatory response to a future act of Libyan-sponsored international terrorism. This only served to embolden Qaddafi to pursue his international terrorist campaign directed against American interests.

Viewed within a broad international political context, Reagan's decision to approve the American air and naval exercises in the Gulf of Sidra was a monumental strategic blunder. It made additional acts of Libyan-sponsored international terrorism inevitable, and guaranteed Qaddafi a strong hand in confronting any American retaliatory military response which might ensue. Indeed, with Qaddafi armed with the support of the rest of the Arab world, Reagan's options in ordering American military action would be severely constrained, as the course of pursuing regime change in Libya would be foreclosed as long as the renegade leader in Tripoli retained the support of his fellow Arab heads of state. In the end, Reagan's get-tough approach against Qaddafi, as manifested in the demonstration of American military force in the Gulf of Sidra, backfired against the president and redounded to Qaddafi's advantage, as it provided the mercurial leader of Libya the support within the Arab world he needed to pursue his confrontation against the United States, making another act of Libyan-sponsored international terrorism against American interests inevitable, and guaranteeing that the ensuing American retaliatory military response would fall short of the achieving regime change in Tripoli. Qaddafi would arguably emerge from his confrontation against the United States as the victor because his regime would survive its conflict with Washington, due to the support Libya had garnered from the rest of the Arab world, and given the asymmetry of power between the two nations, survival was the best possible outcome the irrepressible leader in Tripoli could expect to his bitter and acrimonious confrontation with his archenemy — Ronald Reagan.

Reagan Delivers a Final Warning to Qaddafi

On March 27, 1986, Reagan appeared at a campaign rally in New Orleans on behalf of W. Henson Moore, the Republican nominee in the November election contest for the United States Senate seat in Louisiana held by the retiring Russell B. Long. Addressing the rally on behalf of Moore, Reagan devoted a small portion of his remarks to the growing crisis between the United States and Libya. In those remarks, Reagan gave Qaddafi one final opportunity to avert American military action against Libya which was becoming increasingly imminent.

In his remarks, Reagan announced the end of American air and naval exercises in the Gulf of Sidra. Reagan used his announcement as an opportunity to once again defend his decision to order the military maneuvers, arguing that they were merely routine. Reagan pointedly rejected the claims of critics of the exercises that they represented an American act of provocation against Libya, placing responsibility for the clashes between American and Libyan military forces in the Gulf of Sidra squarely upon the shoulders of Qaddafi.

> Some of those who often "Blame America First" have suggested that the presence of our fleet [in the Gulf of Sidra] was a deliberate act of provoca-

tion. The truth is, this was the seventh time our fleet has operated and had those exercises crossing ... into the Gulf of Sidra.... It was Qaddafi's illegitimate establishment of a line [asserting Libyan sovereignty over] the Gulf of Sidra that violated international law.

Reagan reiterated that the United States would not be deterred from exercising its freedom of navigation rights in the Gulf of Sidra by the threat of Libyan attack, and that American military forces operating off the coast of Libya would retain the full authority to defend themselves should they confront such assaults.

> The United States will continue to defend the basic principles of law, free navigation, and international security. And I've had one rule from the very first day in office: We will never send our young service people anyplace in the world where there is danger [they will be attacked] without them understanding that when somebody shoots at them, they can shoot back.

Reagan concluded his remarks on Libya by delivering a stern, blunt, and ominous warning that he would order American military action against Tripoli unless Qaddafi abandoned his involvement in international terrorism.

> Qaddafi has routinely violated the peace of his region, the borders of his neighbors, and the safety of innocent civilians around the world.
> The United States will not be intimidated by new threats of terrorism [from Libya] against us. We're aware of intensive Libyan preparations that were already underway for terrorist operations against Americans. Mr. Qaddafi must know that we will hold him fully accountable for such actions.[44]

The remarks on Libya Reagan delivered in New Orleans were deceptive. Contrary to his claims, the American air and naval exercises in the Gulf of Sidra were anything but routine. As we have seen, Reagan authorized the exercises in the annex to the NSDD he signed on January 8, 1986, in order to send a clear message to Qaddafi that the United States was prepared to take military action against Libya if he failed to abandon his involvement in international terrorism. And as the memorandum Weinberger sent to Reagan on February 10, 1986, makes clear, the exercises were also designed to convey that same message to the nations of Western Europe which were intent on preserving their extensive economic relations with oil-rich Libya, despite its involvement in international terrorism. Reagan's remarks make it clear that he had abandoned all hope that American economic sanctions would succeed in persuading Qaddafi to cease his involvement in international terrorism, and the president was now prepared to order American military action should another act of terrorism be committed which the United States could directly tie to Libya.

Conclusion

During the winter and early spring of 1986, the United States and Libya moved inexorably toward military confrontation. The critical events which triggered the growing crisis between the United States and Libya were the Rome and Vienna attacks, the most flagrant, bold, and audacious acts of terrorism ever committed by Tripoli to that date. The attacks gave Reagan a basis, whether legitimate or not, to order American military action against Libya. However, fearing that such action would result in a dangerous escalation of tensions between the United States and Libya, Reagan decided instead to choose the more moderate and benign option of economic sanctions in an effort to persuade Qaddafi to abandon his involvement in international terrorism. To this end, on January 7, 1986, Reagan imposed an economic embargo against Libya in response to the Rome and Vienna attacks.

However, American economic sanctions alone were certain to fail to achieve their intended effect of persuading Qaddafi to abandon his involvement in international terrorism. Western Europe enjoyed more extensive economic relations with oil-rich Libya than the United States did prior to Reagan's imposition of sanctions. The nations of Western Europe could easily replace the American goods and services Libya stood to lose from American economic sanctions. Accordingly, if economic sanctions were to succeed in persuading Qaddafi to abandon his involvement in international terrorism, they would have to be part of a comprehensive global economic sanctions regime involving Western European participation. But such a regime was not possible, as the nations of Western Europe had made it clear that they would not join the United States in imposing economic sanctions of their own against Libya. In contrast to the United States, the nations of Western Europe did not regard the threat of Libyan-sponsored international terrorism to be sufficiently grave and menacing that they were willing to sever their extensive economic ties with the oil-rich revolutionary Arab nation.

To induce the nations of Western Europe to abandon their neutrality in the bitter and acrimonious conflict between the United States and Libya, and support their American ally, Reagan ordered the conducting of air and naval exercises in the Gulf of Sidra in March 1986. The Reagan Administration hoped that the exercises would send a clear signal to Western Europe that the president was determined to order American military action against Libya unless Qaddafi abandoned his involvement in international terrorism. The administration hoped that the nations of Western Europe would respond to the looming specter of American military action against Libya by imposing economic sanctions of their own against the Arab nation. The assumption in Washington was that the nations of Western Europe wanted to avert a military confrontation between the United States and Libya at all costs, given the lucrative economic ties they enjoyed with the oil-rich revolutionary Arab nation, which would obviously be threatened should Tripoli come under American attack. Without Western European trade, Libya would face economic strangulation, imperiling Qaddafi's political survival. In order to avert this catastrophe, Qaddafi would have no alternative but to give in to Western European pressure, and agree to abandon his involvement in international terrorism.

However, the American air and naval exercises in the Gulf of Sidra failed to persuade the nations of Western Europe to join the United States in imposing economic sanctions of their own against Libya. Moreover, the rest of the Arab world condemned the exercises as acts of provocation against Libya and pledged its support for Qaddafi in his confrontation against the United States. This only served to embolden Qaddafi to instigate additional acts of Libyan-sponsored international terrorism, recognizing that the rest of the Arab world would come to his side in the inevitable military confrontation between Washington and Tripoli which would ensue.

On March 27, 1986, Reagan delivered a blunt and stern warning to Qaddafi that the president was poised to order American military action against Libya should another terrorist act occur which could be directly tied to Tripoli. Reagan's announcement signaled a fundamental change had occurred in American policy toward Libya. Previously, that policy had been based upon the premise that economic sanctions would ultimately succeed in persuading Qaddafi to abandon his involvement in international terrorism.

However, unable to persuade the nations of Western Europe to join the United States in establishing a comprehensive, credible, and effective international economic sanctions regime against Libya, Reagan ultimately abandoned any hope that sanctions could have their intended effect in inducing Qaddafi to change his behavior. This left American military action as the only viable option left which could achieve this result. All that was needed to spark American military action against Libya was another terrorist act which could be directly tied to Tripoli. On April 5 a Libyan-sponsored terrorist attack occurred at a disco in West Berlin, setting the stage for the climactic phase in the vitriolic and venomous conflict between the United States and Libya, which culminated in Reagan's decision to order the American bombing of Tripoli and Benghazi, as we shall now see.

CHAPTER FOUR

Reagan Orders the Bombing

> *The raid [against Libya] had been a genuine success ... Qaddafi, who had exultantly backed the bombing of others, was terribly shaken when the bombs fell near him.*[1]
> — R.A. Davidson, retired officer, United States Army

On April 5, 1986, a terrorist bomb exploded at the La Belle discotheque in West Berlin, a popular nightclub frequented by American military personnel. The explosion killed an American soldier and a Turkish civilian, and wounded 230 others, including fifty American military personnel. The Reagan Administration quickly came to the definitive conclusion that agents operating from the Libyan People's Bureau in East Berlin planted the bomb.[2]

The West Berlin disco bombing coincided with a fundamental change in American policy toward Libya. Prior to the bombing, that policy was based upon the premise that economic sanctions could be used to persuade Qaddafi to abandon his involvement in international terrorism. However, the United States remained the only nation willing to impose economic sanctions against Libya; the nations of Western Europe continued to balk at the Reagan Administration's appeals that they join the Washington in instituting sanctions of their own, This guaranteed that the American economic embargo Reagan imposed would have no effect upon Libya: Western Europe could easily replace the American goods and services Tripoli stood to lose from American sanctions.

The failure of American economic sanctions left, in Reagan's mind, no alternative but to opt for the use of military force in persuading Qaddafi to abandon his involvement in international terrorism. In his address before a

Senate campaign rally in New Orleans on March 27, 1986, Reagan made it clear that he was poised to order American military action against Libya once another terrorist act occurred which could be directly tied to Tripoli. Once the Reagan Administration determined that Libya was involved in the West Berlin disco bombing, swift American military action against Tripoli became a virtual certainty.

Planning for the American Bombing of Libya Begins

Most of the presidential records pertaining to the American bombing of Libya remain classified. Accordingly, a definitive conclusion regarding how and when Reagan made the final decision to order the bombing remains unknown. However, on April 9, 1986, Reagan held a critical meeting on Libya in the Oval Office. Attending the meeting were Shultz, Poindexter, Crowe, and Casey. Another senior foreign and national security adviser involved in the formulation of American policy toward Libya — Secretary of Defense Weinberger — was on an overseas trip at the time of the meeting. Standing in for Weinberger at the meeting was Deputy Secretary of Defense William H. Taft IV.[3]

On April 8, 1986, three members of the NSC staff — Stark, Teicher, and its deputy director for political and military affairs, Oliver L. North — sent a memorandum to Poindexter marked "top secret." The purpose of the memorandum was to prepare Poindexter for the critical meeting on Libya held the following day. Attached to the memorandum to Poindexter were "themes for your use," which was also marked "top secret." On March 21, 2001, NARA declassified both the memorandum and the attached document. In their memorandum, Stark, Teicher, and North urged Poindexter to "draw from the themes," which essentially amounted to talking points the White House national security adviser was to have used in organizing the agenda for the meeting.[4] Poindexter was to have opened the meeting by making the following points:

1. [We] only have about fifteen minutes to reach decisions on [the] timing and nature of U.S. action against Libya.
2. As I consider this problem, [it is] clear that basic force posture adjustments will be necessary to sustain our capability to act against Libya.
3. We also need to keep in mind whether we will use this opportunity to deal decisively with Qaddafi or whether to engage in escalating conventional American strikes [against Libya] and Libyan terrorism.
4. Although we had hoped to act [in launching the American bombing of

Libya] on Saturday night [April 12], for diplomatic and operational reasons, it now appears we need to wait until Monday [April 14].

During the critical meeting on Libya, Poindexter was to have stressed the following two points:

1. [The] President made clear on Monday [April 7 the] importance of striking targets that would hurt Qaddafi as much as possible without undermining those who may work with us in the future.
2. Depending on Qaddafi's response, we need to be ready when we have levels of follow-on strikes against military, political, and economic targets.

Poindexter was also to have asked Casey the following critical question: "What are the prospects for political alternatives to Qaddafi should we get lucky [in killing him]?"

The talking points Poindexter was to have used in the critical meeting on Libya suggest that Reagan made the final decision to order the American bombing of Tripoli and Benghazi at a meeting he held with members of the NSC on April 7, 1986. Reagan refers to this meeting in his memoirs, noting that "we reviewed maps and photographs of Libya, and weighed various options, including strikes in locations in Tripoli." Poindexter's talking points refer to Reagan having stressed in this meeting the "importance of striking targets that would hurt Qaddafi as much as possible without undermining those who may work with us in the future." In his memoirs, Reagan confirms Poindexter's reflections, noting that he wrote in his diary following the meeting, "I'm holding out for military targets to avoid civilian casualties because we believe a large part of Libya would like to get rid of ... Colonel [Qaddafi]."[5] With Reagan having made the final decision to order the American bombing of Libya during his April 7 meeting with members of the NSC, the conference which occurred in the Oval Office two days later was merely designed to select the Libyan sites to be targeted for the air strikes. This is confirmed by a notation in Poindexter's talking points which observes that "Will [Taft]/Bill [Crowe] to brief [attendees at the meeting] on status of targeting."[6]

Was Qaddafi a Target of the American Bombing of Libya?

Perhaps the most intriguing question regarding the American bombing of Libya concerns the critical question of whether the air strikes were designed to either assassinate Qaddafi or induce his overthrow. The short answer to this question is that there is no evidence that the bombing was designed to hasten the demise of either Qaddafi or his regime. However, as the talking points Poindexter used in the critical meeting on Libya held in the Oval Office on April 9, 1986, make clear, the Reagan Administration would have welcomed Qaddafi's death in the bombing, however unintentional a consequence of the air strikes that might have been. However, in the final analysis, the purpose of the bombing was neither to assassinate Qaddafi nor induce his overthrow, but, rather, to achieve the more limited and modest objective of persuading the renegade leader of Libya to abandon his involvement in international terrorism.

The limited objective the Reagan Administration was committed to achieve through the American bombing of Libya is confirmed by the talking points the White House prepared on April 14, 1986, hours before the United States undertook its air strikes against Tripoli and Benghazi. Reagan Administration spokespersons were to have used the talking points to defend the president's decision to order the bombing. In the talking points, the spokespersons were to have stressed:

> The United States is neither trying to kill Qaddafi nor to replace his regime with a government ... friendly to the United States. What we are trying to do is stop Qaddafi's direction of and support for international terrorism.
> He cannot [be allowed to] carry out terrorist acts with impunity. If he decides to stop his direction of and support for international terrorism, he has nothing to fear from the United States. If, however, he decides to continue or even increase such direction and support, the U.S. is prepared to sustain counter-terrorist operations against Libya as long as it takes to stop Libyan-sponsored terrorism.[7]

In his memoirs, Reagan confirmed the official administration position that Qaddafi was not a target of the American bombing of Libya: "The attack was not intended to kill Qaddafi; that would have violated our prohibition against assassination [of foreign leaders]. The objective was to let him know that we weren't going to accept his terrorism anymore, and that if he did it [engaged in terrorism] again, he could expect to hear from us again." However, Reagan also insinuates that the real reason Qaddafi was not a target of the American bombing of Libya was due to the fact that the administration had no firm evidence regarding his whereabouts at the time of the air strikes, and not because of the American legal prohibition against assassinating foreign leaders. As Reagan notes in his memoirs, "It was impossible to know exactly where he would be at the time of the attack."

Had the Reagan Administration possessed firm evidence regarding Qaddafi's whereabouts at the time of the American bombing of Libya it is reasonable to assume that the rogue leader in Tripoli would have been targeted for assassination, regardless of the legal prohibition against such action. Indeed, the congressional ban against arming the Nicaraguan Contras did not prevent North and Poindexter from developing a scheme to circumvent that prohibition through their involvement in the Iran-Contra scandal. The fact that the administration may have had Qaddafi's death in mind when Reagan made the final selection of the sites which would be targeted in the American bombing of Libya is confirmed by the president himself in his memoirs:

> On April 13 we settled on the principal target: Qaddafi's military headquarters and barracks in Tripoli.... Housed in the compound was the intelligence center from which Libya's worldwide program of state-sponsored terrorism was directed.
> We realized that it was possible, perhaps probable, that he might be at or near the intelligence center when our planes struck.[8]

Perhaps the best answer to the question of whether Qaddafi was targeted in the American bombing of Libya has come from Oliver L. North, who gained fame, and notoriety, as the central figure and mastermind of the Iran-Contra scandal. In his memoirs, North notes:

> Killing him was never part of our plan. On the other hand, we certainly made no attempt to protect him from our bombs. By law, we couldn't specifically target him. But if Qaddafi happened to be in the vicinity of the Aziziyah Barracks [his residential compound] in downtown Tripoli when the bombs started to fall, no one would have shed any tears.[9]

North's reflections regarding whether Qaddafi was a target of the American bombing of Libya are confirmed by Duane Clarridge, a senior official of the CIA, who participated in the selection of the sites targeted in the air strikes. Clarridge notes, "There was certainly no discussion ... that we might get him. Did we think that was a possibility? I'm sure we all did."

But Clarridge maintains that the primary target of the American bombing of Libya was Qaddafi's command-and-control center and not the mercurial leader in Tripoli himself. As Clarridge puts it, "The command center was something to take out.... Was it a way of getting rid of him? I don't think so." Not surprisingly, North agreed with Clarridge: "The target was the terrorist infrastructure [in Libya].... [The] purpose [of the bombing] was not to assassinate Qaddafi."[10]

One could argue that targeting Qaddafi's command-and-control center was tantamount to targeting the Libyan leader himself, as he resided in the compound. However, the Reagan Administration insisted that the two targets were distinct and that, by bombing Qaddafi's command-and-control center, the United States was not seeking to assassinate the renegade leader of Libya, but only to dismantle his terrorist infrastructure. This argument is valid, at least on a superficial level, but as North has taken pains to point out, no tears would have been shed at the White House had Qaddafi's death been an unintentional consequence of the bombing. And these sentiments within the White House were confirmed by three military commanders involved in planning the operational details of the air strikes — General Charles L. Donnelly, commander in chief of the United States Air Force in Europe (USAFE); Major General David C. Forgan, the deputy chief of staff for operations of the USAFE; and Colonel Tom Yax, director of operations for the Air Force unit which bombed Tripoli.

Donnelly insisted, "The purpose [of the bombing] was not to kill Qaddafi." Yax confirmed Donnelly's claim, noting that the Air Force pilots who executed the bombing were "not concerned about structuring a strike to actually catch him." Echoing North's views, Forgan noted that, "If we caught Qaddafi in bed [when the bombs fell on Tripoli] that would be a bonus, but that was not our goal." Indeed, in their final briefing before executing the bombing, the Air Force pilots who launched the air strikes against Tripoli were informed that American intelligence officials had failed to locate Qaddafi's whereabouts.[11]

In the talking points Reagan Administration spokespersons were to have used in defending the president's decision to order the American bombing of Libya, a one-sentence statement was prepared for use in case the air strikes resulted in Qaddafi's death: "If Qaddafi is dead, then this is a fortuitous byproduct of our act of self defense [against Libyan-sponsored international terrorism]."[12]

Walters Fails to Rally Western European Support for the American Bombing of Libya

Poindexter's talking points make a very interesting reference to the fact that the American bombing of Libya was initially scheduled to have been executed on April 12, 1986, but was delayed until two days later "for political and operational reasons." What are the "political and operational reasons" which caused this delay? The most likely answer is Reagan's decision to appoint Vernon Walters as special presidential emissary to Western Europe on April 10. Walters was to discharge his responsibilities by traveling to Western Europe on April 11 in order to gather support from Washington's Atlantic allies for the American bombing of Libya Reagan had ordered.

On April 10, 1986, Stark, North, and Teicher sent a memorandum to

Poindexter informing the White House national security adviser, "Attached ... are memos to Don Regan requesting aircraft support for Ambassador Walters' mission to London, Paris, Bonn, and Rome." The three members of the NSC staff recommended to Poindexter "that you sign the memo."[13] Poindexter quickly signed the memorandum and sent it to Regan. In his memorandum, Poindexter informed Regan, "I recommend that an aircraft be made available to support Ambassador Vernon Walters' mission as Special Presidential Emissary to London, Paris, Bonn, and Rome for consultation with key European heads of state on Libyan terrorism. He will depart for London on Friday, April 11, 1986."[14]

If the White House had any illusions that the Walters mission would result in Western European support for the American bombing of Libya, they were laid to rest when foreign ministers of the EC held a meeting in The Hague on April 14, 1986, hours before the United States launched its air strikes, to consider the growing crisis between Washington and Tripoli. The meeting was designed to enable the EC to undertake an eleventh-hour effort designed to avert the American bombing of Libya, which the governments of Western Europe now recognized was imminent as a result of the advance information of the air strikes they received from Walters. Following the conclusion of their meeting, the foreign ministers issued a statement in which, for the first time, they officially identified Libya as a state sponsor of international terrorism.

> The twelve [member states of the EC] are gravely concerned by the increased tension in the Mediterranean created by the recent acts of terrorism. They met today to concert common action against this scourge. They consider that states clearly implicated in supporting terrorism should be induced to renounce their support and to respect the rules of international law. They call upon Libya to act accordingly. The twelve are convinced that terrorist attacks do not serve whatever political cause the perpetrators claim to be furthering.

In retaliation against Libya for its involvement in international terrorism, the foreign ministers of the EC announced that their governments were ordering a reduction in the staffs of the Libyan People's Bureaus in Western Europe, a restriction on the movement of Libyan diplomats and consular officials in the region, and the imposition of stricter visa restrictions upon Libyans seeking to visit the area. These three measures would undermine the ability of Libyan embassy personnel to use diplomatic immunity to foment terrorist operations in Western Europe, and to prevent Libyan-sponsored terrorists from entering the region to do the same. However, this is as far as the foreign ministers of the EC were willing to go in joining the United States in its campaign against Libyan-sponsored international terrorism. The foreign ministers failed to even consider, let alone approve, the Reagan Administration's request that the nations of Western Europe join the United States in closing all Libyan People's Bureaus in the region, and impose economic sanctions against Tripoli.[15] Moreover, in their statement, the foreign ministers urged the United States and Libya to avoid military confrontation: "In order to enable the achievement of a political solution [to the Libyan-American crisis and], avoiding further escalation of military tension in the region, with all the inherent dangers, the twelve [member states of the EC] underline the need for restraint on all sides."[16] Since the United States was the only one of the two protagonists capable of projecting power in the Mediterranean, the Western European plea for restraint was actually directed against Washington, and designed to serve notice upon the Reagan Administration that the Atlantic allies remained strongly opposed to any American military action against Libya.

Through the measures they adopted against Libya, the governments of the EC intended to serve notice upon Qaddafi that he risked loss of his vital economic ties to Western Europe unless the rogue leader in Tripoli abandoned his involvement in international terrorism. This would hopefully represent a sufficient basis to persuade Qaddafi that his best interests would be served by joining the community of civilized nations in renouncing his support for international terrorism. If this EC strategy was successful, it would preempt any rational basis upon which Reagan could order American military action against Libya.

A Rift Develops Between the Two Sides of the Atlantic Over Policy Toward Libya

Despite the measures adopted against Libya, the Reagan Administration was deeply disappointed, indeed dismayed, by the results of the meeting of the foreign ministers of the EC. The administration essentially regarded the EC's actions against Libya as empty gestures which would do little, if anything, to persuade Qaddafi to abandon his involvement in international terrorism. The administration's dismay at continued Western European inaction in the face of Qaddafi's relentless campaign of international terrorism was revealed in the talking points Reagan Administration spokespersons were to have used in defending the president's decision to order the American bombing of Libya. In the talking points, administration spokespersons were to have acknowledged, "The President was aware of eleventh-hour actions taken at the EC foreign ministers' meeting. These actions included a reduction in the staffs of LPBs (Libyan People's Bureaus); restrictions in the movement of Libyan diplomatic and consular officials; and strengthening of visa application procedures [for Libyans traveling to Western Europe]."

However, Reagan Administration spokespersons were to have criticized the EC's intended actions against Libya as ineffective in confronting the threat posed by Qaddafi's continuing and relentless campaign of international terrorism: "Although these actions are certainly a step in the right direction, in our judgment they do not go far enough to ensure that the future terrorist attacks being planned by Libya in more than a dozen countries will be forestalled. The President felt an urgent responsibility to act decisively in light of the immediate Libyan threat." In an uncharacteristic jab at the nations of Western Europe, the spokespersons were to have insinuated that the actions against Libya taken by the foreign ministers of the EC represented a cynical ploy to forestall the American bombing of Tripoli and Benghazi, and did not represent a real and genuine effort to respond to the threat posed by Qaddafi's continuing and relentless campaign of international terrorism: "The EC did not produce those actions [against Libya] until after the United States had begun to consult with its key allies concerning the possible military action."

Reagan Administration spokespersons were to have concluded that, while the Reagan Administration appreciated the steps the nations of Western Europe had taken thus far, the White House would continue to urge their governments to take more effective measures to counter the threat posed by Libyan-sponsored international terrorism.

> We have been working closely with our allies to counter international terrorism. Some have taken measures [against Libya] and we applaud their efforts. Today the EC foreign ministers, meeting in a special session in The Hague, decided to restrict the movement of Libyan diplomatic and consular officials, reduce the staffs at the Libyan People's Bureaus, and institute stricter visa requirements. [However], much remains to be done and our consultations continue.[17]

The talking points Reagan Administration spokespersons used to defend the president's decision to order the American bombing of Libya contains a very interesting attachment regarding White House reflections on the results of the Whitehead mission. Recall that in January 1986 Reagan dispatched Whitehead to Western Europe in an unsuccessful effort to persuade the nations of the region to join the United States in imposing economic sanctions of their own against Libya. In a paper entitled "Whitehead Results," prepared hours before the American bombing of Libya, the White House noted that

> During his visit to twelve European countries, Mr. Whitehead explained the reasons for the U.S. imposition of unilateral economic sanctions [against Libya]. We encouraged our friends to look at their economic relations with Libya and consider similar peaceful measures, although not necessarily the same ones, to convince Qaddafi to stop his support for terrorism.

The White House noted that Whitehead had produced results from his consultations with Western European leaders: "The visit was an important step toward increased cooperation against international terrorism. European, and some other countries such as Canada, did take helpful steps such as agreeing not to sell arms to Libya and to discourage their companies from filling [in with goods and services] behind the departing Americans." However, the White House could not conceal its disappointment at Whitehead's failure to persuade the nations of Western Europe to join the United States in imposing economic sanctions of their own against Libya: "Overall, however, we were disappointed with the response of the Europeans [to the Whitehead mission] and felt more had to be done [against Libya]." The White House argued that the nations of Western Europe would have to confront the consequences of their inaction in the face of Qaddafi's continuing and relentless campaign of international terrorism, as Whitehead had made it clear to the governments of the region during his trip that the United States would resort to the use of military force if economic sanctions failed to persuade the renegade leader of Libya to change his behavior: "As Mr. Whitehead said during his trip, we prefer to use peaceful measures, but if they are not successful the President reserves the right to use other options."

A notation was inserted at the conclusion of the portion of the White House talking points pertaining to the Whitehead mission which observes, "This was not cleared [for public release] due to a lack of time."[18] However, this is undoubtedly untrue: The other portion of the talking points defending Reagan's decision to order the American bombing of Libya was prepared at the same time as the paper dealing with the Whitehead mission, and was released to the public. The real reason that paper was not released is most likely because it is uncharacteristically critical of Western European policy toward Libya. Indeed, the paper essentially attributes the American bombing of Libya as much to American frustration with Western Europe's determination to retain its extensive economic relations with oil-rich Libya as it does to Washington's exasperation over Tripoli's international mischief-making. The Reagan Administration certainly did not want to antagonize the nations of Western Europe at a sensitive time, as the American bombing of Libya was about to be launched. The United States would need Western European support in response to international condemnation of the bombing which was sure to come. Accordingly, the White House decided to withhold its paper criticizing the nations of Western Europe for the failure of the Whitehead mission.

As the talking points Reagan Administration spokespersons used to defend the president's decision to order the American bombing of Libya make clear, by April 14, 1986, hours before the launching of the air strikes, a complete rift had developed between the two sides of the Atlantic regarding the appropriate steps to be taken in confronting the threat posed by Libyan-sponsored international terrorism. The nations of Western Europe remained committed to a modest policy of limited measures against Libya in the hope that this might persuade Qaddafi to abandon his involvement in international terrorism. By contrast, the United States remained convinced that only the complete isolation of Libya from the rest of the international community could persuade Qaddafi to change his behavior. Because the nations of Western Europe were determined to maintain their extensive economic relations with oil-rich Libya, there was no way that a credible and effective international economic sanctions regime could be established which would inflict damage upon Tripoli and threaten the survival of the Qaddafi regime. The only option left, which would indeed threaten Qaddafi's grip on power and persuade the renegade leader of Libya to change his behavior, was unilateral American military action against Tripoli.

The position taken by the nations of Western Europe with respect to the growing and deepening crisis between the United States and Libya left, in Reagan's mind, no choice but to proceed with his decision to order the American bombing of Tripoli and Benghazi. The purpose of the Walters mission was to rally Western European support for the bombing. This was an impossible mission, as there was no way that the nations of Western Europe would have offered such support, with the notable exceptions of the United Kingdom, which shared American disdain for Qaddafi, and West Germany, the nation where the bombing of the disco in West Berlin had taken place.

However, the nations of Western Europe might have responded to the imminent prospect of American military action against Libya by agreeing to impose economic sanctions against Tripoli. In that event, Reagan would have most likely not proceeded with his order for the launching of the American bombing of Libya. Western European economic sanctions would have delivered such a crippling blow to Libya that the survival of the Qaddafi regime would have been placed in grave jeopardy. Qaddafi would have had no choice but to abandon his involvement in international terrorism.

By pledging that they would continue their extensive economic relations with oil-rich Libya, even in the aftermath of the bombing of the West Berlin disco, the nations of Western Europe deprived Qaddafi of any incentive he may have had to change his behavior. The only action left which had any hope of inducing such a change of behavior was American military action against Libya. Hours after the foreign ministers of Western Europe had announced that there would be no major change in the cordial relations their governments enjoyed with Libya, the United States launched the bombing of Tripoli and Benghazi. Far from achieving its intended effect of forestalling the bombing, the meeting of foreign ministers of the EC in The Hague had the unintentional consequence of hastening the launching of air strikes.

Reagan and His Senior Foreign and National Security Policy Advisers Brief Leaders of Congress on the Bombing of Libya

At 4 p.m. Eastern time on April 14, 1986, less than three hours before the launching of the American bombing of Libya, Reagan and his senior foreign and national security policy advisers held a meeting with leaders of Congress at the White House to brief them on his decision to order the air strikes.[19] North and Craig P. Coy, deputy director of the Office of Counterterrorism and Narcotics, drew up a list of all members of the Reagan Administration and Congress who attended the meeting. Administration officials attending the meeting included Reagan, Bush, Shultz, Weinberger, Crowe, Casey, and Poindexter. Thirteen leaders of Congress attended the meeting, including O'Neill; Senate majority and minority leaders Bob Dole of Kansas and Robert C. Byrd of West Virginia, respectively; House majority and minority leaders Jim Wright of Texas and Bob Michel of Illinois, respectively; Richard G. Lugar of Indiana, chairman of the Senate Foreign Relations Committee; Claiborne Pell of Rhode Island, ranking Democratic member of the committee; Dante Fascell of Florida, chairman of the House Foreign Affairs Committee; and William S. Broomfield of Michigan, the ranking Republican member of the committee. The agenda for the meeting called for Reagan to open the conference, followed by an introduction from Poindexter. Casey would then follow with an intelligence assessment, Shultz would provide a foreign policy analysis, and Weinberger and Crowe would explain the military operations which would commence hours after the conclusion of the conference.[20]

On April 12, 1986, Poindexter received a memorandum, marked "top secret," from five members of the NSC staff—North, Teicher, Stark, Coy, and Robert L. Earl, deputy director of the Office of Counterterrorism and Narcotics. On October 25, 2000, NARA declassified the memorandum, which informed Poindexter:

> Attached ... is a memo from you to the President forwarding details and talking points ... for use in his meeting with the congressional leadership regarding Libya. Arrangements will be made for the participants to arrive [for the meeting] as unobtrusively as possible.
> Talking points for your use during the meeting are attached.
> Ron Sable [special assistant to the president and senior director for legislative affairs for the NSC] concurs.

The five members of the NSC staff recommended to Poindexter "that you initial and forward your memo to the President [and] use the talking points."[21] Poindexter initialed the two blank spaces next to the word "Approve" on the memorandum the White House national security adviser received from the five members of the NSC staff in order to signify his acceptance of the recommendations.

The memorandum to Reagan the five members of the NSC staff prepared for Poindexter included the name of William L. Ball III. On August 6, 2002, NARA partially declassified both the memorandum and the talking points Poindexter used during Reagan's meeting with leaders of Congress, both of which had been marked "top secret." In their memorandum, Poindexter and Ball informed Reagan that he would hold a meeting with leaders of Congress in order to inform them of his decision to order the American bombing of Libya: "This meeting has been called to consult with the congressional leadership regarding the use of U.S. military forces [against Libya]. This meeting fulfills the requirements of the War Powers Resolution."

Poindexter and Ball informed Reagan that his decision to order the American air strikes against Libya was based upon the existence of irrefutable and incontrovertible evidence of Libyan involvement in the bombing of the West Berlin disco. The bombing came following months of efforts by the Reagan Administration to use non-military means in order to persuade Qaddafi to abandon his involvement in international terrorism. Those efforts ultimately proved to be futile.

> The evidence behind Libyan-sponsored terrorism has been building considerably over the last several months. The April 5, 1986, bombing of the West Berlin disco is the latest incident in which we have clear and convincing proof of direct responsibility and support by Libya.
> The decision to strike specific terrorist-related targets in Libya was preceded by political, diplomatic, and economic efforts to persuade Qaddafi to abandon his support for and use of terror. Ambassador Walters is briefing heads of government in London, France, Germany, Italy, and Spain on the

intelligence linking these terrorist attacks. He is advising them of our intent to act and is seeking their support.

Poindexter and Ball concluded their memorandum to Reagan by informing the president that during his meeting with leaders of Congress, "Secretaries Shultz and Weinberger and Admiral Crowe will provide details on diplomatic activity and U.S. military operations [against Libya]. Talking points for your use during the meeting are attached."[22]

The talking points Reagan used to brief leaders of Congress during their meeting regarding his decision to order the American bombing of Libya remain classified. However, as noted, the talking points Poindexter used to brief leaders of Congress during the meeting have been partially declassified. Poindexter's opening remarks make it clear that Reagan had informed leaders of Congress that the purpose of the meeting was to enable the administration to share intelligence information regarding Libyan involvement in the bombing of the West Berlin disco, and to notify lawmakers that the president had decided to respond by ordering American air strikes against Tripoli and Benghazi: "As the President has said, we would like to brief you on what we know about Libya's involvement in international terrorism — and specifically the bombing last week in Berlin — and to tell you what action the United States is taking against this threat."

Poindexter proceeded with his briefing of leaders of Congress by arguing that the Reagan Administration had thus far exhausted all efforts short of the use of American military force against Libya in order to persuade Qaddafi to abandon his involvement in international terrorism; but those efforts had been to no avail. Poindexter reminded the congressional attendees:

> Less than three weeks ago some of you came to the White House as we described how Libyan forces had repeatedly fired missiles at US aircraft over international waters, and how our forces had defended themselves in a measured and proportional manner. Unfortunately, in spite of the Gulf of Sidra action, Qaddafi continued with his plans for terrorist attacks against American citizens and facilities.
> The United States has tried every possible means short of military action to convince Qaddafi to stop his outlaw behavior. Diplomacy, economic sanctions, and even military posture have all been in vain.

Poindexter informed leaders of Congress that the Reagan Administration had reached the firm conclusion that only American military action against Libya would persuade Qaddafi to abandon his support for international terrorism.

> Some would argue that a military response [to Libyan-sponsored international terrorism] only provokes Qaddafi to greater excesses. That's simply not true. We know that Qaddafi uses this as an excuse for [terrorist] actions he has already planned far ahead of time.
>
> In fact, it is our unanimous opinion that [the] failure to respond [to Libyan-sponsored international terrorism] by the world community has encouraged Qaddafi's aggression. Only when he is made to pay an unacceptable price will he stop.

Poindexter made it clear to leaders of Congress that Reagan had made a final and irreversible decision to order the American bombing of Libya, which would commence hours following their meeting: "Very shortly, American aircraft will strike terrorist facilities and headquarters in Libya, together with military facilities which support Libyan aggression. Within forty-eight hours the President will send you a full report of that action. I'll let Cap [Weinberger] and Bill Crowe elaborate on the military operation."

After Poindexter concluded his briefing he introduced Casey, Shultz, and Weinberger and Crowe to leaders of Congress. In three separate introductions, Poindexter informed leaders of Congress:

> Bill [Casey] will be brief you on what we know of Libyan terrorist activity ... George Shultz will review our extensive diplomatic activity and consultations with allies, including the visit by Ambassador Dick Walters to London, Paris, Rome, Bonn, and Madrid, [and] Cap and Admiral Crowe will now describe in more detail the planned military strikes.[23]

In remarks delivered during his briefing of leaders of Congress, Poindexter made it clear that the purpose of the meeting was not to solicit the views of lawmakers regarding whether Reagan's decision to order the American bombing of Libya should proceed, but to inform them that such action would go forward regardless of whether or not they concurred. Indeed, one of the leaders of Congress who attended the meeting, Senate Minority Leader Byrd, charged that the conference did not satisfy the requirements of the War Powers Act because it served "as notification rather than consultation." By that, Byrd meant that Reagan and his senior foreign and national security policy advisers failed to solicit the views of leaders of Congress as to whether the president's decision to order the American bombing of Libya should indeed proceed; rather, as Poindexter's remarks clearly illustrate, lawmakers were merely notified of the impending action. Leaders of Congress were given no opportunity to voice their opinion as to whether they supported or opposed the action. Speaking on the Senate floor on April 15, 1986, Byrd explained that "the purpose of consultation [under the War Powers Act] is [for the president] to seek the best possible advice so that the actions of this nation on the weighty matter of conducting hostile action is given the benefit of thoughtful consideration by responsible public officials in both branches of government."

But in a much larger sense, Byrd's point is really academic: The Reagan Administration fully recognized that the president's decision to order the American bombing of Libya would have the near-unanimous support of members of Congress; accordingly, there was really no need for the White House to solicit the views of lawmakers regarding the impending military action. Indeed, another leader of Congress who attended the meeting with Reagan, Senator Lugar, argued that the conference did indeed satisfy the requirements of the War Powers Act, contrary to Byrd's view. Lugar argued that Reagan would have rescinded his decision to order the American bombing of Libya had any congressional attendee at the meeting strongly objected to the impending military action.[24]

Consistent with Lugar's argument, Whitehead, who did not attend the meeting between Reagan and leaders of Congress, quotes the president as assuring lawmakers that, "At the conclusion of this meeting, I could call off the [military] operation [against Libya]. I am not presenting you with a fait accompli. We will decide at this meeting whether to proceed [with the bombing of Libya]."[25] According to Whitehead, Reagan then turned to leaders of Congress attending the meeting and posed the following question: "I would like to ask if any of you believe we should cancel the operation which I can now do by placing a call from this telephone. Please raise your hands if you believe we should cancel." As Whitehead notes, "No hands were raised."[26]

But, contrary to his assurances, it is inconceivable that Reagan would have actually rescinded his decision to order the American bombing of Libya had any leader of Congress attending the meeting held hours before the launching of the air strikes objected to such action. In all likelihood, Reagan made the offer to rescind his decision only because he fully realized no leader of Congress would oppose the bombing. Reagan's offer represented an empty gesture designed to create the appearance that the president had involved Congress in his decision to order the bombing when, in fact, he had not done so. Contrary to his assurances, Reagan had indeed presented leaders of Congress with a fait accompli: His meeting with lawmakers to inform them of his decision to order the American bombing of Libya was a pro forma exercise designed to create the appearance that he was consulting with them about his action, when in fact he was notifying them of it. Byrd's argument that Reagan had failed to properly involve Congress regarding his decision, consistent with the requirements of the War Powers Act, is correct.

But in the end, assured of strong support in Congress, Reagan permitted the American military to proceed with the administration's carefully planned bombing of Libya. A total of sixteen American F-111 aircraft based in the United Kingdom bombed three targets in Tripoli: Seven attacked Qaddafi's residential compound and command-and-control center, six struck the Tripoli Military Airfield, and three attacked the Murat Sidi Bilal Training Camp. Another total of twelve American aircraft based in the Mediterranean bombed two targets in Benghazi: Six attacked the Benina Airfield, and another six struck the Benghazi Military and Jamahiriyya Barracks. Four of the targets collectively represented the infrastructure supporting Qaddafi's international terrorist campaign. The fifth target—the Benina Airfield—was bombed to prevent Libyan aircraft from threatening the American planes which struck Benghazi. The five separate air strikes lasted approximately twenty minutes, concluding shortly after 7 p.m. Eastern time.[27] Two hours later, Reagan delivered a nationwide television address from the Oval Office explaining why he had decided to order the American military action.[28]

The views of members of Congress regarding the American bombing of Libya were perhaps best expressed by Senate Majority Leader Dole, who attended the meeting with Reagan at the White House hours before the air strikes, and Representative, and future Speaker of the House, Newt Gingrich of Georgia. Responding to the news of the bombing, Dole emphatically declared that, "The President did what he had to do.... He met his responsibilities as Commander-in-Chief.... Now it is up to us [in Congress] to do our part ... to stand together in doing whatever it takes to answer the challenge of international terrorism."[29] Dole's sentiments were echoed by Gingrich. In a letter circulated to House members on April 15, 1986, Gingrich declared, "On Monday [April 14], America challenged state terrorism and committed its forces to the battle for civilized behavior and the rule of law. We must all recognize that ... Qaddafi is a serious enemy of Western civilization and the rule of law."[30] The strong support in Congress for American military action against Libya made involvement of lawmakers in Reagan's decision to order the bombing of Tripoli and Benghazi superfluous and unnecessary.

Democratic Leaders in the Senate Voice Criticism of Reagan

While the American bombing of Libya had the near-unanimous support of members of Congress, Reagan's failure to adequately involve lawmakers in his decision to order the air strikes antagonized at least a few influential Democratic leaders in the Senate. The leading Democratic critic of Reagan's decision not to properly involve leaders of Congress before ordering the bombing remained Senate Minority Leader Byrd. Following the bombing, Byrd joined three other Democratic leaders of the Senate — Claiborne Pell of Rhode Island, ranking Democratic member of the Foreign Relations Committee; Sam Nunn of Georgia, an influential member of the Armed Services Committee; and Patrick Leahy of Vermont, a then influential, and currently chairman of the Judiciary Committee — in sending a letter to Reagan. The purpose of the letter was to protest Reagan's failure to adequately involve leaders of Congress in his decision to order the American bombing of Libya.

The four senators began their letter by expressing their hope that the American bombing of Libya, combined with increased cooperation between the United States and Western Europe in taking steps to isolate Tripoli from the rest of the international community, would ultimately persuade Qaddafi to abandon his involvement in international terrorism.

> We are hopeful that the purposes of the military action you ordered for Monday, April 14, 1986, in regards to Libyan military and terrorist support facilities have been accomplished. Specifically, we join you in the hope that a powerful incentive has been provided for Colonel Qaddafi, as well as other terrorist elements, against the use of their tools of violence against the civilized world. Secondly, it would be a very positive step if our allies could take a second look at the question of sanctions against the Libyan government and join with us in a tightly coordinated policy whereby economic actions provide additional incentive to the Libyan government to renounce the use of terrorism.

After declaring their support the American bombing of Libya, the four senators expressed criticism over how Reagan arrived at his decision.

> In discussions with a number of colleagues, the question of the flow of information between the Executive Branch and the Congress has been repeatedly raised. We are very cognizant of the tight requirements of secrecy needed in order to ensure that operations of this type have the maximum opportunity for success, and in order to safeguard the lives of the courageous men and women who put themselves in harm's way to accomplish the goals of national policy.
>
> Taking all this into account, we would like to call your attention to the following factors: First, advance information as to the intentions of your administration was the subject of continuous press attention for over a week prior to the military action [against Libya], leading to advance defensive action taken by Qaddafi which could have endangered American lives. Much of this was the result of substantial public commentary by administration officials. Second, your special emissary, Ambassador Walters, apparently briefed our [Western European] allies prior to the provision of information to responsi-

ble members of Congress. Third, the first indication [to members of Congress] of your decision [to order the bombing of Libya] was at a meeting Monday afternoon [April 14, 1986] at the White House, after the operation was underway, and this amounted to notification of your actions, rather than consultation required by law; Section 3 of the War Powers Act provides that, "the President in every possible instance shall consult with Congress before introducing United States Armed Forces into hostilities."

The four senators argued that Reagan's alleged violation of the War Powers Act was so egregious that the law should be amended in order to establish a special body, composed of leaders of Congress, whom the president would have to consult before committing the American military to hostile action.

> We believe a strongly bipartisan foundation is the only guarantor of success in our nation's foreign affairs. It is in the spirit of further developing this foundation that we suggest that a consultative body, composed of the Speaker of the House, the President Pro Tempore of the Senate, the Majority and Minority Leaders of both chambers [of Congress], and the Chairmen and ranking minority members of the Armed Services, Foreign Relations, and Intelligence Committees in both chambers, be designated. These eighteen members then would have the responsibility of fulfilling consultative duties required by the [War Powers] Act before introducing United States Armed Forces into hostilities or situations of imminent hostilities, and would be the body to which you could look with more predictability for the purpose of fulfilling the obligations of your office under the Act.

The four senators concluded their letter to Reagan by saying, "We hope you take these views into consideration, and we can discuss making more satisfactory arrangements [for implementing the War Powers Act] than have sometimes been the case in the past."[31] On May 8, 1986, Byrd, Pell, and Leahy announced on the Senate floor that that they were introducing Joint Resolution 340 which would have established the consultative body, composed of leaders of Congress, whom the president would have to consult prior to committing the American military to hostile action. Members of the consultative body would have been the same as those listed in the letter Byrd, Pell, Nunn and Leahy sent to Reagan.[32]

Reagan Responds to Criticism from Democratic Leaders in the Senate

Pell, Nunn, Byrd, and Leahy represented influential members of the Senate. Accordingly, the White House could not politically afford to ignore the stinging criticism they delivered against Reagan in their letter to him. Indeed, the White House was determined to respond to this criticism. To this end, on May 14, 1986, Kathy Ratte Jaffke, director of congressional correspondence for the White House, sent a memorandum to Cathy Thibodeau, director of congressional correspondence for the State Department. In her memorandum, Jaffke wrote:

> I would appreciate your assistance in providing a draft response to the attached letter in which Senators Byrd, Pell, Nunn, and Leahy suggest that a consultative body be designated to refine the section of the War Powers Act on consultation [with Congress].
> Although the letter is undated, it was received shortly after the attack on Libya. Will [Ball] has requested a draft response from [the] State [Department] as quickly as possible. NSC has advised that Abe Sofaer [legal adviser to the State Department] would be the one to provide you the input.
> Thanks for your help.[33]

On May 30, 1986, Platt sent a memorandum to Poindexter, entitled "Response to Letters from Senators Byrd, Pell, Nunn, and Leahy on [the] War Powers [Act]," informing the White House national security adviser, "A draft reply is attached for the President's signature to Senators Byrd, Pell, Nunn, and Leahy on the above subject. (Also attached are the letter to the President from these Senators, and a copy of the bill on this subject introduced by Senators Byrd, Pell, and Leahy)."[34]

Poindexter quickly sent to Reagan the letter the White House national security adviser had received from Platt. Reagan in turn quickly signed and sent the letter the State Department had written on his behalf, which was addressed only to Byrd. In his letter, Reagan expressed his appreciation to Byrd both for the Senate minority leader's support for the president's decision to order the American bombing of Libya, and his commitment to improve the consultative process between the White House and Congress with respect to implementation of the War Powers Act.

> Thank you for your recent letter concerning the U.S. operations against Libya on April 14. I appreciate very much your support for the purposes which those operations were intended to serve, and for our continuing efforts to achieve a coordinated program of action with our allies to deter further support for international terrorism by the Libyan government. I also appreciate your views on how we might improve the flow of information between the Executive Branch and Congress in such cases.

In his letter, Reagan flatly rejected the proposal of Byrd, Pell, Nunn, and Leahy that the War Powers Act be amended to provide for the establishment of a special body, composed of leaders of Congress, whom the president would have to consult before committing American military forces to hostile action. Reagan warned that such a consultative process would jeopardize the ability of the administration to keep secret counter-terrorist military operations patterned after the American bombing of Libya which he might order in the future. This would jeopardize the ability of the current and all future administrations to successfully implement such operations, thereby undermining the capacity of the United States to effectively respond to the threat of international terrorism. Nevertheless, Reagan promised that he would abide by the spirit of the proposal of Byrd, Nunn, Pell, and Leahy, as embodied in Joint Resolution 340 introduced on the Senate floor on May 8, 1986, by consulting with leaders of Congress before committing the American military to hostile action, whenever feasible. However, in introducing the resolution, Reagan noted that Byrd had acknowledged that maintaining the secrecy of the American bombing of Libya in advance of the air strikes was critical to the success of the military operation.

> I have considered the specific proposal to amend the War Powers Resolution to create a formal consultative body of eighteen members of Congress for the purpose of consultation under Section 3. I believe it would be unwise to establish by statute any such rigid formula for prior consultations on specific counter-terrorist operations. Given the high stakes in human life that are at risk, I need as President to maintain as much flexibility as possible to judge how many individuals can be consulted in advance and in what manner, taking into account the facts of each situation. Congressional leaders, you believe, should be consulted, and I will endeavor in good faith to be responsive to your views, but I hope you will not find it necessary to insist on inflexible rules in this regard. As you recognized on May 8, the operation against Libya is one which required "the element of surprise if such actions are to be successful in minimizing American losses and in maximizing chances of the operation's success."

Reagan defended himself against the charge of Pell, Nunn, Byrd, and Leahy that he had failed to adequately consult leaders of Congress before ordering the American bombing of Libya. Reagan noted that he had made it clear since the Rome and Vienna attacks that he would order American military action against Libya if Qaddafi failed to abandon his involvement in international terrorism. Accordingly, the American air strikes against Libya could hardly have come as a surprise after the Reagan Administration determined that Libya was involved in the bombing of the West Berlin disco. Moreover, Reagan noted to Byrd that his decision to order the air strikes enjoyed strong support in Congress, making consultations with lawmakers unnecessary and superfluous, as the president fully recognized that the American military action would have their firm backing.

> I regret that you are not entirely satisfied with arrangements made prior to the April 14 operations for consultations with congressional leaders. Despite the difficulties of consulting in that instance, I believe we fully satisfied this important responsibility. My decision to defend American lives against state-sponsored terrorist acts was clearly signaled to Congress, to the American people, and to the world. I said in January, after the murders of Americans at the Vienna and Rome airports, that we would use force if Libya continued to use terrorists to kill Americans. This policy, I believe, was, and continues, to be overwhelmingly supported by Congress and the American people. I am particularly grateful, in fact, for the bipartisan support we have received [for the American bombing of Libya].

Reagan flatly rejected the argument of Pell, Nunn, Byrd, and Leahy that the meeting he held with leaders of Congress in the White House hours before the bombing of Libya failed to satisfy the provision of the War Powers Act which requires the president to consult with lawmakers before committing American military forces to hostile action. Reagan also summarily dismissed the charge of the four senators that the administration informed America's allies in Western Europe of his decision to order the bombing of Libya before notifying leaders of Congress of the impending action, claiming that only that information required for the success of the American military operation was divulged to Washington's friends in the region.

> The arrangements we made in connection with the April 14 operation ensured an opportunity for congressional leaders to make their views known before any irrevocable action was taken [against Libya]. This fully satisfied both the letter and spirit of the consultation provisions of the War Powers Resolution. The extent of my consultations with Congress in this instance was far greater than that provided by Presidents in prior similar instances, such as the Iran [hostage] rescue mission. Finally I want to assure you that our prior communications with selected allies were limited to that which we considered necessary for the conduct of the mission, and unusual precautions were taken to ensure their security.

Reagan concluded his letter to Byrd by expressing his commitment to working with Congress in order to ensure that the consultative process between the two branches of government required under the War Powers Act would be fully implemented in any future American military action he might order: "I believe, as you do, that full cooperation in this area is vital to maintaining the kind of effective bipartisan foreign policy we all seek."[35]

Reagan's position in his conflict with Byrd over his handling of the sensitive issue of involving Congress in the decision-making process with respect to the American bombing of Libya essentially boiled down to his argument that consulting with lawmakers regarding the air strikes was superfluous and unnecessary: The military action enjoyed strong support on Capitol Hill. Accordingly, Reagan argued that his failure to adequately consult leaders of Congress regarding this decision did not justify amending the War Powers Act in order to create a special body with whom the president would have to confer before ordering future American military action. Reagan's position received the strong support of Congress as lawmakers refused to even consider, let alone act upon, Joint Resolution 340. The inaction by Congress represented a sharp rebuke against Reagan's critics on Capitol Hill, led by Byrd, who charged that the president had subverted the consultative provisions of the War Powers Act in ordering the American bombing of Libya without adequately involving lawmakers in his decision.

The Reagan Administration Defends the American Bombing of Libya

While the White House fully recognized that Reagan's decision to order the American bombing of Libya would have strong support in Congress, this was hardly the case with the international community. Indeed, the White House was prepared for widespread international criticism, if not condemnation, of the bombing. To counter this criticism, on April 16, 1986, Thomas F. Gibson III, special assistant to the president and director of the White House Office of Public Affairs, sent a memorandum to all Reagan Administration spokespersons. In his memorandum, Gibson wrote, "Attached for your use are talking points on the U.S. action against terrorist targets in Libya. If you have any questions concerning these materials, please feel free to call the Office of Public Affairs.... Thanks very much."[36]

In their talking points, spokespersons for the Reagan Administration were to have announced:

> At 7 p.m. EST [Eastern Standard Time], April 14, air and naval forces of the United States launched a series of strikes against the headquarters, terrorist facilities, and military assets that support Muammar Qaddafi's international terrorist activities.
>
> The attack [against Libya] followed clear and irrefutable evidence that Qaddafi had ordered and helped execute the bombing of a West Berlin discotheque that killed two people and injured 230 as well as confirmed reports of Libyan planning and preparation for numerous additional terror attacks.

Given Libyan involvement in the bombing of the West Berlin disco and Tripoli's alleged plan to launch a number of other international terrorist attacks, Reagan Administration spokespersons were to have argued that the president had no alternative but to order the air strikes against the revolutionary Arab nation: "To sit back passively would have been inexcusable and could have cost many American lives. Inaction would have been a clear invitation to proceed [with additional terrorist attacks]."

Reagan Administration spokespersons were to have argued that Libya represented the primary source of international terrorism.

1. Libya has become a textbook case of state-supported terrorism — operating terrorist training camps for instruction in demolition, sabotage, hijacking, and assassination.
2. Libya makes a mockery of international diplomatic privilege to smuggle arms and explosives and store them at its diplomatic missions.
3. Libyan "diplomats" have been directly involved in several recent terrorist operations, including a plot to kill dissident Libyan students in the U.S. last year.

Reagan Administration spokespersons were to have argued that the bombing of the West Berlin disco represented only the first in a number of terrorist attacks against American interests Libya had planned to execute.

Qaddafi and key lieutenants of his terrorist apparatus have ongoing plans for violence against U.S. citizens and facilities in Europe, the Middle East, Africa, and Latin America.

1. U.S. citizens are being followed and our embassies watched by Libyan agents in a number of cities around the world.
2. Reports indicate that Qaddafi intends to attack American citizens and facilities overseas.
3. In Africa Libyans are planning attacks and conducting surveillance of U.S. facilities in no less than ten countries. Just last week three Libyan agents entered one of these African countries intent on bombing the U.S. Chancery and kidnapping our Ambassador.

Reagan Administration spokespersons were to have argued that the bombing of the West Berlin disco had coincided with three other terrorist attacks against American targets Libya had planned to launch in Paris and Beirut, which were either foiled or aborted.

> There is compelling evidence of Libyan involvement in other planned attacks against United States citizens in recent weeks, several of which were designed to cause maximum casualties similar to the Berlin bombing.
> 1. France expelled two members of the Libyan People's Bureau in Paris for their involvement in a planned attack on visa applicants waiting in line at the U.S. Embassy on March 28.

2. Six days later, France expelled two Fatah Force 17 members recruited by Libya to conduct another operation against the United States in Paris.
3. On April 6 a Libyan-inspired plot to attack the U.S. Embassy in Beirut resulted in a near miss when a 107 mm rocket fired at the embassy exploded on launch.

Reagan Administration spokespersons were to have argued that Qaddafi was intent upon carrying out a widespread international terrorist campaign of which the bombing of the West Berlin disco represented only one of a number of terrorist acts Libya had planned. Accordingly, the American air strikes against Libya were designed to forestall Qaddafi from executing the numerous international terrorist attacks against American interests which were to have followed the bombing of the West Berlin disco.

> There is ample evidence that Qaddafi and his key lieutenants have planned to conduct widespread attacks against Americans over the next several weeks and that they are confident they could carry out a series of hostile acts against the United States.
> The President's action [against Libya] has put Qaddafi on notice that terrorist actions will only come at considerable cost.[37]

The talking points Reagan Administration spokespersons used to defend the American air strikes against Libya make it very clear that the military action was less a retaliatory response to Libyan involvement in the bombing of the West Berlin disco, and more designed to forestall future terrorist attacks against American targets Tripoli was allegedly planning. Indeed, the administration saw the bombing of the West Berlin disco as only the tip of the iceberg of a widespread and pervasive international terrorist campaign against American targets Libya was planning to execute.

Given Qaddafi's increasingly reckless and unrestrained embrace of international terrorism, the administration argued that Reagan would have been derelict in his duty had he failed to order the bombing of Libya; indeed, American indifference to the threat Tripoli posed would have been an open invitation for the revolutionary Arab nation to carry out its planned terrorist campaign against American targets. The administration hoped that the international community would share the American view that the bombing represented an act of self-defense in which the United States was seeking to protect the nations of the world from the threat posed by Libyan-sponsored international terrorism. However, as we will see, the international community did not perceive Libya to be anywhere as severe a threat to the nations of the world as the United States did, and remained skeptical, if not disdainful, of the rationale the administration had used to justify the bombing.

The Reagan Administration Assesses the Damage Inflicted Upon Libya

The fundamental objective of the American air strikes against Libya was to impress upon Qaddafi the fact that he stood to pay an unacceptably high price if he pressed ahead with his alleged plan to follow the bombing of the West Berlin disco with additional acts of international terrorism. Indeed, in his nationwide television address announcing the execution of the air strikes, Reagan made it clear that he was prepared to order additional military action against Libya if Tripoli sponsored any additional act of international terrorism. As Reagan put it, "Today we have done what we had to do. If necessary we shall do it again." Reagan expressed the hope that his threat to order additional American military action against Libya would persuade Qaddafi that the costs of launching additional acts of international terrorism would exceed the benefits, providing the rogue leader in Tripoli with the necessary incentives to dismantle his global terrorist enterprise: "We believe that this preemptive action against his terrorist installations will not only diminish Colonel Qaddafi's capacity to export terror; it will provide him with incentives and reasons to alter his criminal behavior."[38]

The American bombing of Libya could have had its intended effect of altering Qaddafi's behavior only if the air strikes inflicted significant damage upon the targets designated for attack. Accordingly, on May 7, 1986, David R. Brown, executive secretary of the Defense Department, sent a memorandum to Platt and McDaniel informing his counterparts in the State Department and NSC, respectively, that, "Attached is a statement we will release at noon today here in the Pentagon regarding the results of the operations against Libya on 15 April."[39] The statement Brown referred to in his memorandum was a comprehensive Defense Department report, released on May 8, which assessed the damage inflicted upon the facilities targeted for attack in the American bombing of Libya. The report began by explaining:

> The military objective of our operations was to inflict damage to the headquarters associated with terrorist activities, terrorist facilities, and military installations that support Libyan subversive activities.

The specific mission was to conduct simultaneous night strikes against five selected targets with surprise and saturation of enemy defenses, while minimizing collateral damage and combat losses. The raid was to damage and destroy the combat swimmer school at the Sidi Bilal Military Complex (terrorist training facility), damage or destroy Qaddafi's terrorist headquarters, and communication, command, and control apparatus at Azizziyah Barracks [in Tripoli] and Jamahiriyah Barracks in Benghazi, and protect the striking U.S. forces from the Libyan MIG-23 air threat at Benina Airfield and damage Libya's IL-75 transport aircraft.

The report concluded: "The results of the strike met established objectives. While complete destruction of each of the five targeted installations was never envisioned, all targets were hit and all targets received appreciable damage. At the same time collateral damage was held to a minimum."[40]

Given the success of the United States in inflicting significant damage upon the five sites targeted in American bombing of Libya, the air strikes did indeed achieve their intended effect in persuading Qaddafi that he stood to pay an unacceptably high price if the renegade leader in Tripoli chose to instigate additional terrorist acts of international terrorism. Indeed, in the weeks and months following the bombing there were no additional terrorist attacks involving Libya, despite the Reagan Administration's contention that Tripoli had already planned to carry out a number of deadly assaults against American targets at the time of the air strikes. The Lockerbie bombing in 1988 was in fact the only known act of international terrorism involving Libya since the air strikes.[41] The reason why Libya abandoned its involvement in international terrorism following the air strikes is no mystery: Confronted with the certainty that additional acts of international terrorism would provoke an American retaliatory military response, Tripoli had no alternative but to dismantle its global terrorist enterprise; to do otherwise, would have invited devastating American military action which would have threatened the existence of the Qaddafi regime.

Accordingly, the American bombing of Libya could not have been more successful in achieving its ultimate objective of all but eliminating Tripoli as the world's primary source of international terrorism. All in all, the American bombing of Libya would have to be judged as an unmitigated success, though one could still legitimately question whether American goals could have been achieved through non-military means. Indeed, one is left to ponder whether Reagan should have given the nations of Western Europe an opportunity to use the significant economic leverage they exerted over Libya in order to persuade Qaddafi to abandon his involvement in international terrorism.

However, as we have seen, hours before the American bombing of Libya, foreign ministers of the EC held a meeting in The Hague in which they made it clear that their governments would not impose economic sanctions against Tripoli. The nations of Western Europe could certainly have been expected to take a harder line against Libya in the face of additional terrorist attacks involving Tripoli. But by April 14, 1986, the Reagan Administration, whether justifiably or not, concluded that it could no longer wait for the nations of Western Europe to join the United States in its campaign to isolate Libya from the rest of the international community.

As we have seen, the Reagan Administration was convinced, whether correctly or not, that Libya had planned to follow the bombing of the West Berlin disco with a number of additional international terrorist attacks against American targets. Accordingly, the administration did not believe Reagan could politically afford to wait for another Libyan-sponsored international terrorist attack to occur in order to provide the nations of Western Europe an opportunity to determine whether their conciliatory policy toward Libya should be abandoned in favor of adopting the American hard-line approach against Tripoli. Rather, the administration believed that Reagan had to order preemptive military action against Libya before Tripoli could carry out additional terrorist attacks against American targets the Qaddafi regime allegedly had planned. Indeed, the American air strikes against Libya were less a retaliatory response to Tripoli's involvement in the bombing of the West Berlin disco, and more an act of preemption in order to persuade Qaddafi to abandon the additional terrorist attacks against American interests he allegedly planned to carry out.

In the end, Reagan had to weigh the costs of military action against the costs of inaction. Military action was certain to provoke international criticism, if not condemnation, against the United States and alienate Washington from its allies in Western Europe and the Arab world. But, as the Reagan Administration argued in its defense of the American air strikes against Libya, the absence of a military response to the bombing of the West Berlin disco would only invite additional acts of Libyan-sponsored international terrorism. Nevertheless, the fact that Reagan felt compelled to order the American bombing of Libya is a testament to the severe erosion in American credibility in the Arab world which had occurred during his presidency.

Reagan had all but abandoned the peace process, providing Qaddafi the opportunity to exploit the resulting loss of American credibility in the Arab world in order to challenge Washington's interests in the region. Qaddafi had every reason to believe, correctly as it turned out, that the moderate Arab nations would support Libya in its inevitable military confrontation with the United States. Indeed, it is reasonable to assume that the moderate Arab nations viewed Reagan's close and open-ended embrace of Israel to be even more distasteful than Qaddafi's involvement in international terrorism. Rather than representing a demonstration of American military power designed to neutralize the world's leading international rogue and menace of the 1980s — Muammar Qaddafi — Reagan's decision to order the bombing of Libya can be viewed as an act of desperation to salvage Washington's lost credibility in the Arab world. And Reagan's strategy to achieve this objective involved, not the use of creative and enlightened diplomacy to advance the peace process, but a demonstration of American military power against Libya designed to make it clear that the United States would use force against its enemies in the Arab world, with Qaddafi serving as the prime example of this.

To be sure, one can legitimately argue that the nations of Western Europe should have taken steps to make it clear to Qaddafi that he risked loss of his vital economic relations with the region unless he abandoned his involvement in international terrorism. This would have both provided Qaddafi incentives to change his behavior and deprived Reagan of any pretext to order American military action against Libya. Indeed, it is unreasonable to have expected the United States to absorb another terrorist blow from Libya in the hope that this might result in Western European adoption of measures designed to persuade Qaddafi to dismantle his global terrorist enterprise.

Accordingly, one can legitimately argue that Western European inaction in the face of Libya's continuing campaign of international terrorism made American military action all the more necessary. As Reagan put it in his nationwide address announcing the execution of the American bombing of Libya, "Self-defense is not only our right; it is our duty. It is the purpose behind the mission undertaken tonight.... I said that we would act with others, if possible, and alone, if necessary, to ensure that terrorists would have no sanctuary anywhere. Tonight we have."[42]

With the nations of Western Europe refusing to join the United States in its campaign to isolate Libya from the rest of the international community, Reagan concluded that he had no alternative but to order unilateral military action against Tripoli in order to preempt the Qaddafi regime from carrying out its alleged plan to instigate additional terrorist attacks against American targets. Nevertheless, the fact that Reagan had come to the sad and sorry point where he found no alternative but to order the American bombing of Libya is testament to his failure to pursue a credible policy in the Middle East: one based upon the preservation of American credibility in the region through the use of diplomacy, not military force. However much Qaddafi deserves condemnation for his involvement in international terrorism, a credible case can be made against the American bombing of Libya based upon the argument that it illustrates the degree to which Reagan wrongfully relied upon the use of military force, rather than creative and enlightened diplomacy, to preserve Washington's interests in the Middle East.

Was the American Bombing of Libya Designed to Instigate the Overthrow of Qaddafi?

Was the American bombing of Tripoli and Benghazi intended to incite Libyan dissidents to overthrow Qaddafi? Was Reagan prepared to order additional American military action against Libya in order to achieve this objective? A definitive answer to these questions must await the full declassification of the presidential records pertaining to the air strikes. However, as we have seen, the available evidence suggests that Qaddafi was not a target of the air strikes. The same could be said concerning the question of whether the air strikes were intended to incite the overthrow of Qaddafi. Indeed, the purpose of the air strikes was neither to kill Qaddafi nor induce his overthrow. However, if either event were to occur as a consequence of the air strikes, it would have been welcomed by the Reagan Administration which had open-ended contempt and disdain for Qaddafi, to say the very least.

Evidence that the Reagan Administration hoped that the American bombing of Libya would incite Libyan dissidents to overthrow Qaddafi comes from a memorandum Robert H. Pelletreau, deputy assistant secretary of Defense for Near Eastern and South Asian affairs, sent to Armitage on April 18, 1986. On August 6, 2002, NARA partially declassified the memorandum, which is entitled "Means by Which to Weaken Qaddafi's Internal Security Apparatus at a Propitious Time." In his memorandum, Pelletreau expressed his belief that the American bombing of Libya was likely to provoke an uprising within its army against the Qaddafi regime.

> In the period immediately following the U.S. retaliation [against Libya], Qaddafi will remain extremely vulnerable to spontaneous uprisings by disaffected army units, and thus is more dependent now than ever before on the loyalty and effectiveness of his state security organizations. Likewise, Qaddafi has always been considered paranoid and is without a doubt increasingly wary and suspicious of his military and security staff.

Pelletreau concluded that the Reagan Administration should take steps to exacerbate the political instability in Libya which the American bombing of Tripoli and Benghazi was likely to unleash.

> We have an opportunity to exploit these circumstances in a very simple and unrisky fashion, which will add to his vulnerability and hopefully provoke further confusion. By use of disinformation and the press, we may be able to, in effect, remove one or more of Qaddafi's key security or military officers. However, it will be Qaddafi himself who, out of fear, will eliminate these officers from his staff.[43]

Additional evidence that the Reagan Administration hoped that the American bombing of Libya would incite dissidents to overthrow Qaddafi comes from a document entitled "Next Steps to Deter Further Libyan Terrorism," which was marked "top secret" and written on April 17, 1986. On April 23, 1999, NARA declassified most of the document, marked "Flower," signifying that it was produced in connection with Operation Flower. As we saw in Chapter 2, Operation Flower was established in response to the presidential finding on Libya Reagan signed on July 29, 1985, which authorized covert action designed to instigate the overthrow of Qaddafi. Since the NSC administered Operation Flower, members of its staff were undoubtedly the authors of the document entitled "Next Steps to Deter Further Libyan Terrorism."

The declassified portion of the NSC document began by arguing that the American bombing of Libya had de-stabilized the Qaddafi regime: "Qaddafi's vulnerability to a coup has never been greater. He is terrified, confused, and unsure of how to stabilize the situation.... Our action has catalyzed elements of the Libyan military to act against him. But their ability to succeed depends largely on fast action." The document urged the Reagan Administration to grant serious consideration to exploiting the alleged chaos existing in the aftermath of the American bombing of Tripoli and Benghazi in order to incite Libyan dissidents to overthrow Qaddafi: "Time is a wasting asset and the U.S. must decide immediately whether and how to act in a manner that will energize rebellious elements [in Libya against Qaddafi]."

The NSC reported that Qaddafi had fled Tripoli following the American bombing of the capital of Libya, and had taken refuge in the desert.

> Yesterday ... photographic intelligence indicated that Qaddafi has most likely departed Tripoli for Sebha in Central Libya. We have seen an unusual number of VIP aircraft at the Sebha Airport and a "flight package," similar to that used by Qaddafi when he travels internally, is now at the Sebha field. Satellite imagery shows unusual security around several facilities and a residence in Sebha.

The NSC noted that the defenses at Sebha had traditionally been modest: "A battery of ZSU-23/4 anti-aircraft machine guns are normally in the area, but usually not deployed." However, since the American bombing of Libya an unusually large number of military assets were deployed in Sebha, serving as additional evidence that Qaddafi had fled Tripoli and taken refuge in the desert city: "There are two SA-2 and two SA-3 sites outside the city.... There are sixteen MIG-25 aircraft imaged on the field, along with several 707s, 727s, and an IL-76 which are normally associated with his movements."

The NSC argued that Qaddafi's focus in the days following the American bombing of Libya would be to restore his authority which had been severely diminished by the air strikes.

> It is likely that his capabilities will improve markedly in the next several days as he re-establishes his communications and relocates his command and control structure. Qaddafi's appearance last night on Libyan television will likely result in a reduction of dissident activity, and he will probably move more quickly to re-establish internal control unless he is further threatened.

The NSC argued that, despite his success in re-building some of his shattered authority, Qaddafi's grip on power remained fragile as the American bombing of Libya had succeeded in inciting domestic dissident activity against the beleaguered leader.

> There are a variety of developments taking place within Libya which may lead to the downfall of Qaddafi. The rebellion of the Libyan Army battalion at Tarhuna, south of Tripoli, and the subsequent civil strife that was evidenced throughout the Tripoli area in the late night of April 16 and early morning of April 17, presents an opportunity that we can exploit. Libyan military officers and intelligence officials in Tripoli are indicating to the opposition that the American bombing created a vacuum in the political leadership that disgruntled army officers are seeking to exploit to overthrow the regime. There are similar reports of army units in Derna rebelling.

The NSC revealed that dissidents in the Libyan Army were requesting additional American air strikes in order to fuel the insipient insurgency against the Qaddafi regime which the bombing of Tripoli and Benghazi had precipitated.

> While Libyan Air Force units appear to have dispersed the rebelling army units yesterday, an additional catalyst is needed to reinforce the rebellion. Libyan officers are asking for more U.S. strikes which would preoccupy the Libyan Air Force, enhancing the capability of the rebellious army units to march against the government. Such actions exacerbate the anarchic situation, and due to the perceived absence of Qaddafi, presents an internal dynamic to other Libyans that the regime can be changed. But this window will close as Qaddafi exerts more control. This control is directly related to the Libyan Air Force's ability to control the skies.

The NSC recommended that Reagan should grant serious consideration to authorizing additional American air strikes against Libya in order to support the incipient insurgency campaign Libyan dissidents were waging against the Qaddafi regime.

> The maximum option would be a U.S. air strike at Sebha, the desert retreat of the Libyan leadership. Alternatively, a strike at Libyan Air Force units in

Tripoli at Uqbah Bin Nafi may allow army units to march on Tripoli unmolested. Evidence that the U.S. is still engaged in Libya in confronting Qaddafi will fuel the unrest and contribute to the demonstrated willingness of the Libyan military to rebel.

The NSC recommended two options Reagan should consider in pursuing American military action to further de-stabilize the Qaddafi regime. The first option would involve placing American aircraft within striking distance of Tripoli in order to demonstrate the incapacity of the Qaddafi regime to protect the capital of Libya from additional bombing. The second option would be an air strike against Sebha, where Qaddafi was believed to be, in order to destroy his residence and military command headquarters. The implicit objective of the second option would be to assassinate Qaddafi.

> In signaling U.S. determination to maintain pressure on Qaddafi, the most effective measures — renewed [air] strikes or demonstrations close to Libyan population centers — would also entail the most risks. One option is to conduct feints against Tripoli, which would keep U.S. aircraft outside Libya's SAM [surface-to-air missile] envelope while still generating ineffective firing from Libyan air defense sites. The effect would be to heighten the sense of threat within the city and maintain the perception of Qaddafi's vulnerability.
>
> A second option, assuming that Qaddafi could be located at Sebha, would be to launch an air strike against his residence and command facility.[44]

Reagan failed to respond to recommendations contained in the NSC document that he consider ordering additional American air strikes against Libya. The reason for this is obvious: The American bombing of Libya served notice upon the Qaddafi that additional military action would be forthcoming unless the rogue leader in Tripoli abandoned his involvement in international terrorism. This threat was sufficient to persuade Qaddafi to change his behavior, and no additional American military action was needed to achieve this objective.

The Reagan Administration's objective remained to induce a change in Qaddafi's behavior and neither to precipitate his overthrow or assassination. The administration fully recognized that Qaddafi's objective was to survive in power, and not to seek martyrdom on behalf of "the Arab struggle against Zionism and American imperialism in the Middle East." Recognizing that Qaddafi was, in the final analysis, a political pragmatist, and not a revolutionary, the administration had every expectation that he would change his behavior once he confronted American military force, and realized that either the overthrow or assassination of the mercurial leader of Libya was unnecessary for the United States to achieve its objectives, which remained the elimination of Tripoli as the world's primary source of international terrorism. Since this objective could be, and ultimately was, achieved without inducing regime change in Libya, the administration was fully willing to peacefully coexist with the Qaddafi government, as long as the renegade leader in Tripoli abandoned his involvement in international terrorism, which he all but did in the weeks and months following the American bombing of Libya.

Did the American Bombing of Libya Actually Result in the De-stabilization of the Qaddafi Regime?

The NSC document quoted in the previous section claims the American bombing of Libya resulted in a significant de-stabilization of the Qaddafi regime. To support this claim, the document makes two rather stunning allegations: that Qaddafi fled Tripoli following the bombing and took refuge in the desert, and that Libyan dissidents launched an incipient insurgency aimed at toppling his regime in the days after the air strikes. Were these rather startling claims, which certainly raised hopes in the White House that the demise of the Qaddafi regime might be imminent, actually accurate? Or did they reflect the wishful thinking of the White House which was frantically searching for any evidence, however flimsy and lacking in credibility, that the ultimate and most momentous consequence of the American bombing of Libya would be the overthrow of Qaddafi?

On the evening of April 16, 1986, Qaddafi did indeed appear on Libyan television before fleeing Tripoli to take refuge in the desert, as the NSC document notes.[45] According to ABC News, American intelligence confirmed that an insurrection had occurred at the army base in Tarhunna, located fifty miles south of Tripoli, and that Qaddafi had ordered the Libyan Air Force to attack the insurgents. This is consistent with the document's reference to an insurrection at Tarhunna.

However, there is no evidence that the American bombing of Libya triggered anything more than scattered and isolated uprisings which did not represent a significant or credible threat to the survival of the Qaddafi regime. Indeed, the NSC's claim that "There are a variety of developments taking place within Libya which may lead to the downfall of Qaddafi" reflected wishful thinking in the White House. There remains no credible evidence that Qaddafi's grip on power was ever threatened by the very weak, scattered, and unorganized uprisings which the American bombing of Libya triggered.

The NSC's claim that "Qaddafi's vulnerability to a coup has never been greater" than was the case in the aftermath of the American bombing of

Libya is certainly true. But this says nothing, as Qaddafi's grip on power has always been secure, and the modest turmoil triggered by the bombing represents an aberration in the high level of political stability Libya has enjoyed under the rule of its supreme leader. Indeed, Qaddafi's rule has been so secure that the bombing failed to even approach the threshold required to incite the internal insurrection aimed at toppling the mercurial leader of Libya the White House had hoped for.

Certainly the NSC's claim that a credible prospect existed for Libyan dissidents to overthrow Qaddafi in the aftermath of the American bombing of Tripoli and Benghazi represented wishful thinking in the White House. Perhaps the Reagan Administration official who was most responsible for raising false hopes concerning prospects for the overthrow of Qaddafi was Secretary of State Shultz. In his news conference held on April 17, 1986, Shultz claimed "there was ... considerable dissidence in the armed forces of Libya with Qaddafi and what he is doing." Shultz issued an open invitation to Libyan dissidents to overthrow Qaddafi, proclaiming that such a development would be "all to the good" for the Libyan people. Shultz added, "We know that there are lots of people in Libya who think that Libya would be better off if Qaddafi was not there."[46] Shultz may have been correct in his argument that a significant dissident community existed in Libya opposed to the Qaddafi regime. But the dissidents posed no significant threat to the Qaddafi regime, and the Reagan Administration's hopes that the American bombing of the revolutionary Arab nation would trigger the overthrow of its irrepressible leader remained an exercise in wishful thinking, to say the very least, and an act of self-delusion at the very worst.

The Reagan Administration Pursues Covert Action to Instigate the Overthrow of Qaddafi

The fact that the American bombing of Libya was not designed to instigate the overthrow of Qaddafi does not mean that the official policy of the United States was not to achieve this objective. As mentioned in Chapter 2, on July 29, 1985, Reagan signed a presidential finding on Libya authorizing covert action to overthrow Qaddafi. On April 10, 1986, Poindexter sent a memorandum to Reagan apprising the president in the progress the United States had made in implementing the finding. The memorandum, marked "top secret," was written in Poindexter's name by Vincent M. Canistrero, director of intelligence programs for the NSC. On March 15, 2001, NARA declassified the memorandum.

In his memorandum, Poindexter revealed that the United States had enlisted Algerian and Egyptian participation in the covert operations to instigate the overthrow of Qaddafi Reagan had authorized through the president's finding on Libya.

> You signed the July 1985 finding ... which authorized support for third countries which are arming and directing anti–Qaddafi Libyan dissidents. The covert activity undertaken since July 1985 has focused its efforts to assist Algerian and Egyptian training and direction of paramilitary operations inside Libya. Problems have arisen in implementing these programs with third countries. Algerian support has diminished since leaks appeared in the press concerning our covert action program. Algeria has withheld some equipment ... intended for the use of the principal Libyan opposition group — the National Front for the Salvation of Libya (NFSL). The NFSL also has an uneasy relationship with the Egyptian government, whose support of the Libyan opposition agenda has waxed and waned depending on the political tides and pressures exerted by Qaddafi on the Egyptians. While unilateral propaganda and psychological operations directed against Qaddafi have been effective, third-party efforts to mold and guide a viable paramilitary force have had only modest success.

Given the obstacles the United States had encountered in building a viable counterinsurgency force against Qaddafi, Poindexter requested that Reagan sign a new finding which would authorize the training of a newly reconstituted and effective NFSL militia.

> We have concluded after extensive review by the Planning and Coordination Group [of the NSC] that direct training and supply of the NFSL for specific covert missions is required to get the program moving. If you approve the finding, upwards of 200 Libyan opposition cadre may be trained for special missions inside Libya. The initial training would take place in the U.S. In addition, we would propose to monitor and guide the implementation of the covert action closely in order to ensure its integration with other U.S. activities directed at Qaddafi and its responsiveness to U.S. policy objectives. The attached ... finding does not add to the existing authorities provided by the July 1985 Finding on Libya.

Poindexter explained that the new presidential finding on Libya which he recommended that Reagan sign was intended to strengthen the capability of the United States to provide the necessary operational and logistical support in order to enable Libyan dissidents to undertake a successful counterinsurgency to overthrow Qaddafi.

> This direct role [for the United States] would include preparation of target assignments for paramilitary operations inside Libya, and would provide a greater measure of U.S. control over opposition activities than is possible under existing restrictions of providing lethal assistance only through third coun-

tries. It will also speed up the covert action program, make it more effective, and telescope the time necessary to field the initial twenty-man special mission to carry out the sabotage activity inside Libya. These activities should be carefully programmed to support U.S. policy objectives.

The Vice President, the Joint Chiefs of Staff, the Secretaries of State and Defense, and the Director of Central Intelligence concur with the new finding. The Attorney General has reviewed the program and concurs with the new finding.

Poindexter concluded his memorandum by recommending that Reagan "approve and sign the new finding." The memorandum contained two lines — "OK" and No" — where Reagan could initial his approval or rejection of Poindexter's recommendation that he sign the finding. However, Reagan failed to initial either box, in effect rejecting the finding.[47]

Why Reagan chose to overrule his senior foreign and national security policy advisers in rejecting the finding presented by Poindexter and how he came to this decision remains unknown, as most of the presidential records pertaining to American policy toward Libya remain classified. But the most likely answer is that Reagan had already ordered the American bombing of Libya when he received the finding from Poindexter four days before the air strikes. Hoping that the bombing would persuade Qaddafi to abandon his involvement in international terrorism, Reagan saw no need to authorize additional covert operations to overthrow the mercurial leader of Libya, as the president was willing for the United States to peacefully coexist with the regime in Tripoli as long as its strongman changed his behavior. Reagan had every hope that the bombing would achieve this effect, making an intensified covert campaign to overthrow Qaddafi, such as that recommended by Poindexter, useless and unnecessary.

The EC Adopts a Hard-Line Policy Against Libya

On April 21, 1986, the foreign ministers of the EC met in Luxembourg in order to reevaluate Western European policy toward Libya in the aftermath of the American bombing of Tripoli and Benghazi. The foreign ministers agreed that their governments would reduce the number of Libyan diplomats to the "absolute minimum necessary" and restrict their movement to the cities of Western Europe where they were stationed. Libyan diplomats would have to obtain special permission from their host governments in order to travel beyond those cities. Limits would be imposed upon the number of Libyan private citizens residing in member states of the EC and they would be placed under close surveillance. Any Libyan expelled from an EC member state for involvement in terrorist activity would be prohibited from entering the remaining eleven nations of the organization as well.[48] The actions taken by the EC were designed to make it clear to Qaddafi that the nations of Western Europe were determined to join the United States in isolating Libya from the rest of the international community unless the rogue leader in Tripoli immediately abandoned his involvement in international terrorism.

The nations of Western Europe saw their adoption of a hard-line policy against Libya as an expedient means to protect their extensive economic interests in the oil-rich revolutionary Arab nation from the threat posed by additional American military action against Tripoli which was certain unless Qaddafi immediately abandoned his involvement in international terrorism. Given Libya's dependence upon Western Europe as a source of goods and services, Qaddafi could not afford to isolate his regime from the nations of the region. Accordingly, the nations of Western Europe had every reason to expect that their adoption of a hard-line policy against Libya would finally persuade its mercurial leader to change his behavior, thereby averting additional American military action against Tripoli. As Stanik puts it:

> In the immediate aftermath of the bombing of Libya, the European allies understood the risks posed to them by Libyan terrorism. They were nervous about the possibility of further hostilities between the United States and Libya, and they were ready to cooperate with the administration in the struggle against international terrorism.

Indeed, the American bombing of Libya was as much designed to convey Washington's exasperation with Qaddafi's reckless embrace of international terrorism, as it was to express American frustration with Western European neutrality in the vitriolic and venomous conflict between Washington and Tripoli. Expressing the Reagan Administration's satisfaction that the American bombing of Libya had finally galvanized the nations of Western Europe into joining the United States in adopting a hard-line policy against Tripoli, Shultz wrote in his memoirs:

> The Europeans, more alert now to the dangers posed to them by Libya, alarmed at the use of force by the United States, and anxious to show cooperation with a [domestically] popular U.S. action took action of their own [against Libya]. We had finally gotten their attention. They forced drastic personnel reduction in the Libyan People's Bureaus [in Western Europe], and the activities of those [Libyans] remaining [in the region] were restricted and watched. This action alone significantly curbed Qaddafi's terrorist capabilities.[49]

Reagan Discusses the Libyan-American Conflict with the Other G-7 Leaders

On May 3, 1986, Reagan arrived in Tokyo to attend the annual meeting of the Group [G] of 7 leaders in Tokyo.[50] Coming less than three weeks following the American bombing of Libya, the bitter and acrimonious conflict between Washington and Tripoli represented a major item on the agenda of the summit meeting. Accordingly, on April 21 the White House prepared two separate lists of talking points Reagan would use in his remarks regarding Libya before members of the international media covering the summit meeting.

In his first list of talking points, Reagan was to have stressed to the international media that he did not intend to order additional American military action against Libya, and was committed to working with the other G-7 leaders attending the summit meeting in formulating a unified policy in confronting the threat posed by Libyan-sponsored international terrorism: "Our military operation was directed against terrorist-related and military targets. We have no bone to pick with the Libyan people. I hope that this sort of action will not be necessary in the future, and I look forward to discussing a collective approach [toward Libya] with our summit partners."

As an additional assurance to the international media that he had no intention of ordering additional American military action against Libya, Reagan was to have affirmed to members of the American and foreign press covering the summit meeting that he was committed to using non-military means to confront the threat posed by Libyan-sponsored international terrorism: "We will stress the importance of the practical economic and diplomatic sanctions which we imposed [against Libya] in January.... We continue to believe that economic sanctions, such as curtailing the purchase of Libyan oil, will be an effective vehicle [against Libya]." Consistent with his new-found commitment to confront the threat posed by Libyan-sponsored international terrorism through non-military means, Reagan was to have expressed his support for the steps taken against the revolutionary Arab nation by the governments of EC which were announced at the meeting of their foreign ministers in The Hague hours before the American bombing of Tripoli and Benghazi: "We hope to build on the positive steps the European Community has taken to reduce the threat of terrorism to Americans and others in Europe by restricting Libyan People's Bureau personnel and by strict visa requirements [for Libyans traveling to Western Europe]."[51]

The second list of talking points Reagan was to have used was designed to provide the president the opportunity to explain to the international media the reasons why he ordered the American bombing of Libya and the criteria which governed his selection of sites targeted in the air strikes. In his talking points, Reagan was to have reiterated to the international media that the American bombing of Libya was designed to preempt a rash of terrorist attacks against American citizens residing abroad which Tripoli planned to carry out in the aftermath of the bombing of the West Berlin disco.

1. I authorized military strikes against terrorist-related targets in Libya to preempt the terrorist attacks then being actively planned by the Libyan government against Americans in Europe, the Middle East, and Africa.
2. I was persuaded that these planned terrorist attacks were not only likely, but imminent, because of the irrefutable proof we had that the Libyan People's Bureau in East Berlin had just executed one of its planned attacks: the bombing of the La Belle disco in West Berlin on 5 April.
3. The objective of our preemptive action was to stop those planned attacks by damaging Qaddafi's ability to plan, direct, and support them.
4. Given these criteria to damage the Libyan terrorist infrastructure while at the same time avoiding collateral damage and the death of innocent civilians as much as possible, five principal targets in Tripoli and Benghazi were selected.
5. I approved the air strikes against those five targets.

In his talking points, Reagan was to have stressed to the international media that Qaddafi was not a target of the American air strikes against Libya despite the fact that the United States Air Force bombed his residential compound in Tripoli.

> One of the targets was the entire Al Aziziyah Barracks compound, a command, control, and planning center for Qaddafi's overseas terrorist acts. While we knew that Qaddafi had one of many personal residences in this compound, we had no knowledge that Qaddafi would even be in Tripoli, let alone in this particular residence, on the night of the air strike. We did not specifically target Qaddafi.[52]

The talking points Reagan used to address the vitriolic and venomous conflict between the United States and Libya, at the summit meeting of the G-7 leaders in Tokyo, clearly show that the president was committed to refrain from ordering any additional American military action against Tripoli. Rather, Reagan had now embraced the position of the nations of Western Europe that non-military measures represented the only realistic hope of successfully resolving this conflict. Why had Reagan significantly moderated his policy toward Libya in the weeks following the American bombing of Tripoli and Benghazi? The likely answer is that the bombing was severely criticized, and in many cases, denounced by almost every nation in the world, including America's allies in Western Europe and the Arab world, as we will see in the following chapter.

Unwilling to risk America's isolation from the rest of the international community, Reagan decided that the best option available was for the United States to join with the nations of Western Europe in adopting a unified approach to addressing the challenge of Libyan-sponsored international terrorism. Consistent with the sentiments of the nations of Western Europe, that approach would eschew the use of American military force in favor of using non-military means to persuade Qaddafi to abandon his involvement in international terrorism. With the notable exception of the American bombing of Libya, Reagan was determined to operate within a global consensus in confronting the threat posed by Libyan-sponsored international terrorism, and address this issue through non-military means.

The G-7 Leaders Adopt a Unified Policy Against Libya

Perhaps the greatest achievement of the summit meeting of the G-7 leaders in Tokyo was the adoption of a unified policy against Libya. This was made possible by the fact that, after months of adopting a neutral stance in the bitter and acrimonious conflict between the United States and Libya, the American bombing of Tripoli and Benghazi finally galvanized the nations of Western Europe, especially the region's four member states of the G-7 (the United Kingdom, France, West Germany, and Italy), into allying themselves with Washington in adopting a hard-line policy against Libya. This policy was unveiled by the nations of Western Europe at a meeting of the foreign ministers of the EC in Luxembourg on April 21, 1986.

Western European adoption of a hard-line policy against Libya made it possible for the G-7 leaders, during their summit meeting in Tokyo, to reach a consensus on a unified policy in confronting the threat of Libyan-sponsored international terrorism. As Reagan's talking points make clear, this was a major objective the president hoped to achieve during the meeting. On May 5, 1986, the G-7 leaders issued a "Statement on International Terrorism," which outlined a unified policy against international terrorism the governments on both sides of the Atlantic would pursue. The statement began with a strong and unequivocal denunciation of international terrorism.

> We, the heads of state or governments of seven major democracies and the representatives of the European Community, assembled here in Tokyo, strongly

affirm our condemnation of international terrorism in all its forms, of its accomplices, and of those, including governments, who sponsor and support it. We abhor the increase in the level of terrorism since our last meeting [in 1985], and, in particular, its blatant and cynical use as an instrument of government policy. Terrorism has no justification. It spreads only by the use of contemptible means, ignoring the values of human life, freedom, and dignity. It must be fought relentlessly and without compromise.

Recognizing that the continuing fight against terrorism is a task which the international community as a whole has to undertake, we pledge ourselves to fight against the scourge. Terrorism must be fought effectively through determined, tenacious, discreet, and patient measures, combining national measures with international cooperation.

To pursue their newly-declared commitment to the war against international terrorism, the G-7 leaders announced a number of measures against states which sponsor terrorism, including the imposition of an arms embargo; restrictions on the size of the staffs assigned to their embassies and consular missions, control over the travel of their diplomatic personnel, and where appropriate, the imposition of substantial reductions in their staffs and closure of their diplomatic offices; the denial of entry to all individuals who have been expelled or excluded from any member nation of the G-7 or EC on suspicion of or conviction for involvement in international terrorism; improved extradition procedures for those charged with acts of international terrorism; the tightening of visa requirements for the admission of citizens of states which sponsor international terrorism; and the ensuring of the closest possible cooperation among police and security organizations involved in combating international terrorism. While the G-7 leaders made it clear that these measures would be applied to any state which sponsors international terrorism, they singled out Libya as the only nation which would be subject to the new sanctions unveiled at the conclusion of their summit meeting in Tokyo.

> We have decided to apply these measures within the framework of international law and in our own jurisdictions in respect to any state which is clearly involved in sponsoring or supporting international terrorism, and in particular Libya, until such time as the state concerned abandons its complicity in, or support for, such terrorism.[53]

The measures taken by the G-7 nations resulted in the expulsion of over 100 Libyan diplomats and businessmen from Western Europe in the three months following the American bombing of Libya. West Germany, the target of the bombing of the West Berlin disco, alone expelled twenty-five Libyans. A substantial number of the Libyans expelled from Western Europe resided in three nations: West Germany, the United Kingdom, and Italy, which along with France represented the four Western European member states of the G-7. On May 29, 1986, the USIA reported that twenty-two Libyans had been expelled from West Germany, twenty-one from the United Kingdom, and nineteen from Italy. The twenty-one Libyans expelled from the United Kingdom were students ordered to leave Britain on April 22. The students were members of militant organizations the United Kingdom deemed a threat to its national security.[54]

The Reagan Administration, which had been deeply chagrined at the failure of the Whitehead mission in January to elicit any substantive Western European cooperation in the American campaign to isolate Libya from the rest of the international community, was pleased at the newly found commitment of Washington's Atlantic allies to act against Tripoli. In commenting on the mass expulsions of Libyans from Western Europe, Whitehead said, "There is a better understanding [among the nations of Western Europe that Libyan-sponsored international terrorism] is a problem to all of us. " Whitehead noted that cooperation between the United States and the nations of Western Europe in confronting the threat posed by Libyan-sponsored international terrorism "is moving along rapidly."[55] By the summer of 1986, the State Department had confirmed that most Libyan intelligence operatives had been expelled from Western Europe, delivering a crippling blow to Tripoli's capacity to instigate terrorist attacks in the region. This represented a devastating setback to Libya's capacity to sponsor acts of international terrorism, as Western Europe represented Tripoli's major theater of terrorist activity.

Insofar as the fight against Libyan-sponsored international terrorism, the summit meeting of G-7 leaders in Tokyo must be judged an unmitigated and rousing success. After months of disarray and disagreement over how to confront the threat posed by Libyan-sponsored international terrorism, the United States and the major industrial nations of Western Europe had finally adopted a unified policy toward Tripoli. This was made possible by Reagan's commitment to refrain from ordering any additional American military action against Libya, and accept the Western European insistence that non-military measures represented the only appropriate means to persuade Qaddafi to abandon his involvement in international terrorism. However, despite this concession from Reagan, the president was able to persuade the major industrial nations of Western Europe to take a hard line against Libya after months of adopting a policy aimed at coddling Qaddafi.

Accordingly, while the Tokyo summit was a victory for Western Europe, insofar as it resulted in Reagan's commitment to refrain from ordering any additional American military action against Libya, it was also a triumph for the president, as it signaled the Western European adoption of a hard-line policy against Qaddafi, albeit one rooted in diplomacy, as opposed to military force. As Stanik puts it:

> The Tokyo summit was a major diplomatic victory for Ronald Reagan. Coming soon after Operation El Dorado Canyon [the code name for the American bombing of Libya], the communiqué provided a powerful follow-up punch in the fight against international terrorism. After the raid, several European governments adopted measures aimed at curbing terrorism, and those measures were beginning to show results.... By significantly reducing the number of Libyans in their countries, the Europeans had effectively weakened Qaddafi's ability to conduct terrorist operations.

The Reagan Administration could not have been more pleased at the results of the Tokyo summit, insofar as its bitter and acrimonious conflict with Qaddafi was concerned. When asked by a reporter what message the statement of the G-7 leaders on international terrorism conveyed to Qaddafi, Shultz responded that the heads of state attending the summit meeting were essentially bluntly telling the strongman of Libya: "You've had it, pal! You are isolated! You are recognized as a terrorist!"[56]

By adopting a unified policy against Libya, the G-7 leaders had effectively isolated Tripoli, if not from the rest of the international community, at least from the industrial world. Given Libyan dependence upon the industrial world, especially Western Europe, as a source of goods and services, the Tokyo summit statement against international terrorism placed Qaddafi on notice that his nation faced economic devastation from the prospect of Western European sanctions, let alone destruction from the possibility of additional American military action, if he failed to abandon his involvement in international terrorism. No longer able to exploit to his own advantage the previous rift between the United States and Western Europe, in light of their adoption of a unified policy against Libya, stung by the devastating blow he suffered from the American bombing of his nation, and with the major industrial nations of Western Europe taking substantive steps to isolate his regime, Qaddafi's back was finally to the wall, and he finally found himself cornered. The mercurial leader of Libya had no option but to abandon his involvement in international terrorism if he had any realistic hope of surviving in power.

Was the American Bombing of Libya Motivated by Domestic Political Considerations?

Thus far, this study has focused on the strategic motivations which governed Reagan's decision to order the American bombing of Libya. Could this decision, which won the approval of 76 percent of the public, according to a *Washington Post*–ABC News poll taken during April 24–28, 1986, have also been motivated by domestic political considerations?[57] This intriguing question arises in response to the inescapable fact that the president could not have been oblivious to the fact that his decision to order the bombing would win widespread public approval. Jane Mayer and Doyle McManus go so far as to allege that the White House used public opinion polls in order enable Reagan to manipulate the Libyan-American conflict to his own political advantage.

> The White House campaign against him [Qaddafi] ... was conducted with more than geopolitics in mind. Concerned that its visible initiatives meet with the public's approval, the White House had ensured that it would be popular too. In fact, the campaign against Qaddafi ... was partly guided by a series of secret polls. Some of these polls were conducted by ... Richard Wirthlin [and] Ronald Hinckley ... for the NSC in general and Oliver North in particular. Both Wirthlin and Hinckley ... sounded out thousands of people on ... how they would feel about a U.S. attack on Libya, and under what circumstances they would support it. By mid–March [1986], public opinion favored military retaliation [against Libya] as long as the strike was seen as a quick and "reluctant" response [to an act of international terrorism], rather than one resulting from U.S. provocation.... The public had been primed for six years for this sort of action, so the bombing [of Libya] was popular at home, as the NSC already determined it would be, based upon its extensive private polling.[58]

Is Mayer and McManus' allegation that the White House used public opinion polls in order to enable Reagan to manipulate the Libyan-American to his own political advantage correct? The answer is yes. The smoking gun confirming this allegation comes from an attachment to a memorandum, entitled "U.S. Public Opinion on Terrorism," St. Martin sent North on March 25, 1986. In his memorandum, St. Martin told North:

> Attached is a brief analysis of U.S. public opinion on an issue in which you have expressed interest. While many surveys taken over the past year were reviewed prior to this analysis, and are referenced in the commentary, most of the information comes from a recent poll.... If you have any questions about the results [of the poll], or would like further information, please contact me.[59]

Attached to St. Martin's memorandum was a White House analysis of recent public opinion polls taken on the issue of international terrorism. The White House focused particular attention on polls which asked those surveyed the following question: "Which of the following do you think the U.S. should do to reduce terrorism that is sponsored by another state?" Ten percent believed that the United States should "take military action against any economic or military target in that country; 39 percent thought that Washington should "take military action against terrorist facilities in that country"; 27 percent felt that this nation should "enact economic sanctions against that country"; 14 percent said that the United States should "enact diplomatic sanctions against that country"; and 7 percent stated that Washington should "take no action." In its analysis, the White House noted that the public was evenly divided between military and non-military action with respect to how Reagan should respond to acts of international terrorism.

> As can be seen from the response statistics, about half the public (49 percent) favor a military response to state-supported terrorism. However, it is clear that most of these people support a military response if it is directed against terrorist facilities, and not aimed at non-terrorist-related targets. The other half of the population (48 percent) looks to non-military options, either in terms of economic or diplomatic sanctions or taking no action at all.

In determining which state sponsor of international terrorism Reagan should target for American military action, a poll, taken in January 1986, found that 53 percent of those surveyed chose Libya as the favored target, leading every other nation on the list of state sponsors of global terrorism the public favored for attack.

The polls taken on the issue of international terrorism had some disturbing news for the White House: The public failed to fully comprehend Reagan's policy toward international terrorism. This is due to the fact that Reagan never clearly articulated such a policy during the first five years of his presidency. To be sure, as we saw at the beginning of this book, Reagan announced his policy only one week after entering the White House, promising "swift and effective retribution" against the forces of international terrorism. But despite the surge in international terrorism, highlighted by the bombings of the American Embassy and Marine barracks in Beirut in 1983, Reagan had failed to implement his policy of "swift and effective retribution" in response to any of the increasingly heinous acts of global terrorism which occurred during his presidency. As Stanik aptly notes, "Reagan pledged that his administration would respond to acts of terrorism with 'swift and effective retribution.' ... Yet he did not act."[60]

Illustrating public doubts concerning Reagan's policy toward international terrorism, one poll, taken in March 1986, asked those surveyed the following question: "When it comes to deciding when and how to respond to terrorist incidents, do you believe officials in the Reagan Administration have been "very unified," "somewhat unified," "somewhat disunited," or "very disunited?" Twelve percent believed that the administration was "very unified" in responding to acts of international terrorism, and 42 percent said "somewhat unified." By contrast, 31 percent of those surveyed believed that the administration "somewhat disunited" in responding to acts of international terrorism, and 14 percent said "very disunited." In analyzing the results of this poll, the White House noted:

> This [poll] appears to reflect a slight perception that the administration lacks coordination on its terrorist policy articulation and implementation. The lumping of responses in the "somewhat" categories shows uncertainty by the public about the administration's position. This serves to diminish the President's ability to lead on this issue, which ... requires good leadership.

The White House analysis of recent public opinion polls on international terrorism concluded:

> These ... polls examined lead to the following conclusions about public sentiment toward dealing with terrorism: Slowly, Americans are becoming more willing than in the past to support military action against terrorism, particularly against nations that sponsor terrorists.... To perceive public support ... the use of military force to respond to terrorist incidents should occur in the following context:
> 1. It is an unwelcome and unsought-for action that has been forced on the nation by an immediate and serious terrorist act.
> 2. It is not the result of the U.S. precipitating the incident that led to the action.
> 3. It is focused as much as possible on the perpetrators of [international terrorism] and their facilities.
> 4. It is necessary because other efforts and sanctions have failed to halt terrorist activities.
> 5. It is a limited engagement, defensive in nature.
> 6. It is conducted, if possible, in conjunction with other nations.
> 7. The administration is publicly united on the need for and execution of the military operation.[61]

The American bombing of Libya met six of the seven aforementioned conditions the White House believed must govern retaliatory military action against international terrorism in order to win public approval. The only such condition the bombing failed to meet was that the United States acted against Libya alone, rather than in concert with any other nation. But the air strikes were in response to a specific unprovoked act of international terrorism — the bombing of the disco in West Berlin; they specifically targeted the facilities which comprised Qaddafi's global terrorist infrastructure; they occurred after American economic sanctions had failed to persuade the rogue leader of Libya to abandon his involvement in international terrorism; they represented a single military operation, limited in time and scope; and they had the strong support of virtually all of Reagan's foreign and national security policy advisers.

It is interesting to note that, in his nationwide television address announcing his decision to order the American bombing of Libya, Reagan stressed that the air strikes had met the most important conditions the White House believed the public wanted the president to adhere to before ordering military action against a nation which sponsors international terrorism. Reagan noted that the bombing was directed against "the headquarters, terrorist facilities, and military assets that support Muammar Qaddafi's subversive activities"; was ordered in response to "the terrorist bombing of the La Belle discotheque [which] was planned and executed under the direct orders of the Libyan regime"; and represented an act of "self-defense [which] is not only our right; it is our duty." Reagan emphasized that the he had ordered the bombing only after all non-military measures designed to persuade Qaddafi to abandon his involvement in international terrorism had failed: "We always seek peaceful avenues before resorting to the use of force and we did [with respect to Qaddafi]: We tried quiet diplomacy, public condemnation, economic sanctions, and demonstrations of military force. None succeeded."

In his nationwide address announcing the American bombing of Libya, Reagan portrayed the air strikes as a regrettable demonstration of military power which was forced upon him by Qaddafi's barbarism and brutality: "Today we have done what we had to do. If necessary, we shall do it again. It gives me no pleasure to say that, and I wish it were otherwise.... I'm sure that today most Libyans are ashamed and disgusted that this man [Qaddafi] has made their country a synonym for barbarism."

The one condition Reagan failed to meet in ordering the American bombing of Libya, which the White House believed was necessary to win public support for military action against state sponsors of international terrorism remains that the air strikes were undertaken unilaterally, rather than in concert with other nations. However, Reagan turned this alleged vice into a virtue. Pointing to his commitment to confront the threat posed by international terrorism, Reagan said, during his nationwide television address announcing the American bombing of Libya, "I said that we would act with others, if possible, and alone, if necessary, to ensure that terrorists have no sanctuary anywhere. Tonight, we have."[62] The point Reagan made — which was fully accepted by an overwhelming majority of the public — is that the United States had no alternative but to act against Tripoli unilaterally, given the gravity of the threat posed by Libyan-sponsored international terrorism, and the failure of the rest of the international community to confront Qaddafi.

To return to our original question: Was the American bombing of Libya motivated to any extent by domestic political considerations? Our answer remains yes, for three reasons. First, the White House analysis of recent public opinion polls on the issue of international terrorism, which St. Martin sent to North, confirms Mayer and McManus' allegation that the White House used polls in order to enable Reagan to manipulate the Libyan-American conflict to his own political advantage. Second, the White House recognized that Reagan needed to clarify public doubts concerning his policy toward international terrorism, as the White House analysis of polls on this issue clearly illustrates; and the only way the president could have done this is to fully implement his vow to take "swift and effective retribution" against the forces of international terrorism. Libya was the convenient target, both for strategic and political reasons. Strategically, Libya was too weak militarily to put up more but token resistance to any American military action Reagan might order. This would ensure that a relatively bloodless American military strike against Libya could be executed which would easily win public approval. Politically, Qaddafi was truly, in the words of Mayer and McManus quoted in the following chapter, the leader "Americans loved to hate," which is no small part why Libya ranked first on the list of state sponsors of international terrorism the public wanted targeted for attack. This alone ensured the American bombing of Libya would be popular in the United States.

A third reason for believing that domestic political considerations represented a factor in Reagan's decision to order the American bombing of Libya can be found in the president's nationwide television address announcing the air strikes. As we have seen, the address was carefully tailored in order to provide Reagan the opportunity to persuade the public that, in ordering the bombing, he had met the conditions the White House believed were necessary to elicit popular approval for American military action against state sponsors of international terrorism. This only strengthens the perception, if not reality, that domestic political considerations represented a factor in Reagan's decision to order the bombing. The White House analysis of public opinion polls on the issue of international terrorism, which St. Martin sent to North, puts Reagan's nationwide television address announcing the bombing in a whole new light, and makes it clear that the speech was designed as much for political purposes — to provide Reagan the opportunity to assure the public that, in ordering the American bombing of Libya, he had met the conditions the White House believed were necessary to win popular support for military action against state sponsors of international terrorism — as it was to allow the president to explain the reasons for the air strikes. And when Reagan failed to meet one of those conditions — that such action be undertaken in concert with other nations — he persuasively explained that he preferred to "act with others, if possible, alone if necessary." It is clear that the White House used public opinion polls in order to carefully tailor Reagan's nationwide television address announcing the American bombing of Libya in a manner which would enable him to gain maximum public support for the air strikes, and ensure that he would gain the greatest possible political dividends from the military action. This is fully consistent with Mayer and McManus' allegation that the White House, armed with internal public opinion polling data, orchestrated the Libyan-American conflict to Reagan's own political advantage.

With the United States representing the only nation willing and able to confront Qaddafi, and the rogue leader of Libya determined to pursue an unrelenting and unabashed international terrorist campaign directed against American targets, an overwhelming majority of the public accepted Reagan's explanation that Washington had no alternative but to take unilateral action against Tripoli. In the end, the American bombing of Libya was motivated to some extent by domestic political considerations, which should surprise no one as Reagan was in the end one of the most skillful and consummate politicians ever to reside in the White House. But one should not exaggerate the domestic political motivations as a factor in governing Reagan's decision to order the bombing. Even the most cynical observer must concede that the dominant reason for the air strikes remains that they were strategically designed to eliminate Libya as the world's primary sponsor of international terrorism. The fact that the bombing would provide Reagan obvious political dividends does not obviate the fact that strategic, rather than domestic political, factors represented the dominant consideration governing the president's decision to order the air strikes. The fact that the bombing was guaranteed to win public support represented an additional incentive for Reagan to approve this decision, but was not the dominant reason for this action.

Conclusion

The American air strikes against Libya represented a preemptive action designed to thwart Tripoli's alleged plan to follow the bombing of the West Berlin disco with a rash of terrorist attacks against American targets. The air strikes were designed to serve notice upon Qaddafi that his regime faced the certainty of destruction at the hands of the United States unless he immediately abandoned his involvement in international terrorism. Indeed, in his nationwide television address announcing the execution and conclusion of the air strikes, Reagan made it clear that he was prepared to order additional American military action against Libya if necessary. The air strikes, combined with the certainty of additional American military action in response to another act of Libyan-sponsored international terrorism, had their intended effect: They persuaded Qaddafi that he must immediately abandon his involvement in international terrorism if his regime had any realistic hope of surviving its vitriolic and venomous conflict with the United States.

The American bombing of Libya was directed, not just at sending a message to Qaddafi, but to the nations of Western Europe as well. Indeed, the bombing was as much a response to the threat to the world community posed by Libyan-sponsored international terrorism as it was to Western European adoption of a neutral stance in the bitter and acrimonious conflict between the Washington and Tripoli. As late as hours before the bombing, the foreign ministers of the EC made it clear, during their meeting at The Hague, that their governments would not join the United States in imposing economic sanctions of their own against Libya. As long as Libya retained its extensive economic relations with Western Europe, the Reagan Administration's campaign to isolate Tripoli from the rest of the international community was doomed to failure. With Libya continuing to function outside the community of civilized nations, and paying little price for its sponsorship of international terrorism, Qaddafi had no incentive to abandon his involvement in terrorism.

The American bombing of Libya served notice upon Western Europe, let alone the rest of the international community, that Reagan would order full-fledged military action against Tripoli unless Qaddafi immediately abandoned his involvement in international terrorism. Given the extensive and lucrative economic relations they enjoyed with oil-rich Libya, any large-scale American military campaign against Tripoli would adversely affect the economic interests of the nations of Western Europe. Accordingly, the major industrial nations of Western Europe concluded that they could no longer retain their neutral stance in the increasingly bitter and acrimonious conflict between the United States and Libya. At the summit meeting of the G-7 leaders in Tokyo in May 1986, the heads of state of the United Kingdom, France, West Germany, and Italy joined Reagan and their colleagues from Japan and Canada in issuing a stern statement, which followed the conclusion of their conference, denouncing international terrorism in the strongest possible terms. The statement was backed by the mass expulsion of Libyan diplomats and businessmen from Western Europe in the weeks and months following the Tokyo summit.

The American bombing of Libya and the results of the Tokyo summit represented fatal blows to Qaddafi's global terrorist enterprise. The bombing served notice to Qaddafi that his regime would face destruction at the hands of the United States unless the mercurial leader of Libya immediately abandoned his involvement in international terrorism. The statement on international terrorism the G-7 leaders issued at the conclusion of the Tokyo summit also made it clear that, after months of coddling Qaddafi, the nations of Western Europe were now prepared to join the United States in taking steps to isolate Libya.

The mass expulsion of Libyan diplomats from Western Europe represented a clear warning that unless Qaddafi changed his behavior, the nations of the region would sever their economic relations with Libya. Given Libya's dependence upon Western Europe as a source of goods and services, such action would result in the economic collapse of the revolutionary Arab nation, imperiling the survival of the Qaddafi regime. With the United States and the nations of Western Europe now united in their determination to stamp out Libyan-sponsored international terrorism by taking steps to undermine, and, if necessary, ultimately destroy the Qaddafi regime, the renegade leader in Tripoli found himself outmaneuvered in his conflict with Washington. No longer able to exploit, to his own advantage, the division between the United States and the nations of Western Europe regarding the most appropriate means to respond to the threat posed by Libyan-sponsored international terrorism, and with the states on both sides of the Atlantic having forged a consensus behind the adoption of a hard-line policy against his regime, Qaddafi had no alternative but to immediately abandon his involvement international terrorism if he hoped to survive in power. Not surprisingly, no Libyan-sponsored acts of international terrorism occurred in the weeks and months immediately following the American bombing of Tripoli and Benghazi.

CHAPTER FIVE

International Condemnation of the Bombing

World reaction to the raid [against Libya] was generally hostile.[1]
— R.A. Davidson, retired officer, United States Army

Perhaps the most perplexing question regarding the American bombing of Libya is this: Why did the Reagan Administration fail to follow the air strikes with additional American military action aimed at toppling the Qaddafi regime? As we saw in the previous chapter, on April 17, 1986, the NSC produced a document which urged that Reagan follow the bombing by ordering additional air strikes against Libya. The NSC argued that such action was needed to support an incipient internal insurrection, which the air strikes had triggered, aimed at overthrowing Qaddafi. The most likely reason Reagan failed to order such action is because American policy toward Libya was designed not to precipitate the overthrow of Qaddafi, but to achieve the more limited objective of persuading the renegade leader in Tripoli to abandon his involvement in international terrorism. And this certainly was true: The Reagan Administration was perfectly willing to peacefully coexist with the Qaddafi regime once the rogue leader of Libya dismantled his global terrorist enterprise.

But the Reagan Administration made no secret of the fact that it would welcome the overthrow of Qaddafi. And the administration may very well have allowed its open-ended contempt and disdain for Qaddafi to result in additional American military action aimed at pursuing regime change in Libya. However, the option of such action was foreclosed by the widespread international criticism, and even condemnation, of the American bombing of Libya. Such criticism was not confined to America's enemies and adversaries, but extended to its closest friends and allies in Western Europe and the Arab world.

The Reagan Administration's entire policy toward Libya was founded upon its attempt to isolate the Qaddafi regime from the rest of the international community. The irony is that the American bombing of Libya threatened to have the opposite effect in potentially rallying international support for Qaddafi, and against the United States.

To prevent this development from occurring, the Reagan Administration abandoned any plan the White House may have had to follow the bombing with additional American military action against Libya. Rather, the administration renewed its original policy, adopted following the Rome and Vienna attacks, to use non-military means to persuade Qaddafi to abandon his involvement in international terrorism. The practical manifestation of this new policy was Reagan's decision to join with the other G-7 leaders in the adoption of a unified policy to respond to the threat posed by Libyan-sponsored international terrorism. The foundation of this policy was substantive action by the nations of Western Europe to begin the process of severing their diplomatic and economic relations with Tripoli through the mass expulsion of Libyan diplomats and businessmen from the region. This would serve as a warning to Qaddafi that a full break in diplomatic and economic relations between the nations of Western Europe and Libya would be forthcoming unless the rebel leader in Tripoli immediately abandoned his involvement in international terrorism.

As it turned out no additional American military action was necessary to persuade Qaddafi to change his behavior: The bombing of Tripoli and Benghazi, combined with the mass expulsion of Libyans from Western Europe, was sufficient to convince the rogue leader in Tripoli to all but dismantle his global terrorist enterprise. But the remarkable fact remains that Qaddafi survived his bitter and acrimonious conflict with the United States. And this is due in no small part to the fact that America's allies in Western Europe and the Arab world were determined to see a peaceful outcome to the bitter and acrimonious conflict between the United States and Libya, and to prevent Washington from toppling the irrepressible leader in Tripoli.

The Reagan Administration had done its best to castigate Qaddafi as a pariah and international outcast who had no right to govern Libya by virtue of the fact that the renegade leader in Tripoli operated completely outside the norms of civilized international behavior. But America's allies in Western Europe and the Arab world rejected this dark view of Qaddafi, considering him to be a rational and legitimate, albeit reckless, leader whose behavior could be changed through peaceful means.

In the end, the Reagan Administration was forced to go along with this more benign view of Qaddafi, and embrace a policy, adopted at the Tokyo summit, wherein the United States and the nations of Western Europe would pursue non-military means to persuade the mercurial leader of Libya to change his behavior. As irrational as the administration believed Qaddafi to be, the irrepressible leader of Libya proved to be sufficiently resourceful and skillful to retain sufficient sympathy, and even support, in Western Europe and the Arab world to survive his vitriolic and venomous confrontation with the United States: a remarkable accomplishment, given the asymmetry in power between Washington and Tripoli, and the open-ended contempt and disdain to which the White House viewed the strongman in Tripoli.

Most Nations of Western Europe Condemn the American Bombing of Libya

Due to the extensive economic interests they had in oil-rich Libya, the nations of Western Europe were quick to respond to the American bombing of Tripoli and Benghazi. As it turned out, most of those nations condemned the bombing. The Netherlands was among the first of those nations to do so. As we have seen, the Netherlands had served as the site of the meeting of the foreign ministers of the EC in The Hague held hours before the bombing.

In urging the United States to exercise military restraint, the foreign ministers intended to make it clear at their meeting that the nations of Western Europe believed that the highly-charged and emotion-laden conflict between Washington and Tripoli could be resolved only through peaceful means. However, this message fell upon deaf ears in Washington, as the United States proceeded with its bombing of Libya, ignoring the EC's demand for a peaceful resolution of the bitter and acrimonious conflict between the two nations. The Dutch government responded to the bombing by issuing a statement declaring, "We deplore this course of events, all the more so because the European Twelve [member nations of the EC] dedicated themselves clearly to a political solution [to the Libyan-American conflict], and to the prevention of military escalation."[2]

Dutch condemnation of the American bombing of Libya was followed by a statement issued by Foreign Minister Karolos Papoulias of Greece.

> We express our intense concern regarding the night raid of American airplanes against Libya.... The Greek government ... must express its disapproval of the American military operation which undermines international legal order and does not contribute to combating terrorism and to the peaceful resolution of the problems of the region, but, on the contrary, will contribute to exacerbated tension and confrontation in this sensitive area of the Mediterranean.

Papoulias reiterated the Dutch government's position that the purpose of the meeting of the foreign ministers of the EC, held in The Hague hours before the American bombing of Libya, was to emphasize the need for a peaceful resolution of the vitriolic and venomous conflict between Washington and Tripoli.

> Greece ... at yesterday's extraordinary ministerial session of the twelve EC member states ... made every effort ... to impress upon its partners the need for cool-headed handling of the situation and obligation of the twelve [member nations of the EC] to work to contribute to the prevention of what finally occurred [the American bombing of Libya]. Greek suggestions were the content of the last paragraph of the statement [issued by the EC] which says that, in order to reach a political solution, without further increasing military tension [between the United States and Libya], the twelve underscore the need for self-restraint from all sides.[3]

Joining the Dutch and Greek governments in condemning the American bombing of Libya was France. Paris made its opposition to the bombing clear even before the air strikes. During his eleventh-hour trip to Western Europe to rally support among the nations of the region for the impending American bombing of Libya, Walters requested that Mitterrand grant British-based American aircraft, which bombed Tripoli, over-flight rights to use French airspace as the most direct route from the United Kingdom to Libya. Mitterrand flatly rejected Walters' request. Following the bombing, the Foreign Ministry of France explained why the government rejected the American request: "Informed of the intentions of the government of the United States, France refused to allow its airspace to be used by American planes. It ... deplores the intolerable escalation of terrorism which has led to an action of reprisal which in itself renews the chain of violence."[4] Joining his government in the issuance of a statement condemning the American bombing of Libya was Mitterrand, who declared, "I don't think you can stop terrorism by killing 150 Libyans who have done nothing." Echoing the French government's warning that the bombing would only inflame, not dampen, international terrorism was Prime Minister Bettino Craxi of Italy who warned, "Far from weakening terrorism, this military action risks provoking explosive reactions of fanaticism and criminal acts."[5]

Adding to the mounting Western European denunciation of the American bombing of Libya was Spain. Like Mitterrand, Prime Minister Felipe Gonzalez had rejected Walters' request that British-based American aircraft, which bombed Tripoli, be granted over-flight rights to use Spanish airspace as the most direct route from the United Kingdom to Libya.[6] The Foreign Ministry of Spain responded to the bombing by declaring its "alarm and concern" over the air strikes. Joining the chorus of Western European condemnation of the bombing was Foreign Minister Sten Andersson of Sweden who called the air strikes a "serious and most dangerous" act.[7]

The intense degree of negative reaction to the American bombing of Libya from the nations of Western Europe was perhaps best summed by the diplomatic correspondent for *The Daily Telegraph*, who noted in its April 16, 1986, edition that, "Britain stood alone in Europe yesterday in condoning America's raid on Libya as NATO [North Atlantic Treaty Organization] appeared to be heading for one of its severest crises.... Britain's European allies reacted with shock, dismay, and outright condemnation of the raid."[8] The Reagan Administration was stung by the outpouring of Western European condemnation against the American bombing of Libya. Reporting on Shultz's news conference held on April 17, 1986, *The Daily Telegraph* diplomatic correspondent wrote, "As the worldwide chorus of protest against the American action in Libya continued yesterday, an unrepentant Mr. George Shultz ... gave a warning at a televised news conference of the dangers of appeasement. Answering questions from correspondents from European capitals, he criticized continental European countries for failing to help America, and praised Mrs. [Margaret] Thatcher."[9]

On April 15, 1986, the Voice of America issued a statement designed for international consumption defending the American bombing of Libya as an act of "self-defense — our response to Colonel Muammar Qaddafi's relentless sponsorship of terrorism."[10] Given the fact that Qaddafi's open-ended and enthusiastic embrace of international terrorism provided a clear cut and unambiguous rationale for the bombing, why did the nations of Western Europe react so harshly and negatively to the air strikes, especially in light of the fact the most recent acts of Libyan-sponsored international terrorism had been conducted in West Berlin, Vienna, and Rome? Perhaps the best answer to this perplexing question was provided by *The Daily Telegraph*, which said in an editorial, published in its April 16, 1986, edition, "It remains difficult for most Europeans to welcome yesterday's American bombing of Tripoli and Benghazi precisely because of our deep doubts concerning whether this will destroy, or even weaken, Qaddafi's power and standing in his own country and the Arab world."[11]

Thatcher and Kohl Express Support for the American Bombing of Libya

The Reagan Administration could take heart in the fact that Western European condemnation of the American bombing was not universal. Indeed, as *The Daily Telegraph* noted, there was one leader of Western Europe who took strong exception to the otherwise harshly negative Western European reaction to the bombing — Prime Minister Margaret Thatcher of the United Kingdom. In sharp contrast to the reaction of other Western European officials, Thatcher expressed strong support for the bombing. This hardly came as a surprise to the Reagan Administration. During his trip to Western Europe, Walters requested that Thatcher grant approval for British-based American aircraft to depart from their airfields to bomb Tripoli. Thatcher granted unconditional approval to Walters' request.[12] Thatcher's decision stands in sharp contrast to Mitterrand and Gonzalez, who refused to allow the British-based American aircraft to use French and Spanish airspace, respectively, to bomb Tripoli.

Thatcher's decision to provide both political and operational support for the American bombing of Libya was condemned by the prime minister's opponents in the United Kingdom, who derided her as "Reagan's poodle." Thatcher's critics pointed out that international terrorist organizations might single out the United Kingdom for attack because Britain stood almost alone among the Western European governments in supporting the bombing. Thatcher responded to her critics by stridently vowing that she would not be intimidated by the fear that her support for the bombing might increase the vulnerability of the United Kingdom to a terrorist attack. Speaking before the House of Commons, Thatcher declared, "If Britain always refused to take risks because of the consequences, then terrorist governments would win and one would only be able to cringe before them. To refuse to take action against terrorism would mean that Britain was supine and passive in the face of that terrorism."[13]

Joining Thatcher as the only other Western European leader to express support for the American bombing of Libya was Chancellor Helmut Kohl of West Germany. Addressing the Bundestag, Kohl revealed that the West German intelligence community had confirmed the validity of the Reagan Administration's claims that the Libyan People's Bureau in East Berlin was behind the bombing of the disco in the western part of the divided city. Kohl defended the American bombing of Libya as "a preventive strike against the further escalation of terrorism." Kohl chided most of the Western European governments which had condemned the bombing: "It is easy to criticize the

United States for resorting to measures we would not have chosen.... If we Europeans do not want to follow the Americans for reasons of our own, we must develop political initiatives [against Libya]. We will not eliminate international terrorism simply by wailing and lamenting."[14]

Kohl's argument that the nations of Western Europe could no longer stand idly by and refuse to take any meaningful action to address the threat posed by Libyan-sponsored international terrorism was a point well taken in the other capitals of the region. While the nations of Western Europe certainly had reasons to reject the use of military force in confronting this threat, they still had a responsibility to take substantive non-military measures to persuade Qaddafi to abandon his involvement in international terrorism. Indeed, one could legitimately argue that, by refusing to take any meaningful action against Libya, the nations of Western Europe left Reagan no option but to order the use of American military force as the only viable means he had available to persuade Qaddafi to change his behavior. As Stanik aptly notes:

> A majority of European leaders privately acknowledged that they bore some of the blame for the conflict between the United States and Libya since they were unable to produce a Libya policy strong enough to dissuade Reagan from taking unilateral action. Reagan's decision to use force strengthened the credibility of his terrorism policy and challenged America's allies to take more resolute steps to deal with the problem and demonstrate that further military action was unnecessary.[15]

As we saw in the previous chapter, following the American bombing of Libya, the nations of Western Europe, after months of adopting a neutral position in the bitter and acrimonious conflict between the United States and Libya, finally decided to pursue a hard-line policy against Tripoli. Over 100 Libyans were expelled from Western Europe, as the nations of the region sent a clear message to Qaddafi that they were prepared to take steps to isolate his regime from the rest of the industrial world, if not the international community, unless the rogue leader in Tripoli immediately abandoned his involvement in international terrorism.

Given the extensive economic relations they enjoyed with oil-rich Libya, the nations of Western Europe had significant non-military leverage they could exert to persuade Qaddafi to renounce his support for international terrorism. Much as Kohl had hoped, the American bombing of Libya galvanized the nations of Western Europe to use this leverage against Qaddafi. Unwilling to risk the loss of his regime's economic ties to Western Europe, Qaddafi finally gave into pressure from the nations of the region, and all but abandoned his involvement in international terrorism in the weeks and months following the bombing. While the nations of Western Europe had every reason to criticize, and even denounce, the bombing, they had no right to continue to turn a blind eye to the threat posed by Libyan-sponsored international terrorism. Much as Kohl argued, the nations of Western Europe had an obligation to, at the very least, take non-military measures to confront to this threat, and they did so — in a very effective manner, as it turned out — following the bombing.

The Soviet Union Condemns the American Bombing of Libya

Perhaps the most interesting aspect of the American bombing of Libya is that it did not provoke a crisis between the United States and the Soviet Union. On the surface, this seems odd: Though Libya was hardly a client state of the Soviet Union, Tripoli retained close and warm relations with Moscow. The Soviet Union served as Libya's largest arms supplier, accounting for half of the $12 billion Tripoli spent on military weaponry during 1979 to 1983.[16] Pursuant to Moscow's commitment to the security of the Qaddafi regime, 2,500 Soviet military advisers served in Libya during the early 1980s.[17] In a gesture of solidarity with Moscow, Qaddafi granted Soviet armed forces access to Libyan military bases, airfields, and ports.[18]

Given the solid and friendly relations existing between Moscow and Tripoli, one might have expected a harsh Soviet response to the American bombing of Libya. Instead the response was mild. To be sure, President Mikhail Gorbachev responded to the American bombing of Libya by sending a letter to Qaddafi. In his letter, Gorbachev informed Qaddafi:

> I would like, on behalf of the leadership of the Soviet Union and all Soviet people, to express to you personally and to the friendly Libyan people feelings of solidarity in the face of this act of piracy committed by American imperialism.... While verbally declaring that they are acting as fighters against "international terrorism," in fact U.S. leaders have once more confirmed their allegiance to a policy of state terrorism.

In an ominous hint that the Soviet Union might intervene to support the beleaguered Qaddafi regime in its bitter and acrimonious conflict with the United States, Gorbachev vowed, in his letter to Qaddafi, "In reaffirming our effective solidarity with you, Comrade Qaddafi, and to the entire Libyan people, the Soviet Union firmly intends to fulfill the commitments it has made with respect to the further strengthening of Libya's defense capability."[19]

In order to ensure that Gorbachev's commitment to the security of the Qaddafi regime was heard in Washington, his letter to the besieged leader of Libya was released to the international community through TASS, the official news agency of the Soviet government. As a practical demonstration of its opposition to the American bombing of Libya, the Soviet Union cancelled a meeting its foreign minister, Eduard Shevardnadze, was to have held with Shultz in May 1986. On April 16 Moscow Radio warned that the bombing had dealt a powerful blow to the dramatic improvement in Soviet-American relations which occurred as a result of the summit meeting held between Reagan and Gorbachev in Geneva during November 19–21, 1985: "When the White House prepared this military operation and ordered it, it knew ... this would be a blow to the spirit of Geneva, and aggravate relations with the Soviet Union. Nevertheless, it went ahead with it [the bombing]. Why?"[20]

The answer to Moscow Radio's question is simple: Reagan proceeded with the American bombing of Libya because he understood that the Soviet Union was not about to sacrifice the improved relations with the United States that accompanied the Geneva summit meeting in order to demonstrate its solidarity with Libya, which was of only marginal strategic value to the Communist superpower.[21] Reagan knew that when given a choice between strengthening relations with the United States or demonstrating solidarity with Qaddafi, Gorbachev would opt for the former and confine himself to rhetorical, rather than substantive, action in conveying his opposition to the bombing. The fact that Reagan could order the bombing without fear that it would have any real adverse impact upon Soviet-American relations was a major factor in his decision to approve the air strikes. The White House all but admitted this. In the talking points defending the bombing, produced hours before the air strikes, Reagan Administration spokespersons were to have said, "The Soviet Union does not have a Treaty of Friendship and Assistance with Libya, and we do not expect the Soviets to provide active military support for Qaddafi."[22]

The Soviet Union's commitment to avoid taking substantive action in support of Libya in its bitter and acrimonious conflict with the United States was consistent with the fact that, despite the existence of firm and solid relations between Moscow and Tripoli, the Communist superpower was determined to maintain some distance from the Qaddafi regime. The Soviet Union made this clear during a visit Qaddafi's senior deputy, Abdel Salam Jalloud, made to the Soviet Union in 1984. As P. Edward Haley notes, Qaddafi used the occasion of Jalloud's visit to propose the negotiation of a formal strategic alliance between the Soviet Union and Libya: "Qaddafi asked for an alliance with the Soviet Union, or at least a 'friendship and cooperation' agreement similar to that between Moscow and Damascus. He was unsuccessful."[23]

The Soviet reluctance to fully embrace the Qaddafi regime was due to Moscow's concerns over the quirky behavior of its renegade leader. As St. John aptly notes:

> The American attack strained Soviet-Libyan relations that could already be described as testy. Due to policy differences and the mercurial nature of the Qaddafi regime, the Soviets remained hesitant, even as relations with Tripoli expanded during the early 1980s, to move too close to Libya. As the American raid developed, Washington kept Moscow informed of its maneuvers, but the Soviets apparently made no effort to intervene on behalf of Libya.[24]

However, despite the comparatively mild Soviet response to the American bombing of Libya, the White House remained concerned that additional military action against Tripoli Reagan might order would indeed create heightened tensions between Washington and Moscow. This concern was conveyed by Jack F. Matlock, special assistant to the president and senior director of European and Soviet affairs for the NSC, in a memorandum, marked "secret," he sent to Poindexter on April 25, 1986. On August 6, 2002, NARA declassified the memorandum, in which Matlock assured Poindexter that the American bombing of Libya would not affect the improved relations between the United States and the Soviet Union that followed the summit meeting between Reagan and Gorbachev in Geneva: "Despite the cancellation of Shevardnadze's visit in May, the Soviets have indicated they want to keep the Libya problem from completely derailing U.S.-Soviet dialogue." However, Matlock also warned that the Soviet Union was likely to take some unspecified, but substantive, action, should Reagan order additional American military operations against Libya. Given its firm and solid relations with Libya, the Soviet Union could not stand idly by and allow Reagan to order such operations without undermining Moscow's credibility in the Middle East: "If the Libyan confrontation escalates, they [the Soviet Union] may fear a loss of face in the Third World — particularly the Middle East — and feel compelled to take further actions [against the United States]."[25]

Matlock's memorandum makes it clear that, while the Soviet Union was willing to confine its opposition to the American bombing of Libya to rhetorical condemnation of the air strikes, Moscow was prepared to take substantive action in support of the Qaddafi regime should Reagan order additional military action against Tripoli. Reagan's desire to avert a potential Soviet-American military confrontation over Libya was certainly a major factor in the president's decision not to order such action. While the Reagan Administration certainly welcomed regime change in Libya, the president was not about to sacrifice the improved Soviet-American relations, which followed the Geneva summit meeting, and risk a confrontation between the two superpowers, in order to pursue his war against Qaddafi beyond the bombing of Tripoli and Benghazi.

The Moderate Arab Nations Condemn the American Bombing of Libya

Perhaps even more significant than the response of the Soviet Union and the nations of Western Europe to the American bombing of Libya was that of the moderate Arab states. Had the moderate Arab nations expressed their support for the bombing, then this would have been the one justification the Reagan Administration may have used to pursue additional American military action aimed at toppling Qaddafi. Absent the support of the moderate Arab nations, Qaddafi would have been sufficiently isolated from his fellow Arab heads of state such that the administration could have exploited the Libyan leader's status as a pariah in the Middle East in order to pursue regime change in Tripoli. As it turned out, Qaddafi was far from isolated in the Middle East: His fellow Arab leaders were quick to condemn the American bombing of Libya, and the denunciation extended to America's closest allies in the Arab world, including Egypt, Jordan, Saudi Arabia, and Kuwait.

Reagan Unsuccessfully Attempts to Elicit Mubarak's Support for the American Bombing of Libya

Perhaps no Arab nation was more critical to the Reagan Administration in supporting its position against Libya than Egypt. As the most populous and militarily powerful Arab nation, which shared a long border with Libya, the support of Egypt was critical to the success of the administration's campaign against Qaddafi. Given the longstanding enmity existing between Egypt and Libya, which stemmed from Tripoli's intense and vociferous opposition to Cairo's decision to sign its peace treaty with Israel in 1979, Mubarak shared the Reagan Administration's open-ended contempt and disdain for Qaddafi. Egypt's military power, its geographical proximity to Libya, and its enmity toward Tripoli were all vital strategic resources the Reagan Administration could use in pursuing its campaign against Qaddafi.

The Reagan Administration had every hope that Egypt would support the American bombing of Libya. Among the nations of the Arab world, Qaddafi had devoted the bulk of his subversive activities in the Middle East to destabilizing and overthrowing the Mubarak regime, which included alleged plots to assassinate the president of Egypt, as we saw in Chapter 2. Given the political and personal threat Qaddafi posed to Mubarak, the Reagan Administration had every reason to believe that the president of Egypt would support the American bombing of Libya.

The White House singled out Mubarak as the one leader whose support for the American bombing of Libya the Reagan Administration desperately wanted to have. To this end, on April 15, 1986, the White House sent a memorandum to Reagan informing him that Shultz, Weinberger, and Poindexter had recommended that the president place a telephone call to Mubarak "between 2:15 and 3:30 pm EST [Eastern Standard Time]." The White House informed Reagan that the purpose of the phone call to Mubarak would be to:

1. Express understanding of [the] sensitive nature of [the] current situation while emphasizing the need [for] Egypt and the United States to stand together against terrorism and Qaddafi.
2. [Note that the] evolving situation may create opportunities for significant [political] change in Libya. [You] will send [a] message later today [to Mubarak].
c. Solicit his views on likely Libyan reactions [to the bombing], and reaffirm U.S. readiness to act again [against Libya] if necessary.

Accompanying the White House memorandum to Reagan were talking points he was to use in his telephone call to Mubarak. Reagan was to have begun the call by expressing to Mubarak his understanding that the American bombing of Libya created the risk of provoking political instability in the Middle East, which represented a threat to the security of moderate Arab nations like Egypt: "I wanted to speak with you about American actions against Libya last night. I understand the sensitive situation that this creates for America's friends in the Arab world. It is thus especially important for us to find ways to stand together against terrorism and Qaddafi if we are to advance our mutual goal of a stable and peaceful Middle East."

Reagan was to have expressed to Mubarak his belief that the American bombing of Tripoli and Benghazi might very well incite Libyan dissidents to the overthrow of Qaddafi: "The situation inside Libya may create opportunities for significant [political] change. I will be sending you additional thoughts on this subject." Reagan was also to have asked Mubarak whether he believed that Qaddafi might instigate additional acts of international terrorism in retaliation for the American bombing of Libya, directly posing the following question to the president of Egypt: "What actions from Qaddafi would you anticipate in the near future?" Reagan was to have made it clear to Mubarak that he would order additional American military action against Libya if Qaddafi instigated any additional act of international terrorism: "Let me reaffirm my determination to act again [against Libya], if necessary, should Qaddafi undertake additional terrorist acts."

Due to the heightened conflict between the United States and Libya, the Reagan Administration wanted to quickly add the battle group of ships, organized around the aircraft carrier *Enterprise*, which was in the Indian Ocean at the time, to the American naval force in the Mediterranean in case the armada was needed in the immediate future for any additional military action against Tripoli the president might order. To expedite the transit of the carrier battle group to the Mediterranean, the administration requested that the Egyptian government grant permission for the armada to sail through the Suez Canal. Reagan was to have emphasized to Mubarak that he considered Egyptian approval of this request to be vital to the strategic interests of the United States in the Middle East.

> U.S. officials have spoken with Foreign Minister [Ismat] Majid and Osama El-Baz [Mubarak's personal advisor] requesting Egyptian permission for the aircraft carrier *Enterprise* and other ships in its group to transit the Suez Canal. I want to emphasize the importance that I attach to this request. It is my hope that we will have your permission by Thursday, April 17.[26]

Pursuant to the White House's request, Reagan placed the telephone call to Mubarak. Following the call, Reagan produced a hand-written note at the bottom of the White House memorandum requesting the conversation. The note recorded Mubarak's responses to some of the questions Reagan posed during their telephone conversation.

In his note, Reagan observed the following thoughts Mubarak had expressed: "He thinks Qaddafi may hold up on terrorist deeds, but isn't certain. He's watching carefully for a favorable change within Libya. As to the *Enterprise*, the matter hasn't been brought up to him yet by his ministers."[27] Reagan's note made it clear that Mubarak did not share Reagan's fear that Qaddafi might retaliate for the American bombing of Libya by instigating a new round of international terrorist attacks, but in fact would do precisely the opposite: The mercurial leader in Tripoli would respond to the air strikes by suspending, at least temporarily, his involvement in any future acts of terrorism. Not surprisingly, given the intense and vociferous enmity existing between Egypt and Libya, Mubarak shared Reagan's hope that the ultimate consequence of the bombing would be the overthrow of Qaddafi.

Given the deep reservoir of animosity Mubarak had for Qaddafi, one would have expected Egypt to express its support for the American bombing of Libya, but in fact the opposite was the case. In a statement issued through the Middle East News Agency on April 15, 1986, Minister of Information Safwat Sherif declared that:

> It was with great disturbance and dissatisfaction that Egypt heard the news [of the bombing]. This action contradicts the commitment of states to refrain from resorting to the use of force in resolving their disputes.... The use of force in any form cannot lead to the solution of international problems and the easing of world tension.

However, Egypt's condemnation of the American bombing of Libya was tempered by its criticism of Qaddafi. As Majid noted, "It is no secret that we have criticized the Libyan leadership." Majid made it clear that Cairo's deep-seated contempt and disdain for Qaddafi was in response to his "attempts to jeopardize the security of Egypt" resulting from the Libyan leader's campaign to destabilize and subvert the Mubarak regime. In a further show of Egyptian solidarity with the United States, in late April Minister of State for Foreign Affairs Boutros Boutros-Ghali reaffirmed Cairo's commitment to preserve its strong alliance with Washington, and condemned Libya for its "policy of destabilization in the Arab world ... and in the world in general."[28]

The fact that Egypt chose, however disingenuously, to denounce the American bombing of Libya should hardly have come as a surprise to the Reagan Administration. As we saw in the previous chapter, Egypt had agreed to train and equip Libyan dissidents committed to the overthrow of Qaddafi as part of Operation Flower. But as Poindexter pointed out in a memorandum sent to Reagan four days before the American bombing of Libya, Egyptian support for the dissidents "has waxed and waned depending upon the political tides and pressures exerted by Qaddafi on the Egyptians." Egypt's less than enthusiastic participation in Operation Flower proved that the Reagan Administration could not depend upon Cairo to support the United States in its bitter and acrimonious conflict with Libya, and this fact was reaffirmed by the Mubarak regime's decision to join the rest of the Arab world in denouncing the American bombing of Tripoli and Benghazi.

Mubarak Approves Reagan's Request for American Naval Access to the Suez Canal

In news which surely was music to the ears of the Reagan Administration, on April 22, 1986, Egypt announced that Mubarak had granted the White House's request that the ships of the *Enterprise* carrier battle group be allowed to transit the Suez Canal for immediate deployment in the Mediterranean.[29] On April 28 members of the JCS transmitted a letter, sent from Weinberger to Mubarak, to the American ambassador to Egypt. Attached to the letter was a message from members of the JCS, marked "secret." On August 6, 2002, NARA declassified the message which told the ambassador, "[We] request that you deliver the following personal letter from Secretary Weinberger to His Excellency, Mohamed Hosni Mubarak." In his letter, Weinberger informed Mubarak:

> I was very pleased to hear of your approval of President Reagan's request for a naval transit to the Suez Canal. Your timely support in this matter will greatly enhance our operational flexibility, and permit us to meet our commitments of peace and security [in the Middle East].
>
> Our nations strive to achieve the same objectives of peace and security. Through continued mutual support, we can achieve these objectives, and create a stable world environment that promotes prosperity for all.
>
> Please accept our deepest appreciation for your support in this important endeavor.[30]

As we have seen, the Reagan Administration gave utmost importance to the issue of Egyptian approval of the White House's request that the battle group of ships, organized around the aircraft carrier *Enterprise*, then in the Indian Ocean, be granted transit rights through the Suez Canal for rapid deployment in the Mediterranean. The ships would be strategically situated for use in any additional American military action against Libya Reagan might order. The *Enterprise* issue was of such great importance to the Reagan Administration that the White House included the matter as an item on the president's agenda during his phone conversation Mubarak held the day following the American bombing of Libya. The fact that Mubarak granted Reagan's request that the *Enterprise* be granted transit rights through the Suez Canal, in the wake of universal Arab condemnation of the bombing, is indicative of the importance Egypt attached to its strategic alliance with the United States. This served to take much of the sting off of Egypt's decision to join the rest of the Arab world in condemning the bombing, and of Cairo's less than enthusiastic participation in Operation Flower.

The Moderate Arab Nations Join Egypt in Condemning the American Bombing of Libya

Egyptian policy toward the Libyan-American conflict attempted to balance its commitment to its alliance with the United States with its need to avoid isolating itself within the Arab world, which would have occurred had Cairo announced its support for the bombing of Tripoli and Benghazi. Indeed, every Arab nation strongly condemned the bombing, and Egypt was not about to be the only such state to sharply depart from this consensus by expressing support for the air strikes. In fact, the other moderate Arab nations were even harsher than Egypt in their condemnation of the bombing.

Leading the Arab chorus of condemnation of the American bombing of Libya was, with the possible exception only of Egypt, America's closest ally in the Arab world — Saudi Arabia. In an announcement broadcast on Riyadh Radio on April 15, 1986, a spokesman for the Saudi government declared its "great regret and condemnation" of the bombing "because violence does not serve the desired goal of the establishment of peace, but escalates the climate of tensions in the Mediterranean and the entire Arab region." The spokesman "reaffirmed" Saudi support for "the Libyan people and indeed for the fraternal Arab people subject to such attack."

Adding to Saudi Arabia's strident denunciation of the American bombing of Libya was Riyadh's ambassador to the United Nations. In a statement broadcast on Riyadh Radio on April 17, the ambassador condemned the American "aggression" against Libya as providing a "license for Israeli terrorism to attack anytime and anywhere" in the Arab world. In a sharp departure from Egypt, which shared the American view of Qaddafi as an international terrorist leader, the Saudi ambassador rejected this characterization of the beleaguered leader of Libya. Instead, the ambassador denounced Israel as "the largest terrorist institution in history." In a tangible sign of Saudi opposition to the American bombing of Libya, Riyadh announced it was canceling a high-level Saudi trade mission to the United States, scheduled for September 1986, citing the lack of sufficient time for planning. However, since Saudi Arabia had five months to plan for the mission — certainly more than ample time — it is clear that the real reason for the cancellation was Riyadh's need to back up its words with some tangible action to make it clear that, in the bitter and acrimonious conflict between the United States and Libya, the kingdom stood squarely behind Tripoli, and against Washington.

Joining Saudi Arabia in its condemnation of the American bombing of Libya was Kuwait. On April 15, 1986, the Kuwait News Agency announced, "Kuwait voices its condemnation and denunciation of these raids. We, on the basis of our pan–Arab responsibilities, feel it is important to stand by and have solidarity with the Arab nation while some of our Arab countries and peoples are subject to this direct aggression." That same day the National Assembly of Kuwait, the legislative body of the emirate, issued a resolution which "denounces this flagrant aggression and appeals to Arab countries and their parliaments to work to end their secondary differences of opinion to defend their dignity and sovereignty" against the United States.

Adding its voice to the Arab chorus of denunciation against the American bombing of Libya was the United Arab Emirates. On April 15, 1986, the president of the United Arab Emirates and emir of Abu Dhabi, Sheik Zayid, announced his nation's support for "the Arab Libyan people who are facing the U.S. attacks." To openly demonstrate his solidarity with Libya, Zayid personally affirmed his support for Qaddafi in a telephone conversation with the beleaguered leader in Tripoli hours after he had survived the American bombing of his residential compound.

In a practical demonstration of its opposition to the American bombing of Libya, the United Arab Emirates, which at the time held a temporary seat on the United Nations Security Council, joined a majority of the members of that body in supporting a resolution condemning the air strikes. Not surprisingly, the resolution was vetoed by three of the five permanent members of the Security Council — the United States, the United Kingdom, and France. In a further signal of its opposition to the American bombing of Libya, the United Arab Emirates suspended contacts between its companies and an American trade mission which was visiting the Persian Gulf nation at the time the air strikes occurred. The United Arab Emirates also canceled its trade exhibition in London in retaliation for Thatcher's decision to provide political and operational support for the bombing.

The strong and unequivocal opposition to the American bombing of Libya voiced by Saudi Arabia, Kuwait, and the United Arab Emirates represented a severe blow to the Reagan Administration. The three monarchies of the Persian Gulf represented close allies of the United States, and collectively accounted for nearly half the world's proven oil reserves. Because the three Persian Gulf monarchies were critical to the economic survival of the entire industrial world, and had adopted oil policies favorable to the economic interests of the developed nations, the Reagan Administration could not politically afford to ignore their strident and vociferous denunciation of the American bombing of Libya. Certainly this denunciation had a sobering effect on the administration as the White House could not politically afford to further alienate the Persian Gulf monarchies with additional American military action against Libya.

Qaddafi's success in garnering the strong and unequivocal opposition of Saudi Arabia, Kuwait, and the United Arab Emirates to the American bombing of Libya represented an unqualified strategic victory for Libya in its vitriolic and venomous conflict with the United States. Reagan could have ordered additional American military action against Libya only at the risk of a complete break in relations between the United States and the three Persian Gulf monarchies. Such a development would potentially have had economically and strategically disastrous consequences for not only the United States, but also the entire industrial world. The denunciation of the American bombing of Libya voiced by Saudi Arabia, Kuwait, and the United Arab Emirates was a certainly a factor in Reagan's decision to abandon any additional American military action against Libya.

In addition to Saudi Arabia, Kuwait, and the United Arab Emirates, another Persian Gulf nation whose response to the American bombing of Libya the Reagan Administration could not politically afford to ignore was Iraq. To be sure, Iraq was hardly a moderate Arab nation under the regime of Saddam Hussein. But during the 1980s, Iraq assumed the role of a surrogate power for American interests in the Persian Gulf, serving as a bulwark against the spread of Iranian-sponsored Islamic radicalism throughout the oil-rich region.

During 1980 to 1988, Iraq was embroiled in a bitter and bloody war with Iran. By thwarting repeated military offensives mounted by the Iranian Army to cross the Iraqi border, Baghdad succeeded in containing the spread of Islamic radicalism emanating from Tehran.[31] While Iraq was hardly an ally of the United States, Washington and Baghdad enjoyed an alliance of convenience during the 1980s as the two nations shared an open-ended contempt and hostility for the Islamic revolutionary regime of the Ayatollah Khomeini. Given the fact that Iraq served the strategic interests of the United States in the Persian Gulf as a counterweight against the threat to the region posed by Iran, the Reagan Administration could not politically afford to alienate Baghdad, and had to be sensitive to its reaction to the American bombing of Libya.

The Reagan Administration actually had greater prospects for procuring Iraqi support for the American bombing of Libya than was the case with Saudi Arabia, Kuwait, and the United Arab Emirates, which served as Washington's closest allies in the Arab world. Libya strongly supported Iran in its war against Iraq. This was consistent with the fact that both Libya and Iran shared an intense and vociferous enmity against the United States. However, if the Reagan Administration believed that Libyan support for Iran would result in Iraqi backing for the American bombing of Tripoli and Benghazi, then the White House was sadly disappointed. Iraq was no less critical of the bombing than was the case with Saudi Arabia, Kuwait, and the United Arab Emirates.

On April 17, 1986, Foreign Minister Tariq Aziz announced that "Iraq strongly condemns this [American] aggression and expresses solidarity with the Arab people in Libya." However, like Egypt, Iraq's condemnation of the American bombing of Libya was tempered by its criticism of Qaddafi: "This obvious condemnation does not at all mean [Iraqi] support for the Libyan regime's stands and policy." Aziz strongly denounced "the Libyan regime's odd stands and deviant policies." As a practical demonstration of its opposition to Qaddafi, on April 18, the Iraqi government, through its official newspaper, *Al Thawrah*, rejected calls for an Arab summit meeting on the Libyan-American crisis, arguing that, "Any Arab meeting ... must first discuss the Iranian aggression against Iraq before the U.S. aggression against Libya."

Iraqi policy toward the Libyan-American crisis was geared toward mobilizing Arab opposition to Iran, not the United States. This certainly served American interests as it deflected Arab attention away from the American bombing of Libya, where the United States found itself strongly denounced by virtually all the Arab nations. But Iraq was seeking to opportunistically exploit the Libyan-American crisis in order to advance its interests against Iran, and Baghdad found itself in the same position as Cairo: The Hussein regime condemned the bombing only because it did not want to be the only Arab government which supported the air strikes.

Like Egypt, Iraq had open-ended contempt and disdain for Qaddafi and its opposition to the American bombing of Libya was a perfunctory exercise and did not represent a serious and genuine revulsion against the air strikes. Both Egypt and Iraq had grievances against Qaddafi, and could take some satisfaction at the punishment the besieged leader of Libya had suffered at the hands of the United States. The Reagan Administration could also take some satisfaction in the fact that Egyptian and Iraqi condemnation of the American bombing of Libya was more designed to ensure that the two nations did not stray away from the Arab consensus against the air strikes, and did not in any way diminish the enmity they had toward Qaddafi. This served as a consolation for the administration in light of the truly harsh and vitriolic denunciation of the bombing which came from Washington's closest and most strategically valuable allies in the Arab world: Saudi Arabia, Kuwait, and the United Arab Emirates.

Joining the list of moderate Arab nations condemning the American bombing of Libya was Jordan. On April 15, 1986, Mohammed Kamal, the

Jordanian ambassador to the United States, declared in Washington, "As an Arab country and member of the Arab League, we have to condemn any attack on an Arab country coming from any source." However, Kamal's condemnation of the American bombing of Libya was tempered by his criticism of the Arab world for having failed to take any steps to resolve the bitter and acrimonious conflict between Washington and Tripoli. Kamal argued that "the United States would not have attacked [Libya] today" had the Arab world been able to "work together to resolve this" conflict.[32] However, unlike Egypt and Iraq, which had coupled their condemnation of the American bombing of Libya with their denunciation of Qaddafi, Kamal's criticism was directed against the Arab world, and not the renegade leader of Libya.

Was the Arab Condemnation of the American Bombing of Libya Really Genuine?

With the Arab world having forged a strong consensus against the American bombing of Libya, Tripoli called for an Arab summit meeting in order to adopt measures against the United States in retaliation for the air strikes. On April 20, 1986, the foreign ministers of the Arab League held a meeting, and issued a statement condemning the bombing. Chedli Klibi, secretary general of the Arab League, argued that the bombing "compromises, perhaps irreversibly, United States relations with the Arab peoples."

However, the foreign ministers of the Arab League rejected a Libyan request for the imposition of unspecified sanctions against the United States in retaliation for the bombing. The sanction Libya was obviously seeking was the imposition of an Arab oil embargo against the United States — the only practical leverage the Arab world wields over Washington. However, in a concession to Libya, the foreign ministers agreed to meet again in Fez during April 30 to May 1 in order to lay the groundwork for an Arab summit conference to consider the highly-charged and emotion-laden conflict between Washington and Tripoli.

However, during their meeting in Fez the foreign ministers of the Arab League could not agree on whether the Libyan-American crisis should be the only issue placed before the agenda of the planned Arab summit conference. Iraq and the Persian Gulf monarchies insisted that what they considered to be the threat from Iran be added to the agenda of the conference. Iran's two allies in the Arab world — Syria and Libya — rejected any inclusion of Tehran on the agenda, insisting that the Arab summit meeting be exclusively devoted to a consideration of the American bombing of Tripoli and Benghazi. Due to sharp divisions among its members over the issue of Iran, the meeting of the foreign ministers in Fez concluded without any agreement to convene an Arab summit conference in order to consider the bombing.

Undaunted by the failure of the Arab League to convene a summit meeting among its member states, Libya took its case against the United States to a meeting of the oil ministers of the Organization of Petroleum Exporting Countries (OPEC) requesting the imposition of an oil embargo against Washington. On April 15, 1986, eight of the thirteen OPEC members issued a statement which "expressed deep concern for [American] acts against international law" and "extended condolences to the Libyan people for the human losses incurred" resulting from the American bombing of Tripoli and Benghazi. However, five non–Arab members of OPEC — Venezuela, Ecuador, Nigeria, Gabon, and Indonesia — refused to support the statement condemning the bombing. And in a further blow to Libya, twelve of the thirteen oil ministers of OPEC flatly rejected the Libyan request for the imposition of an oil embargo against the United States. The only member of OPEC supporting such action was, of course, Libya.

The fact that Libya was unable to procure from the rest of the Arab world anything more than verbal condemnation of the American bombing of Tripoli and Benghazi leads to the following intriguing question: Was the Arab world really sincere in its condemnation of the bombing, or were the Arab nations going through the motions of offering empty and disingenuous rhetorical support for Libya as an obligation required for reasons of maintaining the fiction of pan–Arab solidarity behind a fellow Arab nation which had come under foreign attack? On May 9, 1986, the Washington Institute for Near East Policy sent a paper to the White House, written by Robert Satloff and Jonathan Barkey, entitled "Arab Reaction to the U.S. Air Strikes Against Libya." Satloff and Barkey argued that Arab condemnation of the American bombing of Libya was indeed empty and disingenuous rhetoric as rest of the Arab world had failed to back up its denunciation with any tangible action in support of the beleaguered Qaddafi regime.

In their paper, Satloff and Barkey argued, "Contrary to the opinion of some analysts, Arab world reaction to the U.S. bombing raid on Tripoli and Benghazi has been surprisingly mild. Although all Arab countries have criticized the U.S. air strikes, virtually no substantive actions have been taken to underscore their verbal condemnations." Satloff and Barkey noted, "Bilateral relations between the Arab states and America remain unaffected" by the American bombing of Libya, pointing out:

1. Diplomatically, no Arab state has broken relations with the United States or cancelled a diplomatic mission.
2. Militarily, no Arab state has severed pre-positioning or access agreements, and no Arab state has announced cancellation of future joint military maneuvers.
3. Economically, there has been no interruption in the normal course of business, trade, or finance with any Arab country. Saudi Arabia did cancel a September 1986 trade mission, but gave insufficient time for planning as the explanation.
4. Culturally, there has been no change in exchange programs between America and any Arab country.

Satloff and Barkey argued that Arab condemnation of the American bombing of Libya was mostly a pro forma and perfunctory exercise which many moderate Arab nations had to do for public relations reasons in order to show solidarity with a fellow Arab state which had come under foreign attack.

> Many states, including Egypt, Jordan, Iraq, and Morocco denounced the raid for reasons of "pan–Arab responsibility" and opposition to the use of force as a means to settle disputes. But they drew distinctions between the solidarity they expressed for "the Libyan people" and support for Qaddafi himself. Indeed, editorials in the Egyptian and Iraqi state-controlled press were openly critical of Qaddafi's rule. Only three countries, pro–Soviet Syria and South Yemen and ... Sudan reinforced their [anti–American] rhetoric with offers of material support to Libya.[33]

Satloff and Barkey's claims that the Arab condemnation of the American bombing of Libya represented an empty and disingenuous public relations exercise designed to maintain the fiction of pan–Arab solidarity with Tripoli received critical support from the Israeli newspaper *Haaretz*. In an editorial in its April 17, 1986, edition, *Haaretz* noted that:

> The Arabs did not respond to Qaddafi's call for help. The Arab world did little more than go through the motions of verbal condemnation of America — and for good reason. Having been subjected to Libya's subversiveness, many Arab regimes cannot wait to see Qaddafi go. His downfall would strengthen pro–Western Arab countries.[34]

The argument that Arab condemnation of the American bombing of Libya represented empty and disingenuous rhetoric designed to maintain the fiction of pan–Arab solidarity with Tripoli is supported by Stanik who argues, "Since no Arab leader could openly endorse a U.S. military attack against a brother Arab and expect to survive politically, several moderate Arab governments

... publicly condemned the attack ... but privately welcomed Reagan's use of force against one of the region's biggest troublemakers."[35]

The argument that Arab condemnation of the American bombing of Libya represented an empty and meaningless gesture designed for public relations purposes was fully accepted by none other than the White House itself, at least insofar as Saudi Arabia was concerned. The White House's own cynical view of Arab condemnation of the American bombing of Libya was conveyed by Reagan during a meeting he held with Jewish leaders at the White House on May 19, 1986. On May 15 Stark sent a memorandum to McDaniel telling the executive secretary of the NSC, "Attached ... is a memo from you to David Chew forwarding talking points ... for the President's use in his meeting with Jewish leaders on Monday [May 19]. The talking points have been cleared through the Office of Public Liaison. Ron Sable and Howard Teicher concur."

Stark concluded his memorandum by recommending to McDaniel "that you sign the memo to Chew."[36] McDaniel initialed the blank space next to the word "Approve," and sent the memorandum to Chew on May 16, 1986, informing the White House Staff Secretary, "Attached ... are talking points for the President to use in his meeting with Jewish leaders on Monday, May 19 in the Cabinet Room at 11 a.m. The talking points have been cleared through the Office of Public Liaison."[37]

The purpose of Reagan's meeting with Jewish leaders was to win their acquiescence, however grudgingly it may have been given, to an arms sales package to Saudi Arabia the president had proposed on April 8, 1986, which was pending the approval of Congress.[38] A major argument Reagan's talking points called for him to make was that Saudi Arabia had supported the United States in its bitter and acrimonious conflict with Libya, despite the fact that Riyadh had joined the rest of the Arab world in condemning the American bombing of Tripoli and Benghazi. Reagan was to have told Jewish leaders:

> While the Saudis have ... joined in Arab criticism of U.S. action [against Libya] out of a sense of Arab unity, they have done so in a way which has prevented anything more damaging than verbal criticisms. They do not give support to Qaddafi, and have ensured that no economic or political sanctions were imposed against the U.S. Just two weeks ago, the Saudis torpedoed Qaddafi's efforts to hold an Arab summit to condemn the U.S. strikes on Tripoli.[39]

The White House's claim, conveyed through Reagan's talking points, that Saudi Arabia had supported the United States in its vitriolic and venomous conflict with Libya represents a gross exaggeration of the facts designed to overcome the intense and vociferous lobbying campaign AIPAC had undertaken to block approval of the Saudi arms sales package in Congress. While the White House was correct that Saudi, not to mention other Arab, condemnation of the American bombing of Libya was confined to verbal denunciations of the air strikes, the Arab world would likely have taken substantive action against the United States had Reagan ordered additional military action against Libya. As we have seen, the White House attributed the collapse of efforts to arrange an Arab summit meeting on the Libyan-American conflict to Saudi opposition to the holding of the proposed conference. However, the failure of those efforts was the result not of Saudi opposition to the proposed meeting but of disagreements among the Arab nations as to whether the Iran-Iraq War should be an item on the agenda of the conference. And while the White House is certainly correct in its claim that Saudi Arabia opposed Libyan calls for the imposition of unspecified sanctions — most likely an oil embargo — against the United States in retaliation for the American bombing of Tripoli and Benghazi, so did virtually every other Arab nation. In all likelihood, the White House exaggerated the support Saudi Arabia provided to the United States in its highly-charged and emotion-laden conflict with Libya in order to justify Reagan's argument that Riyadh was a strong and valued ally of Washington. Such an argument was required for Reagan to overcome the substantial opposition in Congress to the proposed Saudi arms sales package which won approval in the Senate by no more than a single vote.[40]

The argument that the Arab condemnation of the American bombing of Libya represented an empty and meaningless gesture designed for public relations purposes is certainly true — but only to a point. To be sure, the Arab world failed to back up its condemnation with any tangible action against the United States, specifically rejecting Libyan calls for the imposition of sanctions — for all intents and purposes, an Arab oil embargo — against Washington. However, the cynical view of the Arab condemnation of the American bombing of Libya misses the point: The purpose of the denunciation was not to lay the groundwork for tangible Arab retaliatory action against the United States. Rather, the purpose was to place the Reagan Administration on notice that the Arab world would not tolerate any additional American military action against Libya.

The condemnation of the American bombing of Libya voiced by Saudi Arabia, Kuwait, and the United Arab Emirates dealt a particularly devastating blow to the United States. Given the economic and strategic value of Saudi Arabia, Kuwait, and the United Arab Emirates to the United States, Washington could not afford to alienate the three Persian Gulf monarchies through its pursuit of additional American military action against Libya.

The desire to avoid a rupture in relations between the United States and those nations was certainly a factor in Reagan's decision to quickly abandon the military option, and renew his commitment to work for a peaceful resolution of the bitter and acrimonious conflict between the United States and Libya following the American bombing of Tripoli and Benghazi. This was manifested in Reagan's decision to join with the leaders of the other G-7 nations during their summit meeting in Tokyo in adopting a unified policy between both sides of the Atlantic aimed at resolving this conflict through peaceful, rather than military, means.

The White House Rejects the International Condemnation of the American Bombing of Libya

If the world community believed that its near universal condemnation of the American bombing of Libya would provoke the Reagan Administration to reassess the wisdom of the president's decision to order the air strikes then the international critics of the military action were sadly mistaken. The administration flatly rejected the condemnation on two grounds: First, the White House did not believe the criticism reflected international public opinion, at least insofar as Western Europe was concerned; and second, the White House challenged the single, central, overriding argument its international critics had used to denounce the air strikes — that they would inflame, rather than dampen, global terrorism.

Perhaps the nation which led the chorus of Western European denunciation of the American bombing of Libya was France. As we saw in the previous chapter, Mitterrand flatly rejected Walters' request that the British-based American aircraft, which bombed Tripoli, be granted over-flight rights to use French airspace as their most direct route to Libya. Mitterrand added insult to injury by harshly condemning the bombing, charging that the United States had slaughtered innocent Libyan civilians through its air strikes.

However, the Reagan Administration did not view Mitterrand as reflecting the sentiments of French public opinion in his condemnation of the American bombing of Libya. Rather, the administration viewed that opinion as being more accurately reflected in the strong support for the bombing expressed by Mitterrand's predecessor, Valery Giscard d'Estaing, who served as president of France during 1974 to 1981. In a statement issued in response to the bombing, Giscard declared unequivocally, "I approve of the American action [which was] justified by repeated acts of [Libyan] aggression against the population in Western democratic countries."[41] Giscard reiterated his support for the American bombing of Libya in a letter he sent to Reagan on April 16, 1986. The letter was transmitted to Reagan by the American ambassador to France.

The White House was gratified by Giscard's support for the American bombing of Libya, especially in light of the fact that it took much of the sting off the French government's harsh condemnation of the air strikes. As a gesture of gratitude, North and Coy prepared a letter in Reagan's name to be sent to Giscard. The letter was attached to a memorandum marked "confidential" North and Coy sent to Poindexter on April 23, 1986. On July 13, 2000, NARA declassified both documents.

In their memorandum, North and Coy informed Poindexter:

> Attached ... is a memo from you to the President requesting that he sign the letter ... to former President Giscard d'Estaing of France thanking him for his support for our action in Libya. This responds to his letter to the President of April 16 ... which was transmitted via AmbEmb Paris.... The State Department will transmit the President's letter via cable to our Embassy in Paris. Ty Cobb [director of international programs and technology affairs for the NSC] concurs.

North and Coy recommended to Poindexter "that you initial and forward your memo."[42] Poindexter responded by marking his initials on the blank space next to the word "Approve," and sending the memorandum to Reagan on April 23, 1986. In his memorandum, Poindexter posed the following question to Reagan: "Should you send a letter of appreciation to former President of France Giscard d'Estaing ... for his public and private message of support for our action in Libya?" In responding to this question, Poindexter noted:

> On April 16 Giscard wrote to you via [the] American Embassy in Paris ... expressing his support for your decision with regard to our action against terrorist-related facilities in Libya.... Although the French government disapproved of our request for over-flight during the air strike on Libya, Giscard has publicly and privately expressed his support for our action.... Your letter ... thanks him for his expression of support (the text of which will be transmitted via cable to our Embassy in Paris).

Reagan responded to Poindexter by marking his initials on the blank space underneath the word "OK" at the bottom of the White House national security adviser's memorandum.[43]

On April 24, 1986, Reagan signed and sent his letter to Giscard. In his letter, Reagan expressed to Giscard:

> I am deeply grateful for your recent letter, expressing your sentiments and those of your countrymen regarding the steps we have taken in the fight against

Libyan-sponsored terrorism. Your support and that of your compatriots in combating the continuing assault against Western democracies is, and will continue, to be very much appreciated.

Reagan expressed to Giscard his hope that the G-7 leaders would agree on a unified policy in confronting the threat posed by Libyan-sponsored international terrorism at their upcoming summit meeting in Tokyo: "I am hopeful that my forthcoming meeting in Tokyo will result in further developments on ways in which we can work together to reduce the threat of terrorism against all our peoples." Reagan concluded his letter to Giscard by reaffirming his gratitude to the former president of France for his strong stand in support of the American bombing of Libya: "Thank you for taking the time to share your thoughts with me."[44]

Reagan's letter to Giscard is remarkable insofar as he insinuated that Mitterrand's position against the American bombing of Libya did not truly reflect French public opinion on the air strikes. Rather, Reagan expressed the belief that Giscard's strong support for the bombing was truly reflective of that opinion. However, Reagan's belief reflected wishful thinking in the White House: Any poll taken of French public opinion of the bombing almost certainly would have shown the overwhelming majority of the French opposed to the air strikes. Indeed, a public opinion poll found that 66 percent of Britons opposed the bombing, despite Thatcher's strong support for the air strikes.[45] The poll is a clear indication of the existence of strong public opposition to the bombing throughout Western Europe.

Nevertheless, the fact that Giscard would express strong support for the bombing illustrated that Mitterrand was by no means speaking for his entire public in his sharp condemnation of the air strikes; and that a large minority of French certainly supported the American military action. And this was no doubt true of the remaining Western European nations whose governments had joined France in condemning the bombing. The Reagan Administration could take solace from this fact, which certainly softened the blow dealt by the sharp condemnation against the bombing voiced by every Western European government, with the notable exceptions of the United Kingdom and West Germany.

The White House Gathers Evidence Demonstrating the Success of the American Bombing of Libya

Perhaps even more important to the White House than the fact that Giscard's support had demonstrated that Western Europe was far from united in its opposition to the American bombing of Libya was the growing evidence that the air strikes had indeed achieved their intended effect. After a period of high levels of Libyan-sponsored international terrorist activity, there were no additional acts of terrorism instigated by Tripoli in the weeks and months following the air strikes. In the White House's view, this fact alone justified Reagan's decision to order the bombing. More importantly, this fact served as a devastating refutation of perhaps the most powerful and persuasive argument international critics had used to condemn the bombing: that it would inflame, rather than dampen, Libyan-sponsored international terrorism.

The White House devoted particular emphasis to gathering intelligence regarding Libya's response to the American bombing of Tripoli and Benghazi. The White House was especially interested in determining whether Libya would indeed retaliate against the bombing with additional acts of international terrorism, a particular concern of the nations of Western Europe, which largely accounts for why most of the governments of the region had voiced their opposition to the air strikes. Initial intelligence gathered in the hours following the bombing suggested that Western European fears that the air strikes would provoke Libyan retaliation were justified. This was reflected in a White House Situation Room Note, marked "top secret," which was written on April 15, 1986. On May 23, 2001, NARA declassified the note, which observed:

> While no specific terrorist incidents or attacks have been noted in response to the U.S. operations [against Libya], Libyan radio is calling on all Arabs to rise up and "destroy all the U.S. bases in the Mediterranean." Tripoli has also called for attacks on all American interests, encouraging Arabs to "tear apart the bodies of Americans, civilian and military, (and) drink their blood."[46]

However, Libyan calls for the perpetration of acts of terrorism against Americans in retaliation for the bombing of Tripoli and Benghazi proved to be empty rhetoric, designed to create the appearance that the air strikes would have no impact upon Qaddafi's determination to aggressively and relentlessly pursue his international terrorist campaign. In fact, the opposite was the case. The bombing clearly had a sobering effect upon Qaddafi, who fully recognized that any Libyan-sponsored retaliatory terrorist attacks in response to the air strikes would invite the United States to launch additional military action against Tripoli, which was sure to deal an even more devastating, and possibly fatal, blow to his regime. Recognizing the dangers of instigating additional acts of international terrorism, Libya specifically instructed its agents and operatives abroad to refrain from launching any retaliatory terrorist attacks in response to the bombing. This was revealed in another White House Situation Room Note, marked "top secret," which was written on April 19, 1986. On May 22, 2001, NARA partially declassified the note:

> According to information of 18 April from a Libyan source, Libyan officials abroad have been instructed to refrain from providing facilities for revenge operations which might lead to the harming of civilians who have no connection with President Reagan's policy on Libya. Libyan officials were told not to meet with anyone who might propose such a thing, and not to go beyond the bounds of their duties, and to respect the laws of the countries in which they were located.[47]

The aforementioned White House Situation Room Note provides conclusive evidence that Western European critics of the American bombing of Libya could not have been more incorrect in their assumption that the air strikes would inflame, rather than dampen, Libyan-sponsored international terrorism. The intelligence the White House gathered clearly shows that the opposite was in fact the case: Libya responded to the bombing by ordering a halt to all international terrorist operations, both in retaliation for the air strikes, or any others that may have been planned at the time of the American military action. This certainly confirmed in the minds of members of the White House staff that the bombing was justified, and that international condemnation of the air strikes was wrongheaded at the very least, and misguided at worst.

The White House Notes the Incorrect Assumptions Underlying International Opposition to the American Bombing of Libya

Satisfaction within the Reagan administration over the results of the American bombing of Libya was evidenced in the enthusiastic White House response to an editorial published in the July 24, 1986, edition of *The Globe and Mail*. Entitled "The Effect on Libya," the editorial assessed the results of the bombing in the setting of the Old American West, in which Reagan was cast as the "lone sheriff" battling the "international outlaw"—Muammar Qaddafi: "About last April ... remember how Sheriff Ronald Reagan emptied his six-shooter at the Tripoli Kid to a chorus of boos from his Western allies? Venerable Canadians ... called the U.S. air strikes on Libya a violation of international law, as if retaliation for the murders of Americans was not [an act of] self-defense."

It is an irrefutable fact that Qaddafi effectively exploited controversial aspects of American policy in the Middle East, especially Reagan's warm and close embrace of Israel, to his own advantage in garnering credibility in the Arab world. But *The Globe and Mail* rejected the notion that a fundamental change in that policy closer to Qaddafi's liking would have prompted the rogue leader of Libya to abandon his reckless embrace of international terrorism as a weapon to undermine American interests in the Middle East: "Others [among Reagan's critics] insisted that the United States should deal with the root causes of the [Libyan-American] conflict, as if Colonel Muammar Qaddafi would be appeased by anything short of the eradication of Israel and the replacement of moderate Arab rulers with radical pro–Libyan ones."

The Globe and Mail argued that international critics of the American bombing of Libya were grossly mistaken in their argument that the air strikes would inflame, rather than dampen, international terrorism.

> Now that the dust has settled, it is instructive to compare the dark prophesies made in mid–April with subsequent events. The trend line since the Tripoli raid indicates that those "rank amateurs" of foreign policy in the White House may have understood what makes the world tick better than the "wise old heads" in allied capitals who stressed the need to take terrorism in stride.
>
> The raid, it was said, would not deter Libya from further acts of terrorism, but would instead provoke it to retaliate. Colonel Qaddafi would try to avenge the blow to his ... honor. In fact, the opposite has occurred: The "Mad Dog" of international terrorism has reacted as a whipped puppy.... The U.S. raids clearly had a sobering effect on him: There has not been one terrorist act attributable to Libya since the U.S. bombers struck.... The U.S. raids effectively communicated to Colonel Qaddafi that his country would not be immune from the consequences of any terrorism he sponsored.

The Globe and Mail noted that the American bombing of Libya galvanized the nations of Western Europe to take a hard-line stand against Qaddafi after months of coddling the renegade leader of Libya.

> The April bombing was ... said to have split the Atlantic alliance, since the U.S. allies in Continental Europe refused to provide co-operation or even approval for the raids. Yes, there were some initial trans–Atlantic tensions, but the Europeans soon came to appreciate that if the alliance did not tackle Colonel Qaddafi collectively, it would force the United States to tackle him unilaterally.
>
> In the following weeks, Libyan diplomats were expelled from West Germany, Italy, France, and Spain in retaliation for their role in terrorism.... The seven-nation summit in May explicitly condemned Libya's mischief.

The Globe and Mail noted that the Arab world had refused to come to the aid of the beleaguered Qaddafi regime following the American bombing of Libya.

It was also predicted in April that the U.S. attacks would inflate Libya's influence in the Middle East; that even moderate Arab rulers would feel obliged to back Colonel Qaddafi in a show of pan–Arab solidarity. For a few days his stock did appear to rise in the Arab world, but this was illusory.

The Globe and Mail concluded that, far from being a disastrous blunder, as international critics charged, the American bombing of Libya proved to be an unqualified success in neutralizing the threat Qaddafi posed to the international community. By proving his international critics wrong in their predictions of disaster they argued the bombing would allegedly inflict upon the world community, Reagan had significantly enhanced his stature as a credible global statesman who had to be taken seriously and reckoned with: "Has the Tripoli Kid been cut down to size? At this point, we still don't know. But Sheriff Reagan, so belittled abroad last April, stands much taller than his critics today."[48]

Not surprisingly, *The Globe and Mail's* editorial praising Reagan, and condemning his international critics, was warmly welcomed at the White House. Recognizing the public relations windfall which the editorial provided to the White House, on July 25, 1986, Cobb sent a copy of the article, along with a memorandum, to Poindexter. In his memorandum, Cobb summarized the editorial's glowing assessment of Reagan's handling of the vitriolic conflict between the United States and Libya, and the erroneous predictions made by the president's international critics regarding the dire implications which would allegedly result from his decision to order the American bombing of Tripoli and Benghazi. Cobb noted to Poindexter that *The Globe and Mail* represented the authoritative newspaper of record in Canada, and was no friend of the Reagan Administration. Indeed, the publication had served as a frequent critic of American foreign policy — lending credibility to its praise of the president's handling of the bitter and acrimonious conflict between the United States and Libya. As Cobb put in his memorandum to Poindexter, "Wonder of wonders! [I] thought you might like to review the attached editorial from the Toronto *Globe and Mail*, the Canadian equivalent to *The New York Times*, and frequent critic of U.S. [foreign] policy."

Cobb went on to summarize the major points of the editorial.

The editorial reassesses the initial condemnation of our strike against Libya, arguing:
1. Criticism of the U.S. strikes as a "violation of international law" were wrong, and suggested erroneously that retaliation for the murders of Americans was not [an act of] self-defense.
2. Suggestions that dealing with the "root causes of the conflict" in the Middle East would mollify Qaddafi were naïve.

3. The downward trend line in international terrorism since the Libyan raid "indicates that those rank amateurs of foreign policy in the White House may have understood what makes the world tick better than the wise old heads in allied capitals."
4. Contrary to conventional wisdom, the "mad dog" of international terrorism has reacted [to the bombing] like a "whipped puppy." The U.S. raid clearly had a sobering effect on him. Further, the expected support of moderate Arabs for Qaddafi never materialized.
5. The raids provoked initial trans–Atlantic tensions, but the allies now agree on the need for collective counterterrorism action.
6. "Sheriff Reagan," so belittled abroad last April, "stands much taller today than his critics."[49]

The editorial of *The Globe and Mail* was certainly music to the ears of the White House staff and only reinforced the Reagan Administration's belief that the American bombing of Libya was justified despite the near-universal international condemnation of the air strikes.

Interestingly enough, *The Globe and Mail* was not the only non–American newspaper to refer to the dramatic and fateful "shoot-out" between Reagan and Qaddafi within the metaphoric setting of the Old American West. In its April 16, 1986, editorial, the French newspaper *Le Matin* did so as well. In reference to folklore regarding the American shoot-out at the OK Corral, the editorial argued:

> Everybody knows that the issue is not a poor remake of a bad movie which could be called "Settling an Account at the OK Tripoli." It is clear, however, that there is a good guy and a bad guy. Reagan is entitled to play the role of sheriff even if it is thought that he sometimes inadvertently pulls out his gun."[50]

Unlike *The Globe and Mail* which portrayed Reagan as a brave sheriff who had courageously subdued the international outlaw, Muammar Qaddafi, *Le Matin* viewed the president as a bumbling sheriff who had chosen to "pull out his gun" at the rogue leader of the Libya at the wrong time exposing himself to international ridicule. These contrasting images of "Sheriff Reagan" represented the differing viewpoints of the two newspapers with respect to the American bombing of Libya, with *The Globe and Mail* praising the air strikes, and *Le Matin* condemning the military action. How the international media viewed the bombing came down to their metaphorical conception of Reagan as a courageous and dependable, or bumbling and simple-minded, sheriff. It was indeed hard for the international media to resist the temptation of casting the momentous and climactic "shoot-out" between Reagan and Qaddafi in the stark metaphorical setting of the Old West, as the world viewed the president as the quintessential American cowboy.

One expert on the Reagan presidency who also has cast the "shoot-out" between the Reagan and Qaddafi in the metaphorical setting of the Old American West is James M. Strock, who was struck by the closing words of the president's nationwide television address announcing the bombing of Libya. Reminding the public of his warnings to Qaddafi, prior to the bombing, that substantive action would be taken against Libya if the rogue leader in Tripoli failed to abandon his involvement in international terrorism, Reagan noted, "I warned that there should be no place on earth where terrorists can rest, and train, and practice their deadly skills. I meant it. I said we should act with others, if possible, and alone if necessary, to ensure that terrorists have no sanctuary anywhere. Tonight, we have." In interpreting the aforementioned words, Strock argues that

> America, in Reagan's presentation, was not only walking tall, it was prepared to walk alone, if necessary. Even if the entire town was paralyzed by cowardice, America was willing to take to the street alone, like Gary Cooper's sheriff in the classic *High Noon*, if that was the only way to deal with armed and dangerous criminals.[51]

Conclusion

If the Reagan Administration believed that the international community would welcome the American bombing of Libya, then the White House could not have been more mistaken. With very few exceptions — the notable ones being the United Kingdom and West Germany — the international community was practically united in its condemnation of the bombing. International condemnation certainly ruled out any possibility that Reagan could even consider ordering additional American military action against Libya, absent further acts of Libyan-sponsored international terrorism.

Rather, Reagan would have to operate within the international consensus which called for a peaceful resolution of the bitter and acrimonious conflict between the United States and Libya. To this end, Reagan joined the other G-7 leaders in forging a unified policy toward Libya, which emphasized the adoption of non-military measures aimed at isolating Tripoli from, if not the rest of the international community, at least the industrial world. The foundation of that policy was the mass expulsion of Libyans from Western Europe, crippling the ability of Tripoli to mount any additional terrorist attacks in the region. More importantly, the expulsion was designed to serve notice upon Qaddafi that the nations of Western Europe were prepared to adopt more draconian measures against Libya, including economic sanctions, unless the renegade leader in Tripoli immediately abandoned his involvement in international terrorism. Such sanctions, coming on the heels of the American embargo, promised to deliver a crippling economic blow to Libya, which was certain to imperil the survival of the Qaddafi regime. Faced with the prospect of additional American military action, and crippling Western European economic sanctions, Qaddafi finally found himself outmaneuvered and with his back to the wall: The mercurial leader of Libya had no alternative but to all but abandon his involvement in international terrorism. Virtually no additional acts of Libyan-sponsored international terrorism occurred in the weeks and months following the American bombing of Tripoli and Benghazi.

Judged by the objectives it was designed to meet, the American bombing of Libya was an unmitigated success: The air strikes all but brought a final end to Qaddafi's global terrorist enterprise. And this was achieved with American military action which stopped well short of a full-fledged operation aimed at pursuing regime change in Libya. All in all, it is hard not to view the American bombing of Libya as an outstanding example of how the limited application of military force can achieve truly momentous strategic objectives, as it can be safely said that Libyan-sponsored international terrorism represented the preeminent threat to the world community during the early months of 1986.

To be sure, one can legitimately argue that Reagan should have deferred American military action against Libya until all diplomatic and economic options, aimed at persuading Qaddafi to abandon his involvement in international terrorism, had been exhausted. But hours before the American bombing of Libya, the foreign ministers of the EC, at their meeting in The Hague, had made it clear that their governments would not take any substantive measures to persuade Qaddafi to change his behavior. It was only after the bombing that the foreign ministers, reconvening in Luxembourg, agreed to take such measures. The bombing had galvanized the nations of Western Europe into taking substantive action against Libya, because they realized that unless Qaddafi immediately changed his behavior, additional American military action against Tripoli would be forthcoming. Given their extensive and lucrative economic ties to oil-rich Libya, the nations of Western Europe had a vital financial stake in averting such action. As it turned out, the mass expulsion of Libyans from Western Europe, coming on the heels of the bombing of Tripoli and Benghazi, was sufficient to persuade Qaddafi that he needed to abandon his involvement in international terrorism, or his regime faced destruction, if not from additional American military action, then from a loss of his nation's vital economic ties to Western Europe. While it is certainly regrettable that Reagan found the need to order the American bombing of Libya, the international community could take heart in the fact that the air strikes were the first and last operation of their kind before the vitriolic and venomous conflict between Washington and Tripoli was finally brought to an end with the Qaddafi's decision to voluntarily dismantle his global terrorist enterprise.

But the fact remains that had Reagan pursued an evenhanded American policy in the Middle East, aimed at resolving the root cause of the political instability in the region — the Arab-Israeli conflict — it is highly unlikely that he would have been placed in the position where he felt obliged to order the American bombing of Libya on April 14, 1986. Qaddafi's unbridled embrace of international terrorism represented a response to the severe loss of credibility the United States had suffered in the Arab world as a result of Reagan's strong and unequivocal support for Israel. The American bombing of Libya was symptomatic of Reagan's determination to salvage that lost credibility — not through the pursuit of creative and enlightened diplomacy in the Middle East, but the exercise of American military force against Washington's preeminent enemy in the region during the 1980s — Muammar Qaddafi. The beleaguered leader of Libya would serve as an example for what those enemies of the United States might expect to face should they choose to challenge American power and influence in the Middle East.

CHAPTER SIX

A Legitimate Response to Terrorism or a Demonstration of Power?

The despicable Qaddafi was a perfect target, a cartoon character Americans loved to hate.... Libya was neither strategically nor militarily formidable. Taking Qaddafi on was the counterterrorism equivalent to invading Grenada—popular, relatively safe, and theatrically satisfying.[1]
— Jane Mayer and Doyle McManus, journalists

There have been suggestions that the White House arbitrarily selected Libya as a target because of its weakness, and there have been insinuations that, to justify itself, Washington manufactured a "Libyan threat," where there was none. To the contrary, Qaddafi very much brought his harsh punishment on himself.[2]
— Brian L. Davis, author

The prevailing view of the American bombing of Libya is that the air strikes represented a legitimate response to Libyan-sponsored international terrorism. This book presents an alternative view: that the bombing represented an act of desperation by Reagan to salvage American credibility in the Arab world which had been severely eroded by his close and warm embrace of Israel. Qaddafi exploited this loss of credibility in order to instigate acts of international terrorism directed against American interests in Western Europe. Through those acts, Qaddafi hoped to emerge as the leader among the forces of Arab radicalism bent upon eliminating American influence from the Middle East.

By April 1986, Reagan saw no alternative to the threat posed by Libyan-sponsored international terrorism than to order the American bombing of Tripoli and Benghazi. In doing so, Reagan hoped to restore Washington's shattered credibility in the Arab world by serving notice upon the nations of the Middle East that the United States stood ready to take military action against its enemies in the region — with Qaddafi serving as the target. Qaddafi would serve as a convenient example of what was in store for Arab radicals who chose to challenge American power and influence in the Middle East. In the end, Reagan attempted to salvage Washington's lost credibility in the Arab world, not through the pursuit of creative and enlightened diplomacy designed to advance the peace process, but the demonstration of American military power, specifically targeted against Qaddafi.

The Prevailing View of the American Bombing of Libya

The prevailing view of the American bombing of Libya — that it represents a legitimate response to Libyan-sponsored international terrorism — has perhaps been best summarized by Stanik, who argues that

> Operation El Dorado ... achieved its principal objectives. The strike inflicted considerable damage to Qaddafi's terrorist apparatus, it deterred a number of terrorist operations targeting American citizens and interests, it forced Qaddafi to revamp his murderous methodology ... and it demonstrated that the United States has the capability and resolve to attack supporters and sponsors of international terrorism.[3]

Stanik's argument that the American bombing of Libya delivered a powerful blow to the forces of international terrorism is endorsed by Brian Jenkins, an acknowledged expert on the subject: "Clearly, the bombing of Libya changed the equation. It suggested to nations that use terrorism as an instrument of policy that they risk retaliation. They may choose to dismiss that risk or accept it, but they're going to have to take it into account." As Davis argues, in supporting Jenkins' view that the American bombing of Libya sent a loud and clear message that that the United States would take military action against state sponsors of international terrorism, "The Reagan Administration wanted to send such a message to America's violent enemies in the Middle East, and a message was indeed delivered; its value is obviously intangible."[4]

Joining the chorus of academic praise for the American bombing of Libya is Dinesh D'Souza who argues that

> Reagan ordered the Libyan air strike because he believed Qaddafi deserved it, and was convinced that only the threat of punishment was likely to deter a maniac like Qaddafi ... Reagan turned out to be right.... Qaddafi seems to have been subdued by the knowledge that his actions would produce a severe

[American] response. After U.S. jets bombed his compound, his provocations and attacks on American targets ceased.[5]

Adding to the academic consensus that the American bombing of Libya had its desired effect in persuading Qaddafi to change his behavior, Robert J. Lieber argues that, "Despite (largely pro forma) outcries in the Arab world ... the administration's action achieved its objective. The Libyan leader appeared shaken by the raid, and Libya seemed to opt for a more cautious set of policies."[6]

Strock notes that Reagan's decision to order the American bombing of Libya carried considerable risks: The president could not have been sure regarding whether Qaddafi might take retaliatory action against the air strike by instigating additional acts of international terrorism. But Strock concludes that Reagan's gamble paid off, precisely because the bombing did indeed have its intended effect in persuading Qaddafi that his interests would be best served by abandoning his involvement in international terrorism: "To appreciate the decisive approach taken by Reagan [against Libya], one must remember the magnitude of the risk and uncertainty he faced.... There was no guarantee Qaddafi and his allies would not choose to escalate their use of terror, perhaps bringing it home to the United States."[7] In noting that there were no additional acts of Libyan-sponsored international terrorism in the weeks and months following the American bombing of Tripoli and Benghazi, Strock concludes that, "Reagan's decision [in ordering the bombing] paid off. He had sent [a] signal of his strength in adhering to his principles [against international terrorism]."[8]

Not surprisingly, senior officials of the Reagan Administration have endorsed the academic consensus in favor of the American bombing of Libya. Perhaps no administration official has been more effusive in his praise for the bombing than Attorney General Meese. In his memoirs, Meese wrote, "Dissenters complained ... that our retaliation [against Libya] would only spur Qaddafi on to greater acts of terrorism. Oddly enough, it did not work out that way."[9] Instead, Meese notes that following the American bombing of Libya, "Qaddafi faded from view, seldom seen or heard from again during the remaining Reagan years."

Meese argues that the American bombing of Libya not only eliminated Tripoli as the world's primary sponsor of international terrorism, but the air strikes restored America's status as a global superpower capable of preserving world security against the threat posed by international rogues and outlaws like Qaddafi. The capability of the United States to use military force in order to preserve its strategic interests had been severely diminished by the Vietnam Syndrome — the reluctance of all post–Vietnam presidents to order military interventions for fear of embroiling this nation in another Vietnam-style quagmire. Meese argues, with much hyperbole, that the American bombing of Libya ended the Vietnam Syndrome.

> Reagan's actions against Qaddafi were of key importance in breaking the "Vietnam Syndrome." Not only did Reagan move against one of the world's most notorious troublemakers, he did so in a situation in which the Carter government had shown visible signs of weakness. The contrast could not have been lost on Qaddafi.[10]

While Meese's argument that the American bombing of Libya ended the Vietnam Syndrome certainly represents a gross exaggeration of the achievements of the air strikes, the attorney general's point that the military action eliminated Tripoli as the world's primary sponsor of international terrorism is beyond dispute, and clearly represents a powerful and persuasive argument that Operation El Dorado Canyon was not only justified, but indeed necessary, despite the worldwide condemnation which followed the execution of the raid.

Presenting an Alternative View on the American Bombing of Libya

However, the conventional view of the American bombing of Libya — that the air strikes represent a legitimate response to Libyan-sponsored international terrorism — fails to take into account the fact that the rise in international terrorism during the 1980s coincided with a stalemate in the peace process, as Reagan tied the interests of the United States so firmly to those of Israel, that Washington essentially abrogated its role as an honest broker in the Arab-Israeli conflict. This development strengthened the hand of the forces of Arab radicalism, which gained real power in the Middle East under Qaddafi's leadership. International terrorism became the weapon of choice for Qaddafi and his radical Arab allies, principally Abu Nidal, as they pressed their campaign to eradicate American influence from the Middle East, however quixotic and impractical that crusade may have been.

By the time he began his second term, Reagan was confronted with two alternatives: either defuse Arab radicalism through diplomatic means — specifically by jump-starting the long-stalled peace process in the Middle East — or ordering the use of American military force against a convenient target in the region designed to deliver a crushing blow to the forces of Arab radicalism. As the center of Arab radicalism during the 1980s, Tripoli, by necessity, would serve as that target. During the early months of 1986, Reagan made his choice concerning how to confront the growing threat of Arab radicalism. By sabotaging the Jordanian-Palestinian peace initiative, the president made it clear he had no intention of breathing new life into the moribund peace process in the Middle East. This would require the United States to deal with the PLO, which Reagan was determined to avoid because it would jeopardize the close and warm relations he had forged between the United States and Israel. Rather, Reagan would deal with the growing threat of Arab radicalism through military means. By ordering the bombing of the very center of Arab radicalism — Qaddafi's residential compound and command-and-control center in Tripoli — Reagan served notice that he would seek to politically marginalize Arab radicals in the Middle East through American military power, not diplomacy. This was, after all, consistent with Reagan's philosophical approach to American foreign policy, which relied heavily upon threat of the use of military force, though the bombing of Libya was a rare instance in which the president actually ordered offensive armed action against a foreign nation. As R.A. Davidson III aptly notes:

> The image that was foremost in everything Reagan did was the projection of American strength.... After taking over from Carter, Reagan's main effort was to show America as a world power once again, and his foreign policy was based on this concept. Power was a crucial factor in Reagan's world of politics, and was probably the single most important element in determining the course of international interactions [during his presidency].[11]

Davidson concludes that Reagan based the credibility of his foreign policy, indeed, of his presidency, upon "public faith in the President and all the good things he symbolized (America Standing Tall)."[12]

Given Reagan's alleged obsession with preserving the credibility of Washington's status as a global superpower, Davidson concludes that the American bombing of Libya was designed to demonstrate to the international community, most especially the rest of the Arab world, that its interests were best served by being a friend, rather than a foe, of the United States: "The final and all-encompassing possibility for the attack on Libya is that Ronald Reagan wanted to show the world that America was once again a dominant world figure ... and that it was worthwhile to have America as a friend."[13]

The motivation Reagan had to demonstrate that the United States was a military power to be reckoned with in the Middle East was greatly strengthened by the fiasco surrounding his disastrously ill-fated decision to establish the MNF in Beirut. The objective of the MNF was to facilitate the restoration of the sovereignty of the Lebanese government throughout its territory, and secure the withdrawal of all foreign military forces from the war-torn nation. However, the MNF — comprised of token contingents of troops from the United States, France, Italy, and the United Kingdom — fell far short of the military force required to achieve these objectives. By restoring political stability to Lebanon, which had been engulfed in a bloody and internecine civil war since 1975, through the MNF's successful completion of its mission, Reagan hoped he could provide Israel with incentives to make the political and territorial concessions required for the establishment of a just and lasting peace in the Middle East. This was consistent with Reagan's decision to introduce his peace plan for the Middle East which was designed to capitalize upon the improved prospects for peace created by Israel's successful expulsion of the PLO from Beirut and South Lebanon.

After languishing aimlessly for a year, American and French members of the MNF fell victim to a well-coordinated pair of devastating terrorist bombings of their respective headquarters buildings in Beirut. Reagan responded to the bombings by vowing that he would not order the American military withdrawal from Beirut, only to do so three months later. The withdrawal dealt a fatal blow to Reagan's strategy for reviving the moribund peace process. Reagan had based his peace initiative in the Middle East upon restoring political stability to Lebanon, and his decision to establish the MNF was designed to serve this objective. But the military assets of the MNF were woefully inadequate to achieve this objective, and the Marines in Beirut served only as an inviting target for a terrorist attack by radical forces bent upon expelling the Americans from the war-torn capital of Lebanon. Reagan pursued a vacillating, irresolute, self-contradictory, and incomprehensible policy in Lebanon which substantially undermined American credibility in the Middle East.

The American bombing of Libya provided Reagan with a welcome opportunity to demonstrate that, despite its humiliating defeat suffered in Beirut, the United States remained a formidable military power in the Middle East which retained both the capability and the will to deal a powerful blow to the forces of Arab radicalism. The United States demonstrated this fact by striking at the leading exponent of anti–Americanism in the Arab world during the 1980s — Muammar Qaddafi. The bombing of Libya allowed Reagan to erase the stain of Beirut and impress upon the Arab world the fact that despite the devastating setback the United States suffered in Lebanon, Washington retained the capability and will to use its awesome military power to punish the forces of Arab radicalism whenever they threatened American interests in the Middle East.

Demonstrating American military might as a means of strengthening Washington's credibility in the Middle East was one major motivation behind the bombing of Libya. Another important motivation was to make it clear that the United States would not tolerate independent Arab leaders who acted out of self-interest, as opposed to doing so on behalf of American interests. Once again, Davidson describes how Qaddafi actually brought his punishment upon himself by defying American interests in the Middle East.

> There [are] two kinds of Arabs: good Arabs and bad Arabs. The good Arabs ... do exactly what the United States [wants].... The bad Arabs ... refuse to do exactly what Washington wants.
> The "baddest" Arab of them all was, of course, Qaddafi. Being a "bad" Arab according to this (Reagan) thought process only ... invites punishment.

As Davidson aptly notes, Reagan enthusiastically embraced the American notion that "Arabs ... have an obligation to take orders from Washington."[14]

Davidson's argument that Reagan's open-ended contempt and disdain for Qaddafi was based upon the Libyan leader's determination to challenge American power in the Middle East is supported by Mansour O. El-Kikhia who aptly notes:

> To President Reagan, General Qaddafi epitomized Third World leaders who had no respect for American power and prowess in the post–Vietnam era. Qaddafi was to Reagan what Castro was to Kennedy, and what Nasser was to Prime Minister Eden — an international pariah bent upon exporting revolution and confronting American and British interests worldwide.[15]

El-Kikhia concludes that through its bombing of Libya, "America appeared to a large number of governments more like a bully than a victim" of Libyan-sponsored international terrorism.[16]

The difference, of course, between how John F. Kennedy handled Fidel Castro and Reagan dealt with Qaddafi is that the 35th president never ordered American military action against Cuba, unlike the case of Libya. But Kennedy, like Reagan in the case of Qaddafi, did authorize American covert action, code named Operation Mongoose, designed to instigate the overthrow of Kennedy's primary nemesis — Fidel Castro.[17] To be sure, Operations Mongoose and Flower both proved dismal failures: As of this day, both Castro and Qaddafi remain firmly entrenched in power, having survived through the Kennedy and Reagan Administrations, respectively. Nevertheless, El-Kikhia makes a cogent and insightful point: Qaddafi was to Reagan what Castro was to Kennedy; both Third World leaders served as international villains who became the object of presidential obsession, with both Kennedy and Reagan determined to reduce to size, if not eliminate, the two enemies of the United States who had served as thorns in their sides. The only difference is that, in ordering the American bombing of Libya, Reagan took his contempt for Qaddafi a step further than Kennedy had done in the case of Castro.

One could argue that Kennedy was constrained from ordering American military action against Cuba due to the risk that such a move would provoke a Soviet-American confrontation, a prospect Reagan did not have to face in the case of Libya. Accordingly, the restraint Kennedy exercised with respect to Cuba may have been more a response to the realities of Cold War international politics than to any natural disinclination to use American military force he may have had. By contrast, Libya, unlike Cuba, was not a client state, much less an ally, of the Soviet Union, and could not rely upon Moscow for military support in any confrontation between Washington and Tripoli which might ensue. This made American military action against Libya far less risky than a similar move against Cuba, which may account for why Reagan was less restrained in confronting Qaddafi than was the case with Kennedy in dealing with Castro.

The Bombing of Libya: A Demonstration of American Military Power

Davidson's and El-Kikhia's observations regarding Reagan's motivations for ordering the American bombing of Libya — that the air strikes were designed to demonstrate the use of American military power against an Arab leader who dared challenge Washington's interests in the Middle East — has more credibility than the alternative prevailing notion that the air strikes represent a legitimate response to Libyan-sponsored international terrorism. Reagan had the option of defusing Libyan-sponsored international terrorism by aggressively pursuing diplomatic means to resolve the longstanding tensions besetting the Middle East, focusing on the core problem of the region — the Arab-Israeli conflict; however, the president chose not to do so. Rather, Reagan chose to use American military force in order to confront the threat posed by Libyan-sponsored international terrorism. In doing so, Reagan made it clear that he would not allow American support for Israel to be compromised in any way in order to appease Qaddafi. Reagan would politically marginalize Qaddafi in the Middle East through military, rather than diplomatic, means which served the president's overall foreign policy strategy of projecting American power wherever Washington's interests were threatened.

To be sure, the moderate Arab nations stridently and vociferously condemned the use of American military force against Libya; however much moderate Arab leaders disdained Qaddafi, they could not politically afford to be seen as approving an attack against a fellow Arab state, especially when executed by Israel's closest ally — the United States. However, through the use of American military force against Libya, Reagan served notice upon the moderate Arab nations that the United States was a global superpower to be reckoned with, and their interests were best served by remaining as friends, rather than adversaries, of Washington. Reagan's strategy to politically marginalize Qaddafi through military, rather than diplomatic, means was indeed a rousing success. Despite their intense and vociferous condemnation of the American bombing of Libya, the moderate Arab nations failed to back up their words with any tangible action to demonstrate, on a practical level, their displeasure with the air strikes. The bombing did indeed have its intended effect of enhancing American credibility in the Arab world because the air strikes served as a practical demonstration of both the awesome military might of the United States and of the willingness of Washington to use that power in order to preserve its economic and strategic interests in the Middle East. Moderate Arab leaders were sure to be determined to avoid Qaddafi's fate by maintaining normal, if not friendly, relations with the United States, however much they disdained American policy in the Middle East, especially Washington's strong and unequivocal support for Israel.

The American bombing of Libya furthered Washington's policy of retaining close and warm relations with both Israel and the moderate Arab nations — despite the enmity existing between the Jewish state and the Arab world, with the exception of two of America's closest Arab allies — Egypt and Jordan. Moderate Arab nations have aligned themselves closely with the United States, despite its strong and unswerving support for Israel, precisely because of America's possession of substantial military power and the willingness of Washington to use that might in order to preserve its economic and strategic interests in the Middle East. The bitter and acrimonious conflict between the United States and Libya provided Reagan a rare opportunity to remind the Arab nations of this fact. The result was that the president succeeded in salvaging American credibility in the Middle East which had been severely eroded by his pursuit of a strong and unswerving pro–Israel policy in the region.

But Reagan's determination to politically marginalize Qaddafi through military, rather than diplomatic, means also meant that there would be no loosening of the strong and close strategic alliance he had forged between the United States and Israel, and that the intractable and long-simmering Arab-Israeli conflict — the core problem of politically troubled Middle East — would remain unresolved. The political instability engulfing the Middle East would ultimately lead during the 1990s and the first years of the twenty-first century to the rise of Al Qaeda and 9–11. Far from representing a permanent solution to the threat posed to the world community by international terrorism, the American bombing of Libya turned out to be a Band-Aid solution to the problem — a short-term palliative which would have no lasting effect in addressing the issue of Arab and Islamic radicalism and extremism. The only permanent solution to the problem of international terrorism remains a reinvigorated diplomatic initiative designed to resolve the long-standing tensions besetting the Middle East, beginning with the core problem of the region — the Arab-Israeli conflict; and from this perspective, the bombing, far from representing the rousing success admirers of Reagan's handling of the Libyan-American conflict believe the air strikes to be, actually turns out to be a dismal failure.

Notes

Introduction

1. Joseph T. Stanik, *El Dorado Canyon: Reagan's Undeclared War with Qaddafi* (Annapolis: Naval Institute Press, 2003), p. 33.

Chapter One

1. William B. Quandt, *Peace Process: American Diplomacy and the Arab-Israeli Conflict Since 1967* (Washington, DC, and Berkeley: Brookings Institution Press and University of California Press, 2001), p. 287.
2. Nicholas Laham, *Crossing the Rubicon: Ronald Reagan and US Policy in the Middle East* (Aldershot: Ashgate, 2004), p. 84.
3. Ibid., p. 61.
4. Noam Chomsky, *Fateful Triangle: The United States, Israel, and the Palestinians* (Cambridge: South End Press, 1999), p. 107.
5. "Remarks to Reporters Announcing the Deployment of United States Forces in Beirut, Lebanon," August 20, 1982, www.reagan.utexas.edu.
6. For an analysis of the Reagan Plan and reasons for its failure, see Laham, *Crossing the Rubicon*, pp. 35–82.
7. Lou Cannon, *President Reagan: Role of a Lifetime* (New York: Simon & Schuster, 1991), pp. 407–08.
8. "Address to the Announcing the Formation of a New Multinational Force in Lebanon," September 20, 1982, www.reagan.utexas.edu.
9. For a thorough and authoritative account of the Lebanese Civil War, see A.J. Abraham, *The Lebanon War* (Westport, CT: Praeger, 1996).
10. Cannon, *President Reagan*, pp. 410–11.
11. "Memorandum of Conversation Between President Reagan and President Gemayel," April 18, 1983, Executive Secretariat, NSC: Records: Country File, Box 91353, Ronald Reagan Presidential Library.
12. "Statement on the Bombing of the United States Embassy in Beirut, Lebanon," April 18, 1983, www.reagan.utexas.edu.
13. Memorandum from William P. Clark to Howard J. Teicher, April 19, 1983, Executive Secretariat, NSC: Records: Country File, Box 91353, Ronald Reagan Presidential Library.
14. Memorandum from William P. Clark to George P. Shultz, April 19, 1983, Executive Secretariat, NSC: Records: Country File, Box 91353, Ronald Reagan Presidential Library.
15. Memorandum from John M. Poindexter to Frederick J. Ryan, April 19, 1983, Executive Secretariat, NSC: Records: Country File, Box 91353, Ronald Reagan Presidential Library.
16. Memorandum from Howard J. Teicher to John M. Poindexter, April 19, 1983, Executive Secretariat, NSC: Records: Country File, Box 91353, Ronald Reagan Presidential Library.
17. "Remarks at a Ceremony Honoring the Victims of the Bombing of the United States Embassy in Beirut, Lebanon," April 23, 1983, www.reagan.utexas.edu.
18. Radio Address to the Nation on the Death of Federal Diplomatic and Military Personnel in Beirut, Lebanon," April 23, 1983, www.reagan.utexas.edu.
19. For an exhaustive and detailed account of the bombing of the Marine barracks in Beirut, see Eric Hammel, *The Root: The Marines in Beirut, August 1982-February*

1984 (St. Paul: Zenith Press, 2005), pp. 287–395.

20. Cannon, *President Reagan*, pp. 440–43.

21. "Remarks to Reporters on the Death of American and French Personnel in Beirut, Lebanon," October 23, 1983, www.reagan.utexas.edu.

22. "Draft Statement," Executive Secretariat, NSC: Records: Country File, Box 91353, Ronald Reagan Presidential Library.

23. "Talking Points for Call to President Mitterrand," Executive Secretariat, NSC: Records: Country File, Box 91353, Ronald Reagan Presidential Library.

24. "The Stakes in Lebanon," Executive Secretariat, NSC: Records: Country File, Box 91353, Ronald Reagan Presidential Library.

25. "Remarks and a Question-and-Answer Session with Regional Editors and Broadcasters on the Situation in Lebanon," October 24, 1983, www.reagan.utexas.edu.

26. "Talking Points for Presidential Address to the Nation: Foreign Policy, Thursday, October 27, 1983," Executive Secretariat, NSC: Records: Subject File, Box 91412, Ronald Reagan Presidential Library.

27. "Presidential Address to the Nation: Foreign Policy," October 27, 1983, Executive Secretariat, NSC: Records: Subject File, Box 91412, Ronald Reagan Presidential Library.

28. Secretary Shultz Statement to Hill," Executive Secretariat, NSC: Records: Country File, Box 91353, Ronald Reagan Presidential Library.

29. "Talking Points for Robert C. McFarlane," Executive Secretariat, NSC: Records: Country File Box 91353, Ronald Reagan Presidential Library.

30. Memorandum from Robert C. McFarlane to George P. Shultz, Caspar W. Weinberger, William J. Casey, and John W. Vessey, October 29, 1983, Executive Secretariat, NSC: Records: Country File, Box 91353, Ronald Reagan Presidential Library.

31. Laham, *Crossing the Rubicon*, pp. 40–41.

32. Cannon, *President Reagan*, p. 422.

33. "National Security Decision Directive Number 111," October 28, 1983, Executive Secretariat, NSC: Records: Country File, Box 91353, Ronald Reagan Presidential Library.

34. Memorandum from John M. Poindexter to George P. Shultz, William J. Casey, John W. Vessey, and W. Paul Thayer, December 2, 1983, Executive Secretariat, NSC: Records: Country File, Box 91353, Ronald Reagan Presidential Library.

35. "National Security Decision Directive 117," December 5, 1983, Executive Secretariat, NSC: Records: Country File, Box 91353, Ronald Reagan Presidential Library.

36. Ralph A. Hallenbeck, *Military Force as an Instrument of U.S. Foreign Policy: Intervention in Lebanon, August 1982-February 1984* (New York: Praeger, 1991), pp. 118–19.

37. *Congressional Quarterly Almanac, 98th Congress 1st Session* (Washington, DC: Congressional Quarterly, 1984), p. 113.

38. "Statement on Signing the Multinational Force in Lebanon Resolution," October 12, 1983, www.reagan.utexas.edu.

39. *Congressional Quarterly Almanac, 98th Congress, 1st Session* (Washington, DC: Congressional Quarterly, 1984), p. 43-S.

40. Ibid., p. 102-H.

41. Thomas J. Downey, Charles E. Bennett, Leon E. Panetta, "A Time for Reappraisal," December 14, 1983, Donald R. Fortier Files, Box 90753, Ronald Reagan Presidential Library.

42. Thomas J. Downey, Charles E. Bennett, and Leon E. Panetta to Thomas P. O'Neill, December 21, 1983, Donald R. Fortier Files, Box 90753, Ronald Reagan Presidential Library.

43. Committee on Foreign Affairs, "Congress to Review Marine Presence in Lebanon Within Context of the War Powers Resolution," December 14, 1983, Donald R. Fortier Files, Box 90753, Ronald Reagan Presidential Library.

44. Memorandum from Howard J. Teicher to Robert M. Kimmitt, Donald R. Fortier, Philip A. Dur, Christopher M. Lehman, Paul Thompson, Robert B. Sims, and Geoffrey Kemp, January 24, 1984, Donald R. Fortier Files, Box 90753, Ronald Reagan Presidential Library.

45. "Implications of MNF Withdrawal — The Stakes," Donald R. Fortier Files, Box 90753, Ronald Reagan Presidential Library.

46. House of Representatives Concurrent Resolution Draft, February 1, 1984, "To bring the prompt and orderly withdrawal of the United States Armed Forces participating in the Multinational Force in Lebanon," Executive Secretariat, NSC: Records: Country File, Box 91353, Ronald Reagan Presidential Library.

47. "LSE [Lawrence S. Eagleburger] Testimony," Draft, February 1, 1984, Donald R.

Fortier Files, Box 90753, Ronald Reagan Presidential Library.
48. "Rumsfeld's Proposed Edits to the Draft Resolution," February 1, 1984, William J. Burns Files, Box 91834, Ronald Reagan Presidential Library.
49. Memorandum from Robert C. McFarlane to George P. Shultz, Caspar W. Weinberger, William J. Casey, David M. Stockman, and John W. Vessey, February 1, 1984, Donald R. Fortier Files, Box 90753, Ronald Reagan Presidential Library.
50. "National Security Decision Directive Number 123," February 1, 1984, Donald R. Fortier Files, Box 90753, Ronald Reagan Presidential Library.
51. Cannon, *President Reagan*, pp. 454–55.
52. "Draft Presidential Statement," Donald R. Fortier Files, Box 90753, Ronald Reagan Presidential Library.
53. Hallenbeck, *Military Force as an Instrument of U.S. Foreign Policy*, pp. 168–69.
54. Bernard Reich, *Securing the Covenant: United States–Israel Relations After the Cold War* (Westport, CT: Praeger, 1995), p. 40.
55. Cannon, *President Reagan*, p. 391.
56. "Rebuilding U.S.–Israel Relations," Donald R. Fortier Files, Box 90753, Ronald Reagan Presidential Library.
57. "National Security Directive 115," November 26, 1983, Executive Secretariat, NSC: Records: Country File, Box 91353, Ronald Reagan Presidential Library.
58. "Remarks of the President and Prime Minister Yitzhak Shamir of Israel Following their Meetings," November 29, 1983, www.reagan.utexas.edu.
59. Reich, *Securing the Covenant*, p. 44.
60. Laham, *Crossing the Rubicon*, p. 75.
61. Ibid., pp. 37–38.
62. Ibid., pp. 93–94.
63. Madiha Rashid Al Madfai, *Jordan, the United States, and the Middle East Peace Process, 1974–1991* (Cambridge: Cambridge University Press, 1993), p. 170.
64. Laham, *Crossing the Rubicon*, pp. 95–98.
65. Ibid., pp. 104–05.
66. Al Madfai, *Jordan, the United States, and the Middle East Peace Process, 1974–1991*, p. 170.
67. Ibid., pp. 174–76.
68. For an insightful and persuasive argument that the United States never served as an honest broker in the peace process, see Naseer Aruri, *Dishonest Broker: The U.S. Role in Israel and Palestine* (Cambridge: South End Press, 2003).
69. Laham, *Crossing the Rubicon*, p. 118.
70. Thomas A. Dine, "The Revolution in U.S.–Israel Relations," Washington, DC, April 6, 1986, James R, Stark Files, Box 91747, Ronald Reagan Presidential Library.

Chapter Two

1. Brian L. Davis, *Qaddafi, Terrorism, and the Origins of the U.S. Attack on Libya* (New York: Praeger, 1991), p. 85.
2. Robert Bruce St. John, *Libya and the United States: Two Centuries of Strife* (Philadelphia: University of Pennsylvania Press, 2002), p. 4.
3. Davis, *Qaddafi, Terrorism, and the Origins of the U.S. Attack on Libya*, p. 27.
4. Ibid., p. 79.
5. Joseph T. Stanik, *El Dorado Canyon: Reagan's Undeclared War with Qaddafi* (Annapolis: Naval Institute Press, 2003), p. 44.
6. Ibid., p. 105.
7. Ibid., pp. 66–72.
8. "Remarks at the Annual Convention of the American Bar Association," July 8, 1985, www.reagan.utexas.edu.
9. Unsigned Memorandum to Donald P. Gregg, Morton I. Abramowitz, Fred C. Ikle, John H. Moellering, John H. Rixse, Undated, James R. Stark Files, Box 91747, Ronald Reagan Presidential Library.
10. Stanik, *El Dorado Canyon*, p. 101.
11. Ibid., pp. 105–06.
12. White House Situation Room Report, December 28, 1985, Elaine L. Morton Files, Box 91758, Ronald Reagan Presidential Library.
13. White House Situation Room Note, December 28, 1985, Elaine L. Morton Files, Box 91758, Ronald Reagan Presidential Library.
14. United States Department of State, "Terrorism: Theme Paper," December 28, 1985, Elaine L. Morton Files, Box 91758, Ronald Reagan Presidential Library.
15. Memorandum from Donald R. Fortier to Ronald Reagan, December 30, 1985, Elaine L. Morton Files, Box 91758, Ronald Reagan Presidential Library.
16. National Security Council, "Responsibility for El Al Attacks," Elaine L. Morton Files, Box 91758, Ronald Reagan Presidential Library.

17. "Remarks at the Welcoming Ceremony for the Freed American Hostages," January 27, 1981, www.reagan.utexas.edu.
18. Elaine L. Morton, "Non-Military Alternatives," December 28, 1985, Elaine L. Morton Files, Box 91758, Ronald Reagan Presidential Library.
19. Memorandum from Donald R. Fortier to Rodney B. McDaniel, December 31, 1985, Elaine L. Morton Files, Box 91758, Ronald Reagan Presidential Library.
20. Central Intelligence Agency, "U.S. and Western Economic Involvement in Libya," December 30, 1985, Elaine L. Morton Files, Box 91758, Ronald Reagan Presidential Library.
21. Memorandum from Howard J. Teicher to William F. Martin, January 7, 1986, Howard J. Teicher Files, Box 91668, Ronald Reagan Presidential Library.
22. Memorandum from William F. Martin to David L. Chew, January 7, 1986, Howard J. Teicher Files, Box 91668, Ronald Reagan Presidential Library.
23. The White House, Office of the Press Secretary, "Executive Order Prohibiting Trade and Certain Transactions Involving Libya," January 7, 1986, Howard J. Teicher Files, Ronald Reagan Presidential Library.
24. Memorandum from William F. Martin to Larry M. Speakes, January 7, 1986, Donald R. Fortier Files, Box 90754, Ronald Reagan Presidential Library.
25. "Libya," January 7, 1986, Donald R. Fortier Files, Box 90754, Ronald Reagan Presidential Library.
26. "Press Conference Opening Statement," January 7, 1986, Donald R. Fortier Files, Box 90754, Ronald Reagan Presidential Library.
27. The White House, Office of the Press Secretary, "Text of a Letter from the President to the Speaker of the House of Representatives and the President of the Senate," January 7, 1986, Howard J. Teicher Files, Box 91668, Ronald Reagan Presidential Library.
28. Ronald Reagan, *An American Life* (New York: Simon & Schuster, 1990), p. 515.
29. United States Information Agency, "Libya Sanctions: Stimulating European Support; Brief Public Diplomacy Strategy," Howard J. Teicher Files, Box 91688, Ronald Reagan Presidential Library.
30. William S. Broomfield to Ronald Reagan, January 6, 1986, Howard J. Teicher Files, Box 91668, Ronald Reagan Presidential Library.
31. United States Department of State, Bureau of Public Affairs, "Libya Under Qaddafi: A Pattern of Aggression," January 1986, William J. Burns Files, Box 91834, Ronald Reagan Presidential Library.
32. United States Department of State, Bureau of Public Affairs, "Chronology of Libyan Support for Terrorism 1980–85," William Burns J. Files, Box 91834, Ronald Reagan Presidential Library.
33. Davis, *Qaddafi, Terrorism, and the Origins of the U.S. Attack on Libya*, p. 79.
34. Stanik, *El Dorado Canyon*, p. 113.
35. Dirk Vandewalle, *A History of Modern Libya* (New York: Cambridge University Press, 2006), p. 148.
36. Stanik, *El Dorado Canyon*. p. 114.
37. Richard W. Murphy, "Review of Developments in the Middle East," William J. Burns Files, Box 91834, Ronald Reagan Presidential Library.
38. St. John, *Libya and the United States*, p. 133.
39. Davis, *Qaddafi, Terrorism, and the Origins of the U.S. Attack on Libya*, p. 87.
40. St. John, *Libya and the United States*, p. 133.
41. Stanik, *El Dorado Canyon*, p. xi.

Chapter Three

1. R.A. Davidson III, *Reagan vs. Qaddafi: Response to International Terrorism?* (R.A. Davidson, 2002), p. 91.
2. Joseph T. Stanik, *El Dorado Canyon: Reagan's Undeclared War with Qaddafi* (Annapolis: Naval Institute Press, 2003), pp. 27–29.
3. Ibid., pp. 51–55.
4. Ibid., pp. 84–85.
5. Ibid., p. 113.
6. Memorandum from Howard J. Teicher to John M. Poindexter, January 7, 1986, Howard J. Teicher Files, Box 91668, Ronald Reagan Presidential Library.
7. "Annex: Acting Against Libyan Terrorism," January 8, 1986, Howard J. Teicher Files, Box 91668, Ronald Reagan Presidential Library.
8. Memorandum from John M. Poindexter to George P. Shultz, Caspar W. Weinberger, William J. Casey, and William J. Crowe, Jr., January 8, 1986, Howard J. Teicher Files, Box 91688, Ronald Reagan Presidential Library.

9. Stanik, *El Dorado Canyon*, pp. 123–24.
10. Memorandum from Caspar W. Weinberger to Ronald Reagan, February 10, 1986, Elaine L. Morton Files, Box 91758, Ronald Reagan Presidential Library.
11. "Libyan Tactics Toward Western Europe," Donald R. Fortier Files, Box 90754, Ronald Reagan Presidential Library.
12. Memorandum from Rodney B. McDaniel to Donald P. Gregg, Nicholas Platt, Sherrie Cooksey, David R. Brown, John H. Rixse, and John Bitoff, February 12, 1986, Elaine L. Morton Files, Box 91758, Ronald Reagan Presidential Library.
13. Crisis Pre-Planning Group, "Participants," February 13, 1986, Elaine L. Morton Files, Box 91758, Ronald Reagan Presidential Library.
14. Crisis Pre-Planning Group, "Libya Agenda," February 13, 1986, Elaine L. Morton Files, Box 91758, Ronald Reagan Presidential Library.
15. Memorandum from Ronald C. St. Martin to Donald R. Fortier, February 12, 1986, Elaine L. Morton Files, Box 91758, Ronald Reagan Presidential Library.
16. "Libya: Talking Points," Elaine L. Morton Files, Box 91758, Ronald Reagan Presidential Library.
17. Memorandum from Ronald C. St. Martin and Elaine L. Morton to John M. Poindexter, February 13, 1986, Elaine L. Morton Files, Box 91758, Ronald Reagan Presidential Library.
18. James A. Baker III to William Von Raab, March 10, 1986, Donald R. Fortier Files, Box 90754, Ronald Reagan Presidential Library.
19. James A. Baker III to Edwin Meese III, March 10, 1986, Donald R. Fortier Files, Box 90754, Ronald Reagan Presidential Library.
20. James A. Baker III to Malcolm Baldrige, March 10, 1986, Donald R. Fortier Files, Box 90754, Ronald Reagan Presidential Library.
21. Sherrie M. Cooksey to Rodney B. McDaniel, March 17, 1986, Donald R. Fortier Files, Box 90754, Ronald Reagan Presidential Library.
22. For an account of the American air and naval exercises conducted in the Tripoli FIR in February 1986, see Stanik, *El Dorado Canyon*, pp. 124–26.
23. Memorandum from James R. Stark and Howard J. Teicher to Donald R. Fortier, March 7, 1986, James R. Stark Files, Box 91747, Ronald Reagan Presidential Library.
24. Memorandum from Donald R. Fortier to Michael H. Armacost, Richard L. Armitage, Robert M. Gates, John H. Moellering, James R. Stark, and Howard J. Teicher, Undated, James R. Stark Files, Box 91747, Ronald Reagan Presidential Library.
25. Crisis Pre-Planning Group, "Libya Military Options Agenda," March 10, 1986, James R. Stark Files, Box 91747, Ronald Reagan Presidential Library.
26. Memorandum from James R. Stark to John M. Poindexter, March 10, 1986, James R. Stark Files, Box 91747, Ronald Reagan Presidential Library.
27. Memorandum from Rodney B. McDaniel to Frederick J. Ryan, March 10, 1986, James R. Stark Files, Box 91747, Ronald Reagan Presidential Library.
28. Memorandum from James R. Stark and Howard J. Teicher to John M. Poindexter, March 12, 1986, James R. Stark Files, Box 91747, Ronald Reagan Presidential Library.
29. Memorandum from Rodney B. McDaniel to Donald Gregg, Nicholas Platt, David R. Brown, Stephen Galebach, John R. Rixse, and John Bitoff, March 12, 1986, James R. Stark Files, Box 91747, Ronald Reagan Presidential Library.
30. National Security Planning Group, "Libya Military Options Agenda," March 14, 1986, James R. Stark Files, Box 91747, Ronald Reagan Presidential Library.
31. Memorandum from Caspar W. Weinberger to John Poindexter, March 13, 1986, Elaine L. Morton Files, Box 91758, Ronald Reagan Presidential Library.
32. "Diplomatic/Congressional/Media Strategy," Elaine L. Morton Files, Box 91758, Ronald Reagan Presidential Library.
33. Memorandum from William J. Crowe, Jr. to Caspar Weinberger, March 12, 1986, Elaine L. Morton Files, Box 91758, Ronald Reagan Presidential Library.
34. Stanik, *El Dorado Canyon*, pp. 127–28.
35. For an account of the clashes between American and Libyan military forces in the Gulf of Sidra, see Stanik, *El Dorado Canyon*, pp. 132–40.
36. Dante B. Fascell to Ronald Reagan, March 24, 1986, James R. Stark Files, Box 91747, Ronald Reagan Presidential Library.
37. Memorandum from Nicholas Platt to John M. Poindexter, March 25, 1986, James

R. Stark Files, Box 91747, Ronald Reagan Presidential Library.
38. Memorandum from Caspar W. Weinberger and John C. Whitehead to Ronald Reagan, March 26, 1986, James R. Stark Files, Box 91747, Ronald Reagan Presidential Library.
39. Memorandum from James R. Stark to John M. Poindexter, March 26, 1986, James R. Stark Files, Box 91747, Ronald Reagan Presidential Library.
40. Memorandum from John M. Poindexter to Ronald Reagan, March 26, 1986, James R. Stark Files, Box 91747, Ronald Reagan Presidential Library.
41. Ronald Reagan to Thomas P. O'Neill, Jr., March 26, 1986 and Ronald Reagan to Strom Thurmond, March 26, 1986, James R. Stark Files, Box 91747, Ronald Reagan Presidential Library.
42. William L. Ball III to Dante B. Fascell, March 25, 1986, James R. Stark Files, Box 91747, Ronald Reagan Presidential Library.
43. Stanik, El Dorado Canyon, p. 142.
44. "Remarks at a Senate Campaign Fundraiser for Representative W. Henson Moore in New Orleans, Louisiana," March 27, 1986, www.reagan.utexas.edu.

Chapter Four

1. R.A. Davidson, *Reagan vs. Qaddafi: Response to International Terrorism?* (R.A. Davison, 2002), p. 89.
2. Joseph T. Stanik, *El Dorado Canyon: Reagan's Undeclared War with Qaddafi* (Annapolis: Naval Institute Press, 2003), p. 146.
3. "Agenda: Oval Office Discussion of Libya," April 9, 1986, Howard J. Teicher Files, Box 91688, Ronald Reagan Presidential Library.
4. Memorandum from Oliver L. North, Howard J. Teicher, and James R. Stark to John M. Poindexter, April 8, 1986, Howard J. Teicher Files, Box 91688, Ronald Reagan Presidential Library.
5. Ronald Reagan, *An American Life* (New York: Simon & Schuster, 1990), p. 518.
6. "Themes," April 8, 1986, Howard J. Teicher Files, Box 91688, Ronald Reagan Presidential Library.
7. "Questions and Answers for Press Spokesmen," April 14, 1986, Howard J. Teicher Files, Box 91688, Ronald Reagan Presidential Library.
8. Reagan, *An American Life*, p. 519.
9. Stanik, *El Dorado Canyon*, p. 152.
10. Deborah Hart Strober and Gerald S. Strober, *Reagan: The Man and His Presidency* (Boston: Houghton Mifflin, 1998), p. 382.
11. Stanik, *El Dorado Canyon*, p. 168.
12. "Questions and Answers for Press Spokesmen," April 14, 1986, Howard J. Teicher Files, Box 91688, Ronald Reagan Presidential Library.
13. Memorandum from James R. Stark, Oliver L. North, and Howard J. Teicher to John M. Poindexter, April 10, 1986, Howard J. Teicher Files, Box 91688, Ronald Reagan Presidential Library.
14. Memorandum from John M. Poindexter to Donald T. Regan, April 10, 1986, Howard J. Teicher Files, Box 91688, Ronald Reagan Presidential Library.
15. Stanik, *El Dorado Canyon*, p. 174
16. White House Situation Room, "Statement by Ministers of Foreign Affairs of the Twelve on International Terrorism and the Crisis in the Mediterranean," April 15, 1986, James R. Stark Files, Box 91747, Ronald Reagan Presidential Library.
17. "Questions and Answers for Press Spokesmen," April 14, 1986, Howard J. Teicher Files, Box 91688, Ronald Reagan Presidential Library.
18. "Whitehead Results, "April 14, 1986, James R. Stark Files, Box 91747, Ronald Reagan Presidential Library.
19. Stanik, *El Dorado Canyon*, p. 180.
20. Oliver L. North and Craig Coy, "Participants," April 12, 1986, James R. Stark Files, Box 91747, Ronald Reagan Presidential Library.
21. Memorandum from Oliver L. North, Howard J. Teicher, James R. Stark, Robert L. Earle, and Craig P. Coy to John M. Poindexter, April 12, 1986, James R. Stark Files, Box 91747, Ronald Reagan Presidential Library.
22. John M. Poindexter and William Ball III to Ronald Reagan, April 12, 1986, James R. Stark Files, Box 91747, Ronald Reagan Presidential Library.
23. "National Security Adviser: Talking Points for Congressional Leadership," James R. Stark Files, Box 91747, Ronald Reagan Presidential Library.
24. Stanik, *El Dorado Canyon*, p. 210.
25. Strober and Strober, *Reagan*, p. 381.
26. Ibid., p. 382.
27. For a vivid and illuminating account

of the operational details of the American bombing of Libya, see Stanik, *El Dorado Canyon*, pp. 181–93.

28. The White House, Office of the Press Secretary, "Address by the President to the Nation," April 14, 1986, James R. Stark Files, Box 91747, Ronald Reagan Presidential Library.

29. Stanik, *El Dorado Canyon*, p. 210.

30. Newt Gingrich to Members of the House of Representative, April 15, 1986, Oliver L. North Files, Box 30, Ronald Reagan Presidential Library.

31. Claiborne Pell, Sam Nunn, Robert C. Byrd, and Patrick Leahy to Ronald Reagan, Undated, James R. Stark Files, Box 91747, Ronald Reagan Presidential Library.

32. "Congressional Record-Senate," May 8, 1986, James R. Stark Files, Box 91747, Ronald Reagan Presidential Library.

33. Memorandum from Kathy Ratte Jaffke to Cathy Thibodeau, May 14, 1986, James R. Stark Files, Box 91747, Ronald Reagan Presidential Library.

34. Memorandum from Nicholas Platt to John M. Poindexter, May 30, 1986, James R. Stark Files, Box 91747, Ronald Reagan Presidential Library.

35. Ronald Reagan to Robert C. Byrd, May 30, 1986, James R. Stark Files, Box 91747, Ronald Reagan Presidential Library.

36. Memorandum from Thomas F. Gibson III to Reagan Administration Spokespersons, April 16, 1986, James R. Stark Files, Box 91747, Ronald Reagan Presidential Library.

37. "White House Talking Points: U.S. Action Against Libyan Terrorists," April 16, 1986, James R. Stark Files, Box 91747, Ronald Reagan Presidential Library.

38. The White House, Office of the Press Secretary, "Address by the President to the Nation," April 14, 1986, James R. Stark Files, Box 91747, Ronald Reagan Presidential Library.

39. Memorandum from David R. Brown to Nicholas Platt and Rodney B. McDaniel, May 7, 1986, James R. Stark Files, Box 91747, Ronald Reagan Presidential Library.

40. "Proposed Press Release: Results of U.S. Military Operations Against Libya on April 15," May 8, 1986, James R. Stark Files, Box 91747, Ronald Reagan Presidential Library.

41. Stanik, *El Dorado Canyon*, pp. 232–36.

42. The White House, Office of the Press Secretary, "Address by the President to the Nation," April 14, 1986, James R. Stark Files, Box 91747, Ronald Reagan Presidential Library.

43. Memorandum from Robert H. Pelletreau to Richard L. Armitage, April 18, 1986, James R. Stark Files, Box 91747, Ronald Reagan Presidential Library.

44. "Next Steps to Deter Further Libyan Terrorism," Howard J. Teicher Files, Box 91688, Ronald Reagan Presidential Library.

45. Stanik, *El Dorado Canyon*, p. 219.

46. Ibid., p. 220.

47. Memorandum from John M. Poindexter to Ronald Reagan, April 10, 1986, Donald R. Fortier Files, Box 90754, Ronald Reagan Presidential Library.

48. Brian L. Davis, *Qaddafi, Terrorism, and the Origins of the U.S. Attack on Libya* (New York: Praeger, 1991), p. 160.

49. Ronald Bruce St. John, *Libya and the United States: Two Centuries of Strife* (Philadelphia: University of Pennsylvania Press, 2002), p. 138.

50. Lou Cannon, *President Reagan: Role of a Lifetime* (New York: Simon & Schuster, 1991), p. 756.

51. "Presidential Talking Points: Press Meeting Regarding Tokyo Economic Summit," April 21, 1986, Howard J. Teicher Files, Box 91688, Ronald Reagan Presidential Library.

52. "Presidential Talking Points: Press Meeting Regarding Targets in Libya," April 21, 1986, Howard J. Teicher Files, Box 91688, Ronald Reagan Presidential Library.

53. "Statement on International Terrorism," May 5, 1986, James R. Stark Files, Box 91747, Ronald Reagan Presidential Library.

54. Stanik, *El Dorado Canyon*, p. 214.

55. United State Information Agency, "Europeans Take Further Steps to Counter Libyan Terrorism," May 29, 1986, OA 17139, Max Green Files, Ronald Reagan Presidential Library.

56. Stanik, *El Dorado Canyon*, p. 215.

57. *The Washington Post*, "76% of Americans Back Bombing of Libya," April 30, 1986, OA 17139, Max Green Files, Ronald Reagan Presidential Library.

58. Jane Mayer and Doyle McManus, *Landslide: The Unmaking of the President, 1984–1988* (Boston: Houghton Mifflin, 1989), pp. 221, 223.

59. Memorandum from Ronald C. St. Martin to Oliver L. North, March 25, 1986, Elaine L. Morton Files, Box 91758, Ronald Reagan Presidential Library.

60. Stanik, *El Dorado Canyon*, p. ix.
61. "Public Attitudes on Terrorism," Elaine L. Morton Files, Box 91758, Ronald Reagan Presidential Library.
62. The White House, Office of the Press Secretary, "Address by the President to the Nation," April 14, 1986, James R. Stark Files, Box 91747, Ronald Reagan Presidential Library.

Chapter Five

1. R.A. Davidson, *Reagan vs. Qaddafi: Response to International Terrorism?* (R.A. Davidson, 2002), p. 93.
2. White House Situation Room, "Dutch Reaction to the U.S. Air Strikes," April 15, 1986, Oliver L. North Files, Box 30, Ronald Reagan Presidential Library.
3. White House Situation Room, "Greek Government Reaction to U.S. Strike on Libya," April 15, 1986, Oliver L. North Files, Box 30, Ronald Reagan Presidential Library.
4. Joseph T. Stanik, *El Dorado Canyon: Reagan's Undeclared War with Qaddafi* (Annapolis: Naval Institute Press, 2003), p. 173.
5. Ibid., p. 213.
6. Stanik, *El Dorado Canyon*, p. 173.
7. "International Reaction: U.S. Retaliation Against Libya," Oliver L. North Files, Box 30, Ronald Reagan Presidential Library.
8. United States Information Agency, "Special Report: Foreign Media Reaction to U.S. Raid on Libya" April 16, 1986, Oliver L. North Files, Box 30, Ronald Reagan Presidential Library.
9. United States Information Agency, "Special Report: Foreign Media Reaction to U.S. Raid on Libya, April 17, 1986, Oliver L. North Files, Box 30, Ronald Reagan Presidential Library.
10. Voice of America, "A Strike in Self-Defense," April 15, 1986, Oliver L. North Files, Box 30, Ronald Reagan Presidential Library.
11. United States Information Agency, "The Early Report: Foreign Media Reaction to U.S. Strike Against Libya," April 16, 1986, Oliver L. North Files, Box 30, Ronald Reagan Presidential Library.
12. Stanik, *El Dorado Canyon*, pp. 172–73.
13. Ibid., p. 211.
14. Ibid., p. 212.
15. Ibid., p. 213.

16. Dirk Vandewalle, *A History of Modern Libya* (New York: Cambridge University Press, 2006), p. 148.
17. Stanik, *El Dorado Canyon*, p. 27.
18. Ibid., p. 84.
19. Ibid., p. 216.
20. United States Information Agency, April 17, 1986, "Special Report: Foreign Media Reaction to U.S. Raid on Libya," Oliver L. North Files, Box 30, Ronald Reagan Presidential Library.
21. For a revealing and illuminating account of the summit meeting between Reagan and Gorbachev, and the significant improvement in Soviet-American relations that resulted from the conference, see Richard Reeves, *President Reagan: The Triumph of Imagination* (New York: Simon & Schuster, 2005), pp. 280–94.
22. "Questions and Answers for Press Spokesmen," April 14, 1986, Howard J. Teicher Files, Box 91688, Ronald Reagan Presidential Library.
23. P. Edward Haley, *Qaddafi and the United States Since 1969* (New York: Praeger, 1984), p. 312.
24. Ronald Bruce St. John, *Libya and the United States: Two Centuries of Strife* (Philadelphia: University of Pennsylvania Press, 2002), pp. 140–41.
25. Memorandum from Jack F. Matlock to John M. Poindexter, April 25, 1986, James R. Stark Files, Box 91747, Ronald Reagan Presidential Library.
26. "Talking Points," Oliver L. North Files, Box 30, Ronald Reagan Presidential Library.
27. "Recommended Telephone Call," April 15, 1986, Oliver L. North Files, Box 30, Ronald Reagan Presidential Library.
28. Robert Satloff and Jonathan Barkey, "Arab Reaction to the U.S. Air Strikes Against Libya," May 9, 1986, OA 17139, Max Green Files, Ronald Reagan Presidential Library.
29. Ibid.
30. White House Situation Room, "Naval Transit of Suez Canal," April 28, 1986, James R. Stark Files, Box 91747, Ronald Reagan Presidential Library.
31. For an incisive and perceptive analysis of how the Iran-Iraq War had profound implications on the security of the Persian Gulf, see Stephen Pelletiere, *Iraq and the International Oil System: Why American Went to War in the Gulf* (Westport, CT: Praeger, 2001).
32. Robert Satloff and Jonathan Barkey, "Arab Reaction to the U.S. Air Strikes Against Libya," May 9, 1986, OA 17139, Max

Green Files, Ronald Reagan Presidential Library.
33. Ibid.
34. United States Information Agency, "Special Report: Foreign Media Reaction to U.S. Raid on Libya, April 17, 1986, Oliver L. North Files, Box 30, Ronald Reagan Presidential Library.
35. Stanik, *El Dorado Canyon*, p. 217.
36. Memorandum from James R. Stark to Rodney B. McDaniel, May 15, 1986, James R. Stark Files, Box 91747, Ronald Reagan Presidential Library.
37. Memorandum from Rodney B. McDaniel to David L. Chew, May 16, 1986, James R. Stark Files, Box 91747, Ronald Reagan Presidential Library.
38. *Congressional Quarterly Almanac, 99th Congress, 2nd Session* (Washington, DC: Congressional Quarterly, 1987), p. 374.
39. "Talking Points," James R. Stark Files, Box 91747, Ronald Reagan Presidential Library.
40. *Congressional Quarterly Almanac, 99th Congress, 2nd Session*, p. 373.
41. Memorandum from John M. Poindexter to Ronald Reagan, April 23, 1986, Oliver L. North Files, Box 30, Ronald Reagan Presidential Library.
42. Memorandum from Oliver L. North and Craig P. Coy to John M. Poindexter, April 23, 1986, Oliver L. North Files, Box 30, Ronald Reagan Presidential Library.
43. Memorandum from John M. Poindexter to Ronald Reagan, April 23, 1986, Oliver L. North Files, Box 30, Ronald Reagan Presidential Library.
44. Ronald Reagan to Valerie Giscard d'Estaing, April 24, 1986, Oliver L. North Files, Box 30, Ronald Reagan Presidential Library.
45. United States Information Agency, April 17, 1986, "Special Report: Foreign Media Reaction to U.S. Raid on Libya," Oliver L. North Files, Box 30, Ronald Reagan Presidential Library.
46. White House Situation Room Note, "Aftermath of Libyan Operations," April 15, 1986, Oliver L. North Files, Box 30, Ronald Reagan Presidential Library.
47. White House Situation Room Note, "Libyan Update," Oliver L. North Files, Box 30, Ronald Reagan Presidential Library.
48. *The Globe and Mail*, "The Effect on Libya," July 24, 1986, James R. Stark Files, Box 91747, Ronald Reagan Presidential Library.

49. Memorandum from Tyrus W. Cobb to John M. Poindexter, July 25, 1986, James R. Stark Files, Box 91747, Ronald Reagan Presidential Library.
50. United States Information Agency, "The Early Report: Foreign Media Reaction to U.S. Strike Against Libya," April 16, 1986, Oliver L. North Files, Box 30, Ronald Reagan Presidential Library.
51. James M. Strock, *Reagan on Leadership: Executive Lessons from the Great Communicator* (Rocklin, CA: Forum, 1998), p. 53.

Chapter Six

1. Jane Mayer and Doyle McManus, *Landslide: The Unmaking of the President, 1984–1988* (Boston: Houghton Mifflin, 1989), p. 221.
2. Brian L. Davis, *Qaddafi, Terrorism, and the Origins of the U.S. Attack on Libya* (Westport, CT: Praeger, 1990), p. ix.
3. Joseph T. Stanik, *El Dorado: Reagan Undeclared War with Qaddafi* (Annapolis: Naval Institute Press, 2003), p. 239.
4. Davis, *Qaddafi, Terrorism, and Origins of the U.S. Attack on Libya*, p. 168.
5. Dinesh D'Souza, *Ronald Reagan: How an Ordinary Man Became an Extraordinary Leader* (New York: Free Press, 1997), p. 232.
6. Robert J. Lieber, "The Middle East," in Larry Berman, ed., *Looking Back on the Reagan Presidency* (Baltimore: Johns Hopkins University Press, 1990), p. 62.
7. James M. Strock, *Reagan on Leadership: Executive Lessons from the Great Communicator* (Rocklin, CA: Forum, 1998), p. 54.
8. Ibid., p. 55.
9. Edwin Meese III, *With Reagan: The Inside Story* (Washington, DC: Regnery Gateway, 1992), pp. 203–04.
10. Ibid., p. 204.
11. R. A. Davidson, *Reagan vs. Qaddafi: Response to International Terrorism?* (RA. Davidson, 2002), p. 34.
12. Ibid., p. 35.
13. Ibid., p. 113.
14. Ibid., p. 63.
15. Monsour O. El-Kikhia, *Libya's Qaddafi: The Politics of Contradiction* (Gainesville: University of Florida Press, 1997), p. 140.
16. Ibid., p. 123.
17. Richard Reeves, *President Kennedy* (New York: Touchstone, 1994), pp. 335–37.

Bibliography

Abraham, A.J. *The Lebanon War*. Westport, CT: Praeger, 1996.
Allain, Jean, ed. *Unlocking the Middle East: The Writings of Richard Falk*. Northampton, MA: Olive Branch Press, 2003.
Al Madiha, Mahida Rashid. *Jordan, the United States, and the Middle East Peace Process*. Cambridge: Cambridge University Press, 1993.
Aruri, Naseer. *Dishonest Broker: The U.S. Role in Israel and Palestine*. Cambridge: South End Press, 2003.
Berman, Larry, ed. *Looking Back on the Reagan Presidency*. Baltimore: Johns Hopkins University Press, 1990.
Bosch, Adriana. *Reagan: An American Story*. New York: TV Books, 2000.
Brownlee, W. Elliott, and Hugh Davis Graham, eds. *The Reagan Presidency: Pragmatic Conservatism and Its Legacies*. Lawrence: University Press of Kansas, 2003.
Cannon, Lou. *President Reagan: Role of a Lifetime*. New York: Simon & Schuster, 1991.
_____. *Ronald Reagan: The Presidential Portfolio*. New York: Public Affairs, 2001.
Chomsky, Noam. *Fateful Triangle: The United States, Israel, and the Palestinians*. Cambridge: South End Press, 1999.
_____. *Middle East Illusions*. Lanham, MD: Rowman & Littlefield, 2003.
Davidson, R.A., III. *Reagan vs. Qaddafi: Response to International Terrorism?* N.p.: R.A. Davidson, 2002.
Davis, Brian L. *Qaddafi, Terrorism, and the Origins of the U.S. Attack on Libya*. New York: Praeger, 1991.
Deaver, Michael K. *A Different Drummer: My Thirty Years with Ronald Reagan*. New York: HarperCollins, 2001.
Druks, Herbert. *The Uncertain Alliance: The U.S. and Israel from Kennedy to the Peace Process*. Westport, CT: Greenwood Press, 2001.
D'Souza, Dinesh. *Ronald Reagan: How an Ordinary Man Became an Extraordinary Leader*. New York: The Free Press, 1997.
El-Kikhia, Mansour O. *Libya's Qaddafi: The Politics of Contradiction*. Gainesville, FL: University Press of Florida, 1997.
Haley, P. Edward. *Qaddafi and the United States Since 1969*. New York: Praeger, 1984.
Hallenbeck, Ralph A. *Military Force as an Instrument of U.S. Foreign Policy: Intervention in Lebanon, August 1982–February 1984*. New York: Praeger, 1991.
Hammel, Eric. *The Root: The Marines in Beirut, August 1982–Feburary 1984*. St. Paul, MN: Zenith Press, 2005.
Hannaford, Peter, ed. *Recollections of Reagan: A Portrait of Ronald Reagan*. New York: William Morrow, 1997.

Laham, Nicholas. *Crossing the Rubicon: Ronald Reagan and US Policy in the Middle East*. Aldershot, UK: Ashgate, 2004.

———. *Selling AWACS to Saudi Arabia: The Reagan Administration and the Balancing of America's Competing Interests in the Middle East*. Westport, CT: Praeger Publishers, 2002.

Little, Douglas. *American Orientalism: The United States in the Middle East Since 1945*. Chapel Hill: University of North Carolina Press, 2002.

Mayer, Jane, and Doyle McManus. *Landslide: The Unmaking of the President, 1984–1988*. Boston: Houghton Mifflin, 1989.

Meese, Edwin, III. *With Reagan: The Inside Story*. Washington, D.C.: Regnery Gateway, 1992.

Neff, Donald. *Fallen Pillars: U.S. Policy and the Arab-Israeli Conflict*. Washington, DC: Institute for Palestine Studies, 2002.

Pelletiere, Stephen. *Iraq and the International Oil System: Why America Went to War in the Gulf*. Westport, CT: Praeger, 2001.

Pemberton, William E. *Exit with Honor: The Life and Presidency of Ronald Reagan*. Armonk, NJ: M.E. Sharpe, 1998.

Quandt, William B. *Peace Process: American Diplomacy and the Arab-Israeli Conflict Since 1967*. Washington, DC, and Berkeley: Brookings Institution and University of California Press, 2001.

Reagan, Ronald. *An American Life*. New York: Simon & Schuster, 1990

Reeves, Richard. *President Reagan: The Triumph of Imagination*. New York: Simon & Schuster, 2006.

Reich, Bernard. *Securing the Covenant: United States–Israel Relations After the Cold War*. Westport, CT: Praeger, 1995.

St. John, Ronald Bruce. *Libya and the United States: Two Centuries of Strife*. Philadelphia: University of Pennsylvania Press, 2002.

Schmertz, Eric J., Natalie Datlof, and Alexj Ugrinsky, eds. *President Reagan and the World*. Westport, CT: Greenwood Press, 1997.

Seliktar, Ofira. *Divided We Stand: American Jews, Israel, and the Peace Process*. Westport, CT: Praeger, 2002.

Shannon, Vaughn P. *Balancing Act: US Foreign Policy and the Arab-Israeli Conflict*. Aldershot, UK: Ashgate, 2003.

Stanik, Joseph T. *El Dorado Canyon: Reagan's Undeclared War with Qaddafi*. Annapolis: Naval Institute Press, 2003.

Strober, Deborah Hart, and Gerald S. Strober. *Reagan: The Man and His Presidency*. Boston: Houghton Mifflin, 1998.

Strock, James M. *Reagan on Leadership: Executive Lessons from the Great Communicator*. Rocklin: Forum, 1998.

Telhami, Shibley. *The Stakes: America and the Middle East*. Boulder, CO: Westview Press, 2002.

Troy, Gil. *Morning in America: How Ronald Reagan Invented the 1980s*. Princeton: Princeton University Press, 2005.

Vandewalle, Dirk. *A History of Modern Libya*. New York: Cambridge University Press, 2006.

Wallison, Peter J. *Ronald Reagan: The Power of Conviction and the Success of His Presidency*. Boulder, CO: Westview Press, 2003.

Zunes, Stephen. *Tinderbox: U.S. Middle East Policy and the Roots of Terrorism*. Monroe, ME: Common Courage Press, 2003.

Index

Abu Nidal: alliance of, with Qaddafi 57, 72–75, 81, 203; directs hijacking of Egypt Air airliner 50; involvement of, in international terrorism 57, 73–74, 75, 77, 203; launches terrorist attacks in Rome and Vienna 53–56, 64, 73, 84–86, 98
Al Madfai, Madiha Rashid 40–41

Baker, James A., III 95–96
Beirut: bombing of American Embassy in 14–17, 157; bombing of American Marine barracks in 4, 10, 17–21, 32, 34–35, 39–40, 46, 157, 205; Congress authorizes American military presence in 26–27, 32; expulsion of PLO from 4, 9, 12–13, 46, 70, 205; opposition in Congress to American military presence in 27–28, 30–33; Poindexter urges Reagan's attendance at arrival ceremony for victims of bombing of American Embassy in 16–17; Reagan addresses arrival ceremony for victims of bombing of American Embassy in 17; Reagan announces formation of MNF in 4, 12–14, 16; Reagan expands rules of engagement in 24–26, 33; Reagan orders American military withdrawal from 4–5, 10, 33–35, 46, 205; Reagan vows to maintain American military presence in 4–5, 10, 16, 18–21, 34, 205; resurgence of political violence in 4, 10, 13, 33, 46; Shultz defends American military presence in 23; Teicher requests American mission to 16; Teicher transmits talking points defending American military presence in 29
Byrd, Robert C.: charges Reagan violated War Powers Act 127–28, 131, 133–35; introduces amendment to War Powers Act in Senate 131, 133; supports American bombing of Libya 130, 132

Cannon, Lou 36
Chomsky, Noam 12
Congress: authorizes American military presence in Beirut 26–27, 32; Fascell recommends review of American policy in Lebanon by 28–29; opposition in, to American military presence in Beirut 27–28, 30–33, 48–49; Poindexter recommends Reagan send report to, on Libyan-American military clashes in Gulf of Sidra 106; Reagan meets leaders of, on Libya 124–28, 131, 134; Reagan receives report to, on Libyan-American military clashes in Gulf of Sidra 104–6; receives report from Reagan on Libyan-American military clashes in Gulf of Sidra 106; refuses to amend War Powers Act 135; supports American bombing of Libya 129–30, 132–35; supports imposition of American economic embargo against Libya 69

Davidson, R.A. 83, 113, 165, 204, 206–7
Davis, Brian L. 49–50, 80, 200–1
Dine, Thomas A. 42–45

European Community (EC): condemns Libya for sponsorship of international terrorism 119; imposes arms embargo against Libya 78–79; imposes travel restrictions against Libyan diplomats 119, 121, 149–50; imposes visa restrictions against Libyans 119, 121, 149–51; orders reduction in number of Libyan diplomatic personnel 119–21, 149–51; Reagan Administration regards actions of, against Libya inadequate 120–21; Reagan supports sanctions of, against Libya 151; refuses to impose diplomatic and economic sanctions against Libya 78, 120, 139, 163; urges United States and Libya to exercise military restraint 120, 167–68

Fascell, Dante B. 28–29, 102–4, 106–8
Fortier, Donald R. 55–56, 91–93, 97–98

Index

Gemayel, Amin 14–16, 47
Giscard d'Estaing, Valery 189–91
Gorbachev, Mikhail 172–73
Group (G) of 7: condemns international terrorism 153–54, 163–64; condemns Libya for involvement in international terrorism 154, 194; summit meeting of members of, in Tokyo 151, 153, 155–56, 189, 191

Haley, P. Edward 173–74

Israel: alliance of, with United States, 5, 10, 35–39, 42–48, 75, 208; American support for 9, 11, 13, 42, 44–45, 207–8; opposes American contacts with PLO 40–41; Qaddafi's opposition to 45, 47, 49–50, 76, 120, 194; Reagan's support for 4–6, 9–12, 35–39, 42–48, 75–76, 140, 193–94, 199–200, 203–4, 208; rejects Reagan's Middle East peace plan 5, 10, 13, 24, 35, 38–39, 46; Shultz's support for 43–44

Kohl, Helmut 170–72

Libya: American bombing of 3–4, 6–7, 9–11, 116, 123–24, 129, 135, 138–39; American public supports bombing of 156–57, 161–62; American public supports military action against 158–59; Arab League rejects request for imposition of sanctions against United States made by 184, 187–88; Arab world condemns American bombing of 6, 152–53, 166, 175, 178–88, 207–8; Arab world fails to hold summit meeting on 184–85, 187–88; Baker orders enforcement of American economic embargo against 95–96; Congress supports American bombing of 129–30, 132–35; Congress supports imposition of American economic embargo against 69; EC condemnation of, for sponsorship of international terrorism 119; EC imposes arms embargo against 78–79; EC refuses to impose diplomatic and economic sanctions against 78, 120, 139, 163; EC urges exercise of military restraint by 120, 167–68; economic relations with United States 58–60, 81; economic relations with Western Europe 6, 59–61, 64, 66–68, 80–82, 84, 89–90, 110–12, 122–24, 141, 150, 163–64, 167, 171, 198; engages in clashes with American military forces in Gulf of Sidra 102; failure of American bombing of 209; Fortier holds CPPG meeting on 91–93; G-7 condemnation of, for involvement in international terrorism 154, 194; Giscard supports American bombing of 189–91; Gorbachev condemns American bombing of 172; involvement of, in bombing of West Berlin disco 3, 112–14, 125–26, 133, 135–38, 140, 159–60, 162, 170; involvement of, in terrorist attacks in Rome and Vienna 6, 47, 49–53, 58–59, 63–64, 73, 75–77, 111; JCS recommends American bombing of 53–54, 65; Kohl supports American bombing of 170; Kohl urges Western European action against 170–72; maintains friendly relations with Western Europe 6, 124; Mitterand condemns American bombing of 168, 189, 191; NSC considers recommending American bombing of 56; NSC recommends additional American air strikes against 144–45, 165; OPEC rejects request for imposition of oil embargo against United States made by 185; Poindexter recommends Reagan sign new Presidential Finding on 148–49; Reagan Administration considers EC actions against, inadequate 120–21; Reagan and Mubarak confer on 176–78; Reagan announces American bombing of 3, 129, 138, 141, 160–63, 197; Reagan fails to sign new Presidential Finding on 149; Reagan holds Oval Office meeting on 114–15; Reagan imposes economic embargo against 57–58, 62–66, 69–70, 77, 81, 84, 90, 111; Reagan imposes economic sanctions against 51, 55, 58, 60; Reagan meets leaders of Congress on 124–28, 131, 134; Reagan orders American bombing of 3, 7, 115, 121–23, 125–30, 135–36, 140–41, 149, 151–52, 156–57, 160–62, 173, 198–202, 204, 206; Reagan sends letter to Giscard on 190–91; Reagan signs Presidential Finding on 51, 143, 147–48; Reagan supports EC sanctions against 151; Stark and Teicher announce holding of NSPG meeting on 99–100; Stark and Teicher request contingency plan from Fortier for American military action against 97–98; Stark requests NSPG meeting on 98–99; success of American bombing of 139, 194–96, 198, 201–3, 205, 208–9; Thatcher supports American bombing of 170; Teicher transmits annex to NSDD on 85; Teicher transmits documents imposing economic embargo against 61–62; Weinberger transmits contingency plan for American military action against 100–1; Western Europe condemns American bombing of 6–7, 152–53, 166–71, 189, 191; Western Europe refuses to impose sanctions against 49, 55, 67, 78–82, 90, 111–12, 122; Whitehead urges Western European imposition of sanctions against 78–79, 82, 91–92, 121–23, 155

Mayer, Jane 157, 161–62, 200
McFarlane, Robert C. 18, 23–24, 31
McManus, Doyle 157, 161–62, 200
Meese, Edwin, III 95, 202–3

Mitterand, François: condemns American bombing of Libya 168, 189, 191; confers with Reagan on Lebanon 18–19; rejects American request for over-flight rights to use French airspace 168, 189

Mubarak, Hosni: confers with Reagan on Libya 176–78; grants Reagan's request for American transit rights through Suez Canal 179; opposes Qaddafi 175, 177–78; Qaddafi's opposition to 71–72, 176; Weinberger's support for 179

Multinational Force (MNF): dissolution of 4, 34; Reagan announces formation of 4, 10, 13–14; Shultz holds discussions on 19

Murphy, Richard 40–41, 77–79, 82

North, Oliver L.: denies American involvement in possible assassination attempt against Qaddafi 117; prepares Poindexter for meeting with leaders of Congress on Libya 124–25; prepares Poindexter for Oval Office meeting on Libya 114–15; receives polling data on international terrorism 157, 161; recommends Reagan sign letter to Giscard on Libya 190

Palestine Liberation Organization (PLO): expulsion of, from Beirut 4, 9, 12–13, 46, 70, 205; Israel opposes American contacts with 40–41, 46; peace initiative of 5, 10, 40, 42, 46–47, 75–76; Reagan's opposition to 11, 40–42, 46–47, 204

Poindexter, John M.: attends meeting with leaders of Congress on Libya 124–27; attends Oval Office meeting with Reagan on Libya 114–15; circulates draft of NSDD 117, 25; opposes Qaddafi 126–27; receives Defense Department's contingency plan for American military action against Libya from Weinberger 100–1; receives documents on Libyan-American military clashes in Gulf of Sidra from Stark 104–5; recommends Reagan send report to Congress on Libyan-American military clashes in Gulf of Sidra 105–6; recommends Reagan sign letter to Giscard on Libya 190; recommends Reagan sign new Presidential Finding on Libya 148–49; recommends Reagan's attendance at arrival ceremony for victims of bombing of American Embassy in Beirut 16–17

Qaddafi, Muammar: alliance of, with Abu Nidal 57, 72–75, 81, 203; American involvement in possible assassination attempt against 115–18; Arab support for 6, 45, 47, 76, 86–87, 108–9, 112, 140; disingenuousness of Arab support for 178, 183, 185–88, 194–96, 207–8; failure of, to elicit Soviet support 173–74, 207; flees Tripoli 143, 146; Gorbachev's support for 172; insurrection against 143–47, 165; involvement of, in international terrorism 3, 6–7, 10, 45–48, 50, 55, 58–59, 61–71, 74–82, 84, 86–91, 93, 96, 102–3, 108, 110–13, 116, 120–23, 125–27, 130, 133, 135–41, 145, 149–50, 152–53, 155–56, 159–60, 162–66, 169, 171–72, 177, 192, 194, 197–203; Mubarak's opposition to 175, 177–78; NSC supports overthrow of 144–45; opposes Israel 45, 47, 49–50, 76, 120, 194; opposes Mubarak 71–72, 176; opposes United States 49–50, 76, 86–87, 89, 91, 101, 108, 205–6; Poindexter's opposition to 126–27; Reagan Administration supports overthrow of 142–45, 147, 165–66; Reagan denies American involvement in possible assassination attempt against 116, 152; Reagan supports overthrow of 176–78; Reagan's opposition to 7, 47–48, 51, 62–65, 110, 138, 160, 176, 193, 196–97, 199, 200–1, 206–8; Shultz supports overthrow of 147; Shultz's opposition to 150, 156; suspends involvement in international terrorism 7, 139, 146, 164, 192–94, 198–99, 201–3; Weinberger's opposition to 86

Quandt, William B. 9

Reagan, Ronald: addresses arrival ceremony for victims of bombing of American Embassy in Beirut 17; announces American bombing of Libya 3, 129, 138, 141, 160–63, 197; announces formation of MNF 4, 12–14, 16; approves American air and naval exercises in Gulf of Sidra 97, 108, 111; authorizes Operation Flower 51–52, 143, 206; Byrd charges violation of War Powers Act by 127–28, 131, 133–35; cancels Murphy's meeting with joint Jordanian-Palestinian delegation 40; confers with Gemayel 14–16; confers with Mitterand on Lebanon 18–19; confers with Mubarak on Libya 176–78; defends American air and naval exercises in Gulf of Sidra 106; Defense Department recommends invocation of War Powers Act by 101, 103–4; denies American involvement in possible assassination attempt against Qaddafi 116, 152; expands rules of engagement in Beirut 24–26, 33; fails to sign new Presidential Finding on Libya 149; Fascell charges violation of War Powers Act by 103–4, 106–8; Fascell urges invocation of War Powers Act by 102–3; holds Oval Office meeting on Libya 114–15; holds summit meeting with Gorbachev in Geneva 173; holds summit meeting with Shamir 5, 37–39, 42–43; imposes American economic embargo against Libya 57–58, 62–66, 69–70, 77, 81, 84, 90, 111; imposes American economic sanctions against Libya 51, 55, 58, 60; international stature of 195–97; Israel rejects Middle East peace plan of 5, 10, 13, 24, 35, 38–39, 46; meets leaders of Congress on Libya 124–28, 131, 134; Middle East peace plan of 5, 9–10, 13, 15, 17, 22, 24, 35, 38–39, 41, 46, 205; Mubarak grants request of, for American naval transit rights through Suez Canal 179; opposes amending War Powers Act 132–33; opposes PLO 11, 40–42, 46–47, 204; opposes Qaddafi 7, 47–48, 51, 62–65, 110, 138, 160, 176, 193, 196–97, 199, 200–1, 206–8; opposes Soviet influence in Middle East 22–23, 39; orders American bombing of Libya 3, 7, 115, 121–23, 125–30, 135–36, 140–41, 149, 151–52, 156–57, 160–62, 173, 198–202, 204, 206; orders American military withdrawal from Beirut 4–5, 10, 33–35, 46, 205; Poindexter and North recommend signing of letter to Giscard by 190; Poindexter recommends report to Congress on Libyan-American military clashes in Gulf of Sidra by 105–6; Poindexter recommends signing of new Presidential Finding on Libya by 148–49; policy of, toward international terrorism 3, 57–58, 158, 161; receives memorandum on Rome and Vienna attacks from Fortier 55–56; receives report to Congress on Libyan-American military clashes in Gulf of Sidra from Weinberger and Whitehead 104–5; requests Mubarak grant request for American naval transit rights through Suez Canal 177; sends letter to Giscard on Libya 190–91; sends report to Congress on Libyan-American military clashes in Gulf of Sidra 106; signs NSDD 24–26, 31–32, 37–38, 111, 115, 117, 123; signs Presidential Finding on Libya 51, 143, 147–48; supports EC sanctions against Libya 151; supports Israel 4–6, 9–12, 35–39, 42–48, 75–76, 140, 193–94, 199–200, 203–4, 208; supports Lebanese government 16–17, 31–32; supports overthrow of Qaddafi 176–78; vows to maintain American military presence in Beirut 4–5, 10, 16, 18–21, 34, 205; Weinberger rejects invocation of War Powers Act by 89

Reich, Bernard 39

Rumsfeld, Donald 30–32

St. John, Ronald Bruce 49, 126, 174

Shamir, Yitzak 5, 37–39, 42–43

Shultz, George P.: announces formulation of NSDD 111, 23–24; defends American military presence in Beirut 23; holds discussions on MNF 19; opposes Qaddafi 150, 156; supports Israel 43–44; supports overthrow of Qaddafi 147

Stanik, Joseph T. 3, 81–82, 150, 156, 158, 171, 186, 201

Stark, James R.: announces holding of NSPG meeting on Libya 99–100; prepares Poindexter for meeting with leaders of Congress on Libya 197–98; prepares Poindexter for Oval Office meeting on Libya 180–81; requests contingency plan for American military action against Libya from Fortier 97–98; requests NSPG meeting on Libya 98–99; transmits documents on Libyan-American military clashes in Gulf of Sidra to Poindexter 104–5

Strock, James M. 197, 202

Teicher, Howard J.: announces NSPG meeting on Libya 99–100; prepares Poindexter for meeting with leaders of Congress on Libya 124–25; prepares Poindexter for Oval Office meeting on Libya 114–15; requests American mission to Beirut 16; requests contingency plan for American military action against Libya from Fortier 97–98; transmits annex to NSDD on Libya 85; transmits documents imposing economic embargo against Libya 61–62; transmits talking points defending American policy in Lebanon 29

Thatcher, Margaret 169–70

United States: alliance of, with Israel 5, 10, 35–39, 42–48, 75, 208; American public supports bombing of Libya by 156–57, 161–62; American public supports military action against Libya by 158–59; Arab League rejects Libyan request for imposition of sanctions against 184, 187–88; Arab world condemns bombing of Libya by 6, 152–53, 166, 175, 178–88, 207–8; bombing of Libya by 3–4, 6–7, 9–11, 116, 123–24, 129, 135, 138–39; conducts air and naval exercises in Gulf of Sidra 83–84, 92–94, 96–110, 112; Congress supports bombing of Libya by 129–30, 132–35; EC urges exercise of military restraint by 120, 167–68; economic embargo against Libya by 57–58, 62–66, 69–70, 77, 81, 84, 90, 111; economic relations with Libya 58–60, 81; economic sanctions against Libya by 78, 120, 139; engages in clashes with Libyan military forces in Gulf of Sidra 102; failure of bombing of Libya by 209; Giscard supports bombing of Libya by 189–91; Gorbachev condemns bombing of Libya by 172; involvement of, in possible assassination attempts against Qaddafi 115–18; Israeli opposition to contacts with PLO by 40–41; JCS recommends bombing of Libya by 53–54, 65; Kohl supports bombing of Libya by 170; Mitterand condemns bombing of Libya by 189, 191; NSC considers recommending bombing of Libya by 56; NSC recommends additional air strikes against Libya by 144–45, 165; OPEC rejects Libyan request for imposition of oil embargo against 185; Qaddafi's opposition to 49, 50, 76, 86–87, 89, 91, 101, 108, 205–6; Reagan announces bombing of Libya by 3, 129, 138, 141, 160–63, 197; Reagan orders bombing of Libya by 3, 7, 115, 121–23, 125–30, 135–36, 140–41, 149, 151–52, 156–57, 160–62, 173, 198–202, 204, 206; Reagan orders military withdrawal from Beirut by 4–5, 10, 33–35, 46, 205; success of bombing of Libya by 139, 194–96, 198, 201–3, 205, 208–9; supports Israel 9, 11, 13, 42, 44–45, 207–8; Thatcher supports bombing of Libya by 170; Western Europe condemns bombing of Libya by 6–7, 152–53, 166–71, 189, 191

Weinberger, Caspar W.: anticipates Libyan-American military clashes in Gulf of Sidra 101; opposes Qaddafi 86; recommends air and naval exercises in Gulf of Sidra 87–88; recommends Reagan not invoke War Powers Act 89; supports Mubarak 179; transmits Defense Department's contingency plan for military action against Libya to Poindexter 100–1; transmits report to Congress on Libyan-American military clashes in Gulf of Sidra to Reagan 104–5

Western Europe: condemns American bombing of Libya 6–7, 152–53, 166–71, 189, 191; economic relations with Libya 6, 59–61, 64, 66–68, 80–82, 84, 89–90, 110–12, 122–24, 141, 150, 163–64, 167, 171, 198; Kohl urges action against Libya by 170–72; maintains friendly relations with Libya 6, 124; mass expulsion of Libyans from 7, 154–56, 163–64, 166, 171, 194; Reagan Administration's distrust of 89–96, 152; refuses to impose diplomatic and economic sanctions against Libya 49, 55, 67, 78–82, 90, 111–12, 122; Whitehead urges imposition of diplomatic and economic sanctions against Libya by 78–79, 82, 91–92, 121–23, 155

Whitehead, John C.: transmits report to Congress on Libyan-American military clashes in Gulf of Sidra to Reagan 104–5; urges Western European imposition of diplomatic and economic sanctions against Libya 78–79, 82, 91–92, 121–23, 155

www.ingramcontent.com/pod-product-compliance
Lightning Source LLC
Chambersburg PA
CBHW032050300426
44116CB00007B/680